AF255612

THE HIPPO LECTURES

The Hippo Lectures

THE CATHOLIC CATALINE ORATIONS

GRACJAN KRASZEWSKI

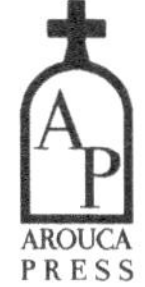

AROUCA PRESS

ISBN: 978-1-990685-81-1 (pbk)
ISBN: 978-1-990685-82-8 (hc)

Arouca Press
PO Box 55003
Bridgeport PO
Waterloo, ON N2J 0A5
Canada
www.aroucapress.com
Send inquiries to info@aroucapress.com

Warmly dedicated to each and every
single person on the Palouse.

CONTENTS

0.A Introduction and Acknowledgements & Scope
    & Everything/Anything Else, etc.   1

0.B On Beauty   11

1 Why Catholic Art–Catholic Literature in
    Particular–Matters; especially Today   25

2 Faith & Athletics: Chasing Impossible Perfection as
    Preparation for the Only Perfection that Matters.   39

3 Should American Catholics Demand a True
    Third Party Political Option?   49

4 Frozen Music: How the Architecture We
    Build Explains What We Believe   61

5 Stupid, Silly Superheroes: Why Comic Book Heroes
    and Silver Screen Strongmen are Woefully
    Inadequate Substitutes for Men and Women
    of Heroic Virtue; the Saints   72

6 The Church and the Environment(alism);
    or, Idaho Hot Springs as Heaven on Earth   83

7 On Beer: Love and Responsibility   96

x.i 1st Fiction Intermission: Maybe, Probably, Definitely, Yes:
    The Tyranny of Relativism   105

8 On Theology of the Body and the Sexual Ethic   122

9 Logos and Human History   132

10 Catholicism and Film: Why Mormon-made *Napoleon
    Dynamite* is a very Catholic Movie   144

11 In Search of a Catholic Economic System   159

12 On What a Catholic College Should Be   174

13 A Conversation Among Friends/The Hope
    We Have in Jesus Christ   189

x.ii 2nd Fiction Intermission: Margaux Himmel:
    Out of Dystopia, Hope   200

14   Between Covid and Me & Humility   221

15   Christianity and Conspiracy Theories   231

16   Label Catholics   243

17   Catholicism, Cults, Fake and Real Religion   257

18   The Necessity of Failure   267

Appendix and Epilogue I: On Scholasticism
   and Saint Thomas   279
Appendix and Epilogue II: A Brief, Biblical Exegesis
   on Three Principles for Perfection   286

About the Author

O. A.

Introduction and Acknowledgements & Scope & Everything/ Anything Else, etc.

I STARTED MY JOB AS DIRECTOR OF INTEL-lectual Formation at the University of Idaho's St. Augustine Center (also known as Vandal Catholic) in August 2019. Although a Pennsylvanian with Polish roots—my father is an American, my mother Polish—it was not my first time to Idaho or Moscow. While living in Boise in 2015–16, finishing up my dissertation at distance from what was then home in Starkville, Mississippi, a time when distance meant miles on a map nothing more, no "social," no "learning," no nothing else Covid-related, my wife, Kate, herself a Mississippi State Ph.D. already done and on a post-doc in the capital city, I was invited to Moscow to give a talk about Walker Percy, Flannery O'Connor, and G.K. Chesterton by the then priest at the center who is still, and praise God, the priest at the center now, my friend, Father Chase Hasenoehrl.

This talk in February 2016 was also not the first time I had to come to Moscow. That would be in the spring of 2010 when Kate, we then but two months married, took me on a lovely week-long road trip up from the Treasure Valley through the mountains and rapids around towns like Council, Riggins, and White Bird unto the distinct region up here, the Palouse, to show me her alma mater and the surrounding environs. We even made it seven miles across the state line to Pullman, Washington, where we currently live and, if that's not cool, aimlessly strolling about your future city/cities totally unaware a decade prior to moving there/here for good, I don't know what is. But still, yet, still the most accurate *first time* I came to Moscow was near the turn of the century, now

I

two decades plus in the past. Fascinated by the uniqueness of the Kibbie Dome, the Idaho Vandals football stadium, I played many a game on PlayStation's *NCAA Football 2002* turning off injuries and fatigue, choosing the easiest difficulty, and creating superhero-like players with impossible size and even more unbelievable abilities. I passed many a high school afternoon, *actually* in Pennsylvania, *virtually* in Moscow, ID, winning imaginary football games by scores such as 273-10. This I would never admit publicly.

Back to February 2016. I owe the invitation to another dear friend, Gabriela Harrison (née Portillo), then a student at the U of I. It was she who put me in contact with Father Chase. Gabriela, I am forever grateful and in your debt. To you, the first proper acknowledgement of this book belongs; thank you.

Kate and I came to Moscow with our then two-year old son, Søren. We stayed with Kate's brother Lars in the downtown Old Moscow Hotel. Prior to the talk, Father Chase and I bonded over burgers and beers and, most especially, discussion of Walker Percy's hilarious book, *Love in the Ruins.* The talk went great. Fifty, maybe even 72, people attended. It was neither livestreamed nor Zoomed; just live. What glorious times. Afterwards, Father Chase heard my confession on a park bench in Friendship Square, the two of us sitting outside in the dark, the cold, the silence, a few people still milling about beneath the nighttime sky. Tomorrow was Ash Wednesday and I wanted to start Lent off on the right foot. Glorious times.

I earned my Ph.D. in August 2016. Kate and I accepted positions at the University of Illinois at Urbana-Champaign. Illinois was like that moment when Kevin Costner's ghost father asks him if the cornfield they are standing in is heaven and Costner says, no, it's Iowa. But imagine a sound edit to the film and when he's supposed to say "Iowa" the dialogue cuts weirdly to a robotic, text to speech voice saying "Illinois." Illinois: open plains as romantic as mountains and seas, corn so tasty it's called sweetcorn, Fighting Illini sports, farm to table breakfasts good enough to make environmentalists, organic purists, vegetarians and vegans violate every ounce of their personal codes, living in the city that was David Foster Wallace's childhood home, teaching history in an old brick building circa 1306 while Kate taught Landscape Architecture in Walter Gropius'/Mies Van der Rohe's Bauhaus-International style ideal; a second son, Bjørn, born, this the best part of all, plus another Father Chase on the scene, Hilgenbrinck, cementing in my mind that naming one's son "Chase" portends greatness of the highest degree should they be called to the priesthood. To both Father Chases, the next, and most heartfelt, acknowledgements and gratitude. You're freaking legends, the two of you. To their parents: a toast, Pope Benedict style beer mugs raised skyward and clinked sufficiently until high tide beer foam is on us, on them, and on you too.

In the summer of 2019 we moved to the Palouse. Kate accepted an assistant professorship in the Washington State School of Design + Construction. I teach there too. (And in the WSU history department, too). That's it, long story short.

And so shortly after that I started giving sort of long talks, monthly, many on long nights short on sunlight. Then not long after that, Father Chase (Hasenoehrl) and I decided we should make something of these talks, a book, but one short enough for no one to accuse it of being too long. That's what this is, that's what you're holding in your hands. It's called *The Hippo Lectures* because our patron, St. Augustine, was from Hippo in Africa, was the Bishop of Hippo, and that's low hanging fruit enough. And if you were to ask if the name of our on-site coffeeshop, *Monica's*, whose baristas do know how to make a good cup of coffee but go above and beyond that by miles each order, has anything to do with Augustine's own mother being named (St.) Monica, you already know the answer. That ancient Hippo is now called Annaba is one of those depressing facts of historical change over time.

This book, what is it exactly? "Collection of essays" is a fair description. That's why I put that, verbatim, in the title. A collection of essays that were also orations (hence the subtexted see alternate title shout out to Cicero), texts so rich, their constituent words so electric like a livewire still hot on Mississippi macadam like crispy bacon sizzling on the griddle that they begged, and do beg still, to be read aloud; and so I did, I read all this aloud, to real people who listened, with their ears, and then posed questions afterwards. And I did my best to answer their questions because that's what you do. (Once, a young woman named Charlotte, from Coeur d'Alene, had the talked recorded by her fiancé, a guy named Eli, so she could listen to it later on because she could not attend in person and I remember thinking, that's really smart of her to do that, that's good planning there, that). And that's cool and nice, I think, because how often do you find yourself in a hammock one hand on a book the other on a drink, the glass cold and filled with ice, reading something that is simultaneously speech and (mini-) saga? How often do you get to have your cake and eat it too?

Herein you will find thoughts on literature, politics, beer, sex, and the environment; a Biblical exegesis, right at the very end, and opinions on economics, film, sports, and architecture. The very first essay is on beauty because beauty matters and maybe even more than people realize. Above all, **t**his book is about the Palouse. You'll hear enough in the coming pages about how Catholics must rediscover the principle of subsidiarity: that which can be done locally should be. Subsidiarity: pro Co-op, the local community, the baker and barber next door. And, like the Benedictine monks and their *ora et labora* philosophy (You're going to hear a whole lot about the Benedictines in this book for there is nothing in life as sublime as prayer and work. If you want to achieve anything of value in this life and the next, you must pray and you must work. There are no substitutes for either.), love the real places they reside and the real people that live there, for love of neighbor only has one command before it, and if in doing so others can do the same, love and work to perfect their own local region, what an archipelago of beauty might yet arise in these well-worn, tried and tired United States were they to be illuminated once more by true Christian values colligated to, rather, catalyzed by, subsidiarious focus.

So this book is about the Palouse and dedicated to the Palouse and its people.

Moscow, and therefore the University of Idaho and the Saint Augustine Center, is on the Palouse. Pullman, and their Cougs, is/ are on the Palouse. Saint Boniface, Neo-Gothic style Cathedral in Uniontown, WA, is on the Palouse. The Palouse region even includes a city called Palouse, go figure. And while the Palouse is often described in straightforward terms as being a "distinct region" in the Pacific Northwest wherein one can see many a green rolling hill and many more wheat sheaves and legumes in addition, and without a cent extra added to the bill, this accurate but not quite *true* description leaves out so much of the ultimate coffee grounds and silt essence to be found here.

Because it's a feeling; a feeling that is something like driving on Brown road south of the Old Moscow-Pullam Highway and it's gravely beneath the tires and the sky is a clean blue, cloudless, and the road is desolate and properly lonely ringed by all those wheat and lentil farm fields upbreaking onto those endless hills about and around and the sun is shining quite bright the force of it confusing to the senses for it looks to be warmer than the high 40s one can feel on the skin on this late March afternoon, if one would let down a window in the car, but that is not a possibility because to let down would be to let in so much of that dust being kicked up about the wheels, because that's what happens on dirt roads, and speaking of dirt roads there are so many of them on the Palouse that one can even stich together a self-made travel itinerary old school from a printed atlas not some online search and use only dirt roads to travel from either Pullman or Moscow to Easter Sunday Mass at Saint Boniface, the dirt roads granting you the privilege of driving past Saint Gall's in Colton on the way to Boniface where so much accoutrement and festive assortment plus put onto the church on this the Sunday of all Sundays does nothing to make it more beautiful for it is always, in and out of season, as beautiful as beautiful gets on this the most beautiful region on Earth. And then a/the final thought comes that post Mass and post Mass brunch back in Pullman or Moscow it would really connect the lost threads of time and space like a solid slap together of dreams and plans planned to the finest detail found realized to go back out near Brown Road but this time on the Old Moscow Pullman Highway and driving and smiling wanting nothing more out of life find a hot spring—a bona fide hot spring like Jerry Johnson off mile marker 152 on US 12 almost to Lolo Pass and the Montana border and the rickety bridge you have to cross to cross over the Lochsa River and then turn right and hike two and a half miles into the forest Warm Creek Spring on your right, cold, but soon you reach the pools, hot, and its lots of people and lots of dogs and evaporating heat and tall trees and maybe snow but always paradise; the views, the water, the squishy pool bottoms exfoliating you down to the soul—dug out on the side of the road about one-hundred feet away from the road therefore sufficiently far away from the dust but not sacrificing a single ray of the sun or that green-hilled view still all about you there as you disembark and enter the bubbling water and laying in the warm water you realize it's not warm but hot, 106 degrees Fahrenheit in fact, but that whoever had made this had made sure to mind his manners and left you a little wooden bench to get out and cool off upon and two bottles of water below it and even a bottle which turns out upon closer inspection to be two bottles of locally brewed beer from somewhere here made just for the sitting and sipping and the getting out/getting in you do until the sky turns orange and the sun sets beneath those hills you yourself tired eventually exhausted unto eyes as heavy as the carbon and manganese I-beam railroad rails crisscrossing these parts lately out of use but still useful fodder for thoughts about the Old West, how the West was won, and what everyone lost in the process. Yes, thoughts like these, you thinking them as you set yourself down on the Palouse ground by the shore of the hot spring and sleep away a dreamless night under the open sky bedazzled by stars far away yet closer than you think, dreamless because you're living that here, and perhaps have in this experience outlived the wildest unconscious speculations in a place so non-descript it's nearly Eden.

This book is dedicated to that.

And, also, if you ask yourself why so many of the chapters deal with Idaho, Idaho themes, Idaho in temporal reality and abstract thought, the formula

> → *subsidiarity [the philosophical principle]* + *subsidiarity's
> expression [for the writer, me, meaning the Palouse] creates Idaho
> × Catholic social teaching's 2nd plank [solidarity] (therefore)* =
> *Idaho & the Palouse in the light of the Universal [Church]* ←

will hopefully be helpful.

The point of the book?

Twofold.

First, I hope, and pray, that in each essay, and the book in sum, readers will find things that nourish their faith and inform them further on that topic. You knew a lot about topic X? Maybe now you know one more thing. You knew nothing beforehand? Now that's no longer the case. And, super critically *and,* perhaps it's the first time, or the first time in a long time, you thought about X in the light of your Catholic faith or under the umbrella of Christian thought generally defined.

Point number two is less obvious. The book is at times absurd (artistically so as in *absurdist,* not colloquially so, see: nonsensical) and free and fun. This because it's also been designed as an antidote to a particular disease prolific at times yet present even in downswings in this the world of Catholic things. And this thing is something unclassifiable as in impossible to be reduced to a singularity but certainly real and easily discernable when the slightest effort is made to add up the A and the B and the C factors into one, even blurry, therefore hazy picture. And that picture is titled, respectively in respect to A, B, and C, "predictable (a.) and wow, really? (b.) and boring (c.)." Sure, we all know the many pitfalls of post Vatican II Catholicism in America: the ghastly architecture, the thin on spiritual sustenance homilies, the general lack of reverence, dropping Mass attendance, widespread rejection of traditional morality, one could go on and on until melting in a puddle of tears. What people don't often point out is that one of the greatest sins of the postmodern era is that what is so incredibly and unbelievably and breathtakingly exciting—the holy Catholic Faith—has been made, or at least many an Old College Try attempts have been made in this direction, dull and sterile and, worst of all, yeah again, yeah, C: boring.

Catholicism is not only true as in True and necessary, it is very much not boring. But so many Catholic authors today try their best to make it boring. Is this an ecumenical initiative? That having pulled out the communion rails and whitewashed the walls clean of iconography we might finally get all the Protestants to swim the Tiber by mimicking the unimaginative, artless, and automobile repair manual level prose they, the Protestants, mastered so many years ago? Is it because many Catholics are Americans and Americans are all about "science" and "efficiency" and especially "*the* science" and so have no clue that writing a book is more than *the 4 things you need to increase your faith 7-fold in a simple 21-step process over 5 months just 9 minutes a day 3 times a week?*

This book is not like that and it is certainly not like that other thing. I hope you like this book. I hope you love it, quote it, Tweet it, and take it with you many a place. Then I hope you recommend it to others and when they won't buy it because they're cheap freeloaders and always have been you lend it to them, but, they being mannerless space cadets too, forget they borrowed it like they often forget which side of their underwear goes front and which back and they don't back, as in give it. Failing that, I hope you despise it, hate its guts. Be hot or cold, Our Blessed Lord Himself said. Not liking it I hope you rip out its pages one by one and burn it in a bonfire you roast mid-summer marshmallows off of. But if you do do this, I sincerely hope you burn your marshmallows and that they taste terrible because you deserve it.

Regarding other unmentioned acknowledgments, a special thanks to Amy McNelly, former Executive Director at St. Augustine's but someone who one can easily imagine as Chief Executive of a nation. Amy McNelly: the maybe future Giorgia Meloni of these United States. To the Deacons Dennis and Verne: thank you. Thank you too Meg Clark, Wendy Karr, Nicole Koepl, Martha Mendez, Nicole Poxleitner and francophone siblings Anna and Sam Kreslins. Thank you, FOCUS denizens Luke and Mika Russell, Allie Friesen of Manhattan (KS), Andrew and Jordan Gogl, Natalie and John Pawelek. To the First Family of the Palouse, the Schmidts, Dave, Trish and Becca, thank you and, Dave, c'mon, announce your campaign already! Run, the people are with you. To the Meyer family: you're quintessential "good people," and I'm honored and blessed to know you. To Sophia and Peter Wieber, Barbara and Earl Aston, Brad King, Betsy Johnson, Maria Swartz, Ryan Alexander, Tom and Janet Richards, Tori Blommer-O'Malley, Hunter Pribyl-Huguelet and Marie Pribyl-Huguelet, Dominic Schmid, Lenah Matz, Clayton Zimmerman,

Brad King, Molly Schwartz, RaeAnn Kirk, Eli Lowman and Wes Nagel—thank you.

A most special thank you to my friend, the veterinarian and philosopher, Cecily Kreslins (née Parell). Before many Hippo Lectures it was Cecily who was the "opening act," reading introductions in Spanish, or about the veracity slash dubious nature of the Moon Landing, or even about a petition to garner support, and public plaudits, for acorn gathering squirrels in Pullman. I, and the most outstanding squirrel, the Tsar of Tree-nut Tower himself, thank you; the Hippo Lectures would not be the same without you. And no less a thank you to Carmen Eggleston who stepped in (to rave reviews) to do the opening act when Cecily had to, I don't know, fix a dog's broken leg or something, work stuff, who knows. P. S. She's a veterinarian, how cool is that? Thank you both!

And as everyone knows, and as authors can attest to from direct, personal experience, no book, no matter how original or sprung from individual genius is ever simply that: an individual effort. I'd like to express a most sincere thanks to the proofreaders of these pages—Kate Kraszewska, Claire Vassia, and Cecily Kreslins—whose critiques, suggestions, and otherwise eagle eyes have improved all that needed to be improved. Top of the list, as far as gratitude goes, is reserved for my editor, Alex Barbas. Alex is the old school editor, in the mold of a Robert Giroux, every author wishes he had, full stop. Working with him, now on this second book with Arouca Press, has been a pleasure. Thank you, Alex.

Next, but nearly most importantly, to my family, all my family, thank you. To my parents, Charles and Aleksandra, as well as to my parents-in-law, Bill and Theresa, to my brother, Konrad, his wife Colby and their daughter, Evy, my Aunt Claire, and to all my brothers and sisters and aunts and uncles besides, to my two sons too, Søren and Bjørn, and to my wife and muse, Kate, thank you. I love you all. Kate: I dedicated this book to the "people of the Palouse" but it's, most likely, dedicated to you; like everything I do. (The book is also dedicated to—at the time of publication—Washington Nationals outfielder Lane Thomas. Because, I mean, man, he really hits lasers, I mean heat seeking missiles, to every part of the ballpark and it's really cool to behold that).

Finally, and most importantly, an acknowledgement and a dedication. This book is also dedicated to, and in thanksgiving to for her unfailing intercessory helps, the Blessed Virgin Mary, Mother of God, Queen of Heaven and Earth, Queen of the Universe. My hope being that those into whose hands this work will fall will themselves follow the advice of her last spoken words in Scripture at the Wedding at Cana, that setting of Our Blessed Lord's first miracle turning water into wine, when she, setting firm the foundation of all true Marian devotion in its essential Christocentricism said to that luckiest waiter—yeah, he was waiting on God Himself and God's Mother and all in one event, not just that but at one singular table, talk about a story to tell your granddkids someday—and to each and every one of us, to all of humanity: "Do whatever He tells you."[1]

Gracjan Kraszewski

(from a basement room equipped with a
keyboard and a bunch of yardwork tools
and a picture of the Sacred Heart of Jesus
and a water heater with a warning in Spanish

*No trate de instalar ni de operar este
calentador de agua si no entiende…*)

*Pullman, Washington, (the) Palouse, United States of America
February 2022*

---

1   John 2:5.

On Beauty

YOUNG CATHOLICS, PROTESTANT CHRIS-tians too, often pose the following questions. "How do I translate the love I have for God to others? How do I evangelize? How do I, a convinced Christian, help others become so themselves?"

I'm here tonight to put forth a simple suggestion: it's not being done as good as it could be, and there's an easier way, and its obviousness is a strength. I'm talking about evangelization by way of beauty. It is not in the eye of the beholder, but something more sublime still, something objective. Being factual, real, even measurable the way a grandmother can turn a blind eye to her granddaughter putting in three times the called for amount of sugar into the chocolate chip cookie dough, so too should we turn eyes, open not closed, into, not away from, beauty. And beauty is the reason the grandmother allows the extra sugar anyways. Her granddaughter is beautiful, and she loves her, and there is a strong connection between love and beauty.

If you are now thinking that you, from your perspective "me," the you "I," I too am beautiful because made in the imagine and likeness of God, that's right, that's theologically and practically correct. You are all beautiful. But, if you are now thinking that this is going to be part of the forthcoming talk, you are mistaken. There are plenty, URL copy and paste thousands of truckload slash boatload online Catholic channels, forums, and talks where you can find so many people happy to tell you so many nice things about how special, wonderful, and incredible you are. This isn't the place, sorry. Also, if I've got to be honest, and we should be honest, when I look out at this crowd and try to thinsplice assign a first impression grade concerning how quote-unquote awesome you all appear to be, I'd say, 34 out of 100, maybe, like, 11, I don't know.

Imagine a Canadian man.

6 foot 3 let's say, 210 pounds.

A descendant of some heroic and duty bound soul who braved the rains and cottage cheese like mud pits of Passchendaele fighting then, during that then the Great War, for the British Empire, for an alliance of Britain and France and Russia and late to the party us, the Americans, against the German speakers in former Prussia and glorious Vienna but in what was and should be remembered as the greatest tragedy of modern times. For, as Pope St. Pius X of happy memory correctly identified, he dying a month into the hostilities, in August of 1914, but so why is Europe, fin de siècle beautiful architecture and avenues and even more beautiful manners and mannerisms, committing suicide, why are Christians killing Christians and for what? No one has yet produced a satisfactory answer.

He, our Canadian man, 6'3, 210 pounds, 4.58 40, 700 pound squat, 375 bench press max, 225 × 22 reps when he's going for that, reps, is from southeastern British Columbia. He's jacked, he's fast, he's from Canada, he's ripped and truly a very nice guy, he's Canadian, from somewhere between Creston and Lister but, above all, not too far from us; not even 200 miles away. He made it across the border, passed the Palouse by in no time, and seeing Boise on green signs pointing south, kept on driving. He made it to the Treasure Valley but, alas, lasted less than half a day. The pretentious attitudes of those in the capital—"we're the new New York City of the Intermountain West!"—alongside the way the formerly empty space between Meridian, Eagle, and Nampa had been eaten up by fast food chains, big box stores, discount cellphone shops, an $8 Oil Change in 8 minutes or your money back, a Stinker gas station, the fortieth one of those, 65 billboards per mile, some of them important like *Have you checked on your dog's emotional wellbeing lately? Call us, Canine on the Couch,* below that, on the one and same billboard, *Hablamos Espanol para que tu perro no tenga que hacerlo. Ya tiene suficientes preocupationes,* a $7 dollar oil change in 90 seconds or, well, we tried, and pop up communities named "Sherwood Forest by the Sea" was just not beautiful to him, see, it came down to beauty, the lack of it, and so he left.

And what *sea* by the way? he thought to himself, yelled aloud as he laid on the horn in thick, California like traffic on I-84 East, stuck between a Prius affixed with the bumper stickers *Blue Girl in a Red State* and *Trees have Dreams Too* and, to his right, a large truck with 32 oversized Trump flags. He counted them all and the total was 32. The truck also had a bumper sticker. *Guns build walls for speech freedom Mexico will pay in Euros BadHombre.com/TodosmisAmigosareMuchoBadBaldEagleHombres.* He shook his head, he didn't get it, *probably because I'm Canadian,* lost in translation, he deduced.

By the sea; were people in Boise so delusional they thought the blue football field of their now irrelevant team counted as an actual body of water? Ducks do, but they're stupid. Is that how Boiseans wanted to measure intelligence? The man had been listening to Shania Twain all the way down—yeah, she's Canadian—but that had been when the traffic had been sparse, the skies high, blue, and open, and the sun warm enough to roll down the window halfway. Shania Twain weather conditions.

Now he was just sitting here, not moving, hot, the windows and the A/C both up, it being one hundred fourteen degrees outside, the oft repeated claims of "yeah, but it's a dry heat" more like mockery than mitigation, and so he put on a rap remix of *Itsy Bitsy Spider* and turned the volume up to max. Sometimes the response to non-beauty is doubling down. Here, it worked. It made him feel better. They did get moving, eventually. Soon after he took a left turn prompted by the signs speaking of Horseshoe Bend and Banks beyond, and left the Treasure Valley, and got into the winding road of 55 north carving a path between deep forests on the right and Payette River rapids down and to the left and, not long after that, he was able to lower the window and put Shania Twain back on. As the orange tint in the sky was slowly receding to something of a dark, purplish hue, he resolved to stop for the night.

And so here he is, imagine him, this Canadian man, sitting, whittling around a campfire in Smiths Ferry, Idaho, hamlet right turn past Cougar Mountain lodge, one bridge over sandy bottomed, icy cold river water unto a dirt road where you can visit Packer John Cabin, still standing site of the first Idaho Territorial Convention in the 1860s. If you have to ask *did he have time to go for a swim in the river before the sitting, the whittling, the fire crackling some meat, some s'mores thing* he's doing now I think you already know the answer. And boy does he feel refreshed, having washed all the Boise away. And that's a beautiful thing, cold water on the skin, and you might surmise he, this Canadian man, is beautiful himself from one anecdote alone. He once walked into a bank and said to the teller,

"Excuse me, can I ask you—

She didn't let him finish but just blurted out, "Yes, I'll marry you." He was going to ask if there was an ATM outside. They got married three weeks later. Turns out she had been named Miss Canada twice while in college. And that's pretty cool. From Regina, Saskatchewan but, go figure, a diehard fan of the Calgary Stampeders. Drop dead gorgeous. Tens marry tens, for them it was 61s marry 61s. They honeymooned north of Calgary.

But when you are imaging this Canadian man, and this is now the third time I've asked you to do that, I don't want you think about beauty but, rather, the absence of it. Things, more precisely definitions, that are not beauty. These non-beautiful, not beauty things, imagine them as flecks of wood he's whittling off, one by one, into the fire in front of him.

Beauty is not *people will just see the joy in my heart and then ask me why I'm so happy and the rest will take care of itself.* Maybe you've heard this one before. I have, a few times. If you haven't, please don't feel bad. Most likely you know a lot less things than I do. Anyone here know the best way to walk a pet armadillo? I didn't think so. I hear this a lot from Protestants and it's well-meaning and makes sense on the surface. If you're filled with God's love that will radiate off you naturally and attract other people. Now, I'll concede here, if this was *actually* the case, the literal definition no more, that would be something we could call "beauty." However, the well-intentioned but fallen and frail beings we are means this approach often comes off as annoying or fake.

Also, armadillos are biological reservoirs for mad amounts of disease; copious carriers, prodigious incubation agents, like, a lot. I don't know about you, but if I walked into a run of the mill Wednesday night Protestant style small group slash Bible study and everyone's wearing ear to ear high voltage smiles and constructing sentences with heavy word choices of: "happy," "joy," "thrilled," "amazing," I might leave before the good stuff gets underway. I'm saying probably don't ever touch an armadillo unless you are one and, if that's the case, it's probably okay but you won't be able to understand this reassuring message due to your lack of language skills in the hear-process-store capability interface owing to your essential armadillo nature i.e., general "armadilloness."

Beauty is not just being nice.

Beauty is not making others feel special by saying the special things that make them feel special.

Beauty is not necessarily classical art or architecture as much as it is not necessarily that latest fad the newest thing the cutting edge whatever soon to be passé done in by its own over-reliance on the time sensitive now.

Beauty is not simply physical beauty, whether on photographic representation or in the flesh. Someone who is considered by the world to be "not attractive" physically might, by the operating effects of God's grace in their soul, and the good works and humility and charity and holiness flowing therefrom, have rendered their soul exceedingly brilliant, supernaturally beautiful. So the definition here certainly cannot be reduced to the physical.

Beauty is not lust.

We've whittled enough for one night. And that guy's got to get back to Canada first thing in the morning because Justin Trudeau just gave a speech. And when Trudeau says things well, never mind, he's just got to get home, that's what he's thinking.

Now, what beauty is, is a transcendental. Transcendentals are properties of being, both foundational, well spring sources for and connected to all in existence, therefore of our realm, while, simultaneously, gateways to the higher, heavenly, essential metaphysical realm. You often hear the transcendentals thrice grouped:

the good,
the true,
the beautiful.

And the essential word there, for all three, is the most common: *the.* Not simply some good, or a true thing maybe true for you, a type of beauty; no, rather, the very form of *the* good, *the* true, *the* beautiful.

These being infinite in their conception and reach they ultimately spring from the one non-contingent Being, the Unmoved Mover who is the way, the truth, and the life and in whom rest all perfections perfectly tuned for all time. This Being that all men call God beholds the very essential form of Beauty by His very nature. That's why we, as we go out into the world, really need to be tapping into this evangelically: evangelizing towards the Beautiful God by way of the transcendental beauty which is His, fully and totally. Transcendentals being transcendental, literally transcending in their activity, means they are universal and accessible to all people, capital A all people, everyone, no matter their age or culture or native language, all people can just get it, immediately, that's what transcendentals do and are. And the ultimate beauty of God leads to appreciation and pleasure in all the lesser beauties connected to God.

What makes you want to listen to this one song more:

a. that it's stunningly beautiful or

b. it doesn't exactly 'sound good' but will give you a nice window into 1980s suburban angst?

Maybe you like angst more than beauty, you probably drink black coffee even though you hate it for the sophistication you assume this gives you. Black coffee plain is rarely good. But the more we can talk about beauty simply vis a vis its own beauty, beauty because it's beautiful, the better you'll evangelize because the closer you'll bring people to the God who is beauty personified. Good black coffee is all about the person making it and most people make it to a quality you'd expect at a Pilot Rest stop on I-40 W headed out from Oklahoma City destination Kingman, Arizona or even headed the other direction on I-40 E towards Memphis[1] or Little Rock. That's not good; the coffee and those places. But with beauty, keep it simple, keep it basking from within beheld from

---

[1] I once had a blue Memphis Tigers T-shirt. Simple design, very nice and full, rich blue color with 'Memphis' and a handsome Tiger logo in white print. It was a great shirt. I lost it at some point and I miss it still. It was a great shirt to workout in.

without. I'm also saying don't you think black coffee is improved with a few subtle dollops of well foamed whole milk and honey poured from the plastic bear's head if you can't get a farmer to deliver it straight from the source?

Beauty for its own sake, because it's beautiful, springing from a Transcendental base, pointing to God, this being good evangelization; a few examples:

The movie you make doesn't have to be like Protestant cinema where some guy beats up a computer he had used for pornography with a baseball bat under the building, dulcet tones of praise and worship music. A review in a secular newspaper rightfully called it "as subtle as a bulldozer." Christ calls us to be sly like serpents, so, when you make your movie, make it subtle, make it simply beautiful—a story that is true, characters that are authentic, and the ever old, ever new human tragicomedy of falling away then returning to the good, to God, by God's grace. Make your movie beautiful and people will know it's ultimately about reality, about God's reality, the only one.

On the other hand, you can make *The Passion of the Christ* like Mel Gibson did, a movie that is not subtle but is beautiful and certainly has led many to Christ and His Church. I heard someone once say, and I'm heavily paraphrasing here, "Mel Gibson has said and done a lot of sketchy stuff. But, he made *The Passion,* so as far as I'm concerned, all is forgiven." I wholeheartedly agree.

The book you write, like the movie you might have made, same rules; beauty first, beauty last, evangelization flowing, naturally and unimpeded therefrom. People think writing a "Christian story" has to be copy and pasting Bible verses. But we've got so much material at our fingertips; sin, repentance, despair in the face of our failures but then the joy of being healed in Christ, triumph, all and every facet of the complexity of the human person; the sacred, the profane, the fallen, the redeemed, all under the umbrella of the messiness of the real. There's a reason that Flannery O'Connor is considered by some to be the best Catholic writer of recent memory even though Walker Percy is definitely better and David Foster Wallace too. She wrote about the real, however painful it was, and so her work was both beautiful and good. Also, tons of Catholics nowadays will cite Ms. O'Connor as their favorite author, or worse still, worse like "Well, nurse, you can mark it on the official records: death by cringe," wear T-shirts with her face or quotes from her books without ever having read even a single page of her literary corpus. This is absolutely unacceptable. Don't wear a T-shirt with Flannery O'Connor's face on it until you've read something she wrote. But I bet when you read anything she wrote you'll realize you should never wear such a shirt. It's unacceptable.

Back to movies, look at the Clint Eastwood film *Gran Tornio*. Lots not to like here. There's some blasphemy in the film, which is horrible, much like much too many a film nowadays, which is horrible, and a good reminder to us that when hearing blasphemy to offer some form of silent reparation, the classic and simple "Blessed be God forever" an excellent remedy. There's lots of ethnic jokes in *Gran Torino*. I'm Polish, part of a people whose navy had to build glass bottom boats to see the old Polish navy which had sunk due to installation of screen doors on their submarines, so I get it, I understand people being offended by these types of jokes. *Gran Torino* has plenty of them and here is an example in highly censored, edited form, which Eastwood's character delivers over beers post work. FYI, again: Please note he actually names certain ethnic groups and says something other than the censored word I provide here for offense taking mitigation purposes. "Ethnic group A, Ethnic Group B, and Ethnic Group C walks into a bar and the bartender looks up and says, 'Get the bleep out of here.'"

You compare this to your non-subtle, computer destroyed, happy praise and worship music movie and you conclude what an awful, useless movie *Gran Torino* is. But I'll pose this counter-question: The state of mankind since the Fall, has it been poppy bubble-wrapped music nice and easy or something so horrible it's often hard to look at? Is sin just kinda bad or really, really awful? Why is it such a grace, such a blessing, that Christ came to redeem us from our sins? Because we needed it just a little bit, us being basically good and nice and smiling happy people, or because we deserved hell and yet dying He destroyed our Death, Rising He Restored our Life? The awfulness of our sin accentuates the beauty of Christ's

Redemptive work all the more. Blessed be God forever indeed. And so Eastwood's character is awful, that's the point, he's fallen, a fallen away Catholic, bitter, filled with venom, horribly racist and just an altogether "bad guy" as we might call him. But Christ died for him all the same, hope remains for him, all the same.

That's beautiful. That's real beauty.

And so when at the end of the movie when he willingly offers his life in defense of a girl who is from an ethnic group he had previously derided, facing his death in a hail of bullets, arms outstretched in cruciform pose, his death leading to her escape from the people who intended to harm her, we can almost see the biblical verse jump onto the screen, John 15:13: "No man has greater love than this, to lay down his life for his friends."

Beauty for beauty's sake because it's beautiful pointing to the Beautiful God.

When you dress yourself, dress beautifully. Certainly under the modest instructions of Scripture—whose adorning let it not be the outward plaiting of the hair, or the wearing of gold, or the putting on of apparel. But the hidden man of the heart in the incorruptibility of a quiet and a meek spirit, which is rich in the sight of God. (1 Peter 3:4)—but in keeping with you being the Image and Likeness of God respectfully reflecting that. I think St. Thomas More said it best, if it was indeed *him* who said it. I might be misremembering but, one of these grand saints, and, again, I think him, once said: "I wear the hair shirt for myself, the gold for the people." Interiorly, in the inner room of prayer visible to God alone, he was doing penance, but in the handsome garments of his outer appearance he was proclaiming, by beauty, by sight, that the interior comeliness God was cultivating in him was matched by a visible and appreciable congruence.

Don't misunderstand what I'm saying here. A thousand dollar plus, custom suit with matching shoes and an expensive watch can look cheaper than the brown habit of a Franciscan, if well cleaned, neatly pressed, perfectly befitting this symbol of living renunciation. But beauty in fashion can be a gift from God—even if the fashion industry was probably placed in some circle of hell by Dante—because someone with it, fashion sense, can make some great looks out of a few twenty dollar bills at the thrift store whereas those without it would remain without it even with millions of dollars at their disposal. So, it's not about money, it's not about bling or ostentatiousness, for we are always supposed to be humble, period, rather it's about respect, especially towards God. He made you in His own Image, try to look the part.

For if you ever find yourself looking in the mirror having given no thought to your appearance and maybe, worse still, tried to look bad on purpose out of some false modesty just think about this. If you asked a waitress in France to bring you the best wine they have then write down her number on the napkin next to it, would it work? You, an accountant from Iowa who knows the tax code back and front, who used to wear pocket protectors and thick rimmed glasses, but now you run three times a week, got Lasik five years ago in Des Moines, visit the dentist annually, have learned how to relax, how to think positive thoughts, how to be nice to yourself, you even call your Aunt in Chicago not infrequently, do you stand a chance? What are the odds she'll go for a coffee with you next door, a black coffee?

If you're going to play a musical instrument, do it beautifully. No one cares about your technique or sight reading skills. Bring forth beauty or leave. If you're going to write a country song write a lyric like Kenny Chesney did in *Back Where I Come From.* "We learned in the Sunday School/Who made the Sun shine through/I know who made the moonshine too/Back where I come from." Why do you bother with basketball if you're not training, each and every workout, to dunk? Dunk or die trying. Make your penmanship as calligriphous as it can be. When you clean your house, your apartment, your frat, clean it so it looks beautiful at the end. I don't just mean clean, that's not enough and I think you know that by now. Speak beautifully to others.

Pray beautifully, and this one is so easy because the prayers themselves are so beautiful in and of themselves. It's like the packet says, just add water, just start praying and you'll see the beauty start bubbling up and frothing all about you. Speaking of prayer, let's all of us here tonight commit to praying for one another forever. I'm serious, add something to your daily intentions like "and for everyone who was at that Hippo talk at St. Augustine's that night, Lord. Please bless them." So easy, so beautiful. Study beautifully, good grades are like a clean frat, good but not enough, go beyond, fall into beauty and learn so as to partake of the fullest intellectual pleasures the good and beautiful God has given you to enjoy. Then, make a beautiful career, a beautiful return of your talents to the demanding Master, as we have read and heard so many times in Matthew 25. Make a beautiful life, by God's grace, and people will be drawn to it and, ultimately, to Him, to God.

It's like a sermon I recently heard at a 7:15 a.m. Communion Service at Sacred Heart in Pullman on a warm August morning, the last gasps of a summer whose pre-5:00 a.m. sunrises will soon surrender to Palouse winters chock full of snow, of ice, snow and ice from late October through April but still no one knows how to drive on all the snow and ice and why? The deacon talked about a woman who confessed to being quote "stuck in a rut with my faith," at least spiritually dry if not like Mother Teresa's years of darkness, feeling far from God, prayer a chore, we've all been there. And then she started taking photographs of the sky around her home; at dawn, at dusk, probably a few of those pitch-black skies that would be like a black hole if not for the shimmering stars speckled about. "I looked at them," she told the deacon, "and I was struck by their beauty, by the beauty of God's creation. And getting lost in this beauty I made my way back to God."

Okay, so, before I conclude, let me give you the takeaways some of you have come for and, reasonably enough, in bullet point format.

• God is beautiful. So being beautiful, acting beautifully, however imperfect our beauty and beautiful acts are, can be a form of honoring God, of growing more like Him, just as we do the same by our penances, prayer life, humility, and love.

• Beauty is a Transcendental, along with the Good and the True, therefore its form and implementation is practically endless and, therefore

• like our Catholic faith it is universal, a universal language, understood and appreciated by people the world over, therefore,

- Use the 1 and 2 connection to God and the flexibility of beauty along with 3, its universality, to, as we started this essay: EVANGELIZE, to bring people to God, to the faith, to the Truth, and that's why

- As this essay has shown, beauty can be so fun, so diverse, so many things because it being transcendently universal and related to God it cannot fail to accomplish number 4, it will evangelize. Whatever you do, if you do it beautifully, whatever it is, it will, by its own accord, because God designed it that way, draw people closer to God, the source of all beauty.

Now, in actual conclusion, not the previous *before I conclude*, we should value beauty because of its relation to the happy end, the beatific vision, towards which we are called, for which we have been created. When we cultivate beauty, appreciate and promote it, we are already enjoying a foretaste of the glory to come. Listen to the following accounts of angels and the Blessed Mother appearing to people and tell me what stands out.

When appearing at Knock, Ireland in 1879, the Blessed Mother was said to be standing a few feet above the ground, wearing a white cloak, eyes raised to Heaven in prayer; but she was first described as simply beautiful. St. Bernadette Soubirous described Our Lady's appearance at Lourdes, in 1846, as standing in front of a dazzling light emanating from the Grotto behind her. More than 300 years earlier, a peasant named Juan Diego was ambling about when he heard beautiful music, akin to the warbling of birds, and soon saw a radiant cloud upon which stood what he took to be an Indian maiden yet dressed, and as striking as, royalty, like an Aztec princess. At Fatima in 1917, the three shepherd children, Jacinta, Francisco and Lucia, spoke of seeing the Blessed Virgin Mary thusly:

> brighter than the sun, shedding rays of light clearer and stronger than a crystal goblet filled with the most sparkling water and pierced by the burning rays of the sun.

A summer earlier, in 1916, when visited by the Angel of Peace who taught them the Fatima prayer—*My God I believe, I adore, I hope, and I love you and I beg pardon of those who do not believe, do not adore, do not hope, and do not love you*—the Fatima seers saw him as a pure, vivid, perfect white light, translucent, radiant, ineffably beautiful and inspiring an awe close to fear, his appearance furthermore "like snow that the sun shines through until it becomes crystalline."[2] At the Resurrection of Jesus Christ, an angel of the Lord, who descended from Heaven to roll back the stone securing the tomb, is described possessing an appearance like lightening and his clothes as white as snow. So impressive, so overwhelming, is the angel that "the guards were shaken with fear of him and became like dead men."[3]

Suffice to say, that other, higher world, Heaven, is a beautiful place, an unblemished place of perfect beauty and of every type of beauty. And so, to put it as simply as I can, we should appreciate and strive for beauty—in the soul above all, spiritually above all—for in doing so we participate, however imperfectly now in this vale of tears, in the perfect Kingdom to come. I'll leave you with a few quotes from a book I highly recommend. It's by the Jesuit priest Father F. J. Boudreaux and the title says it all: *The Happiness of Heaven, and how to Attain the Joys That Await you There.*[4]

"First," Father Boudreaux states early in the book, "we shall endeavor to obtain a definite idea of the Beatific Vision, which is the essential constituent of heavenly bliss." And it really is all bliss and beauty going forward from there. Henceforth exclusively quoting from the text, even if but a few snippets thereof,

> It is the sight and knowledge of God as He is that
> produces this love, because it is impossible for the soul
> to see God in His divine beauty, goodness, and unspeakable love for the soul without loving Him with all the
> power of its being. It would be easier to go near an
> immense fire and not feel the heat, than to see God in
> His very essence and yet not be set on fire with divine

---

2   Warren Carroll, *1917: Red Banners, White Mantle* (Front Royal, VA: Christendom Press, 1981), 26.

3   Matthew 28:3–8.

4   F. J. Boudreaux, SJ, *The Happiness of Heaven, And How to Attain the Joys that Await you There* (Manchester, NH: Sophia Institute Press, 1999).

love ... in the Beatific Vision, God enables the soul to see Him in all His surpassing beauty...[in heaven] the soul becomes bright with His brightness, beautiful with His beauty... the soul, united to God in the Beatific vision, is possessed of a dazzling splendor and unearthly beauty.[5]

---

5   Boudreaux, SJ, *The Happiness of Heaven*, 9, 11, 22.

Why Catholic Art—
CATHOLIC LITERATURE IN PARTICULAR—
Matters; especially Today[1]

"WHAT DO YOU SEEK—GOD? YOU ASK with a smile? I hesitate to answer, since all other Americans have settled the matter for themselves and to give such an answer would amount to setting myself a goal which everyone else has reached—and therefore raising a question in which no one has the slightest interest." Binx Bolling, protagonist-pilgrim of Walker Percy's 1961 novel, *The Moviegoer,* cannot escape the invisible yet crushing weight of life's most pressing question. "As everyone knows, the polls report that 98% of Americans believe in God and the remaining 2% are atheists and agnostics which leaves not a single percentage point for a seeker. Am I, in my search, a hundred miles ahead of my fellow Americans or a hundred miles behind them? Have 98% of Americans already found what I seek or are they so sunk in everydayness that not even the possibility of a search has occurred to them? On my honor, I do not know the answer. What is the nature of the search, you ask? The search is what anyone would undertake if he were not sunk in the everydayness of his own life...to become aware of the possibility of the search is to be onto something. Not to be onto something is to be in despair."[2]

Binx eventually commences the search; his own, personal search. It is something we all must do, set out to find ultimate reality,

---

1   This article was published in the June 2022 issue of *Catholic Stand.*
2   Walker Percy, *The Moviegoer* (New York: Vintage International, 1998; org. 1961), 13-14.

truths and the Truth itself, if we have any designs on lasting happiness and fulfillment. Not much has changed in the fifty-eight years since Percy penned these words. Religion, we are often told, is a private matter. People have long decided whether to believe or not to believe and as such wouldn't it be nice to just not think, not talk, and not fight about religion? It does not matter if you believe or not, just keep it to yourself. And, by the way, what do you mean "seeker"? Sounds like some New Age, used bookstore, self-help guru shtick. Seeking what, exactly? Don't you know there is nothing to find? No truth, no meaning, no purpose. Maybe we'd all be happier if we just followed the advice of Richard Dawkins' "Atheist Bus Campaign," which plastered the following slogan on buses about London: "There's probably no God. Now stop worrying and enjoy your life."[3]

Put aside the fact that if God does not exist life is nothing *but* worry and the complete lack of enjoyment for since there is no good or evil there is no moral standard neither here nor in a next life judgment that will never come and, alas, as Dostoevsky is reported to have said,[4] "without God, all is permitted"; genocide, ethnic cleansing, infidelity, robbery, each morally equivalent to feeding the hungry or curing diseases or baking cookies for the Main Street Bazaar, for the categories "good" and "bad" do not exist outside of their relative, pragmatic utility. Good becomes what works, bad what does not. Joseph Stalin and Mother Teresa are both people who "did things," equally good, or equally bad, or equally nothing or everything or something or anything, whatever you want it and them to be. For what is then mistakenly called "evil" is nothing more than an offended party unhappy that an idea or group opposed to them has seized ground they wished to claim for themselves.

And this is precisely the outlook of the Nietzsche-Foucault postmodern acolytes who have scuttled the rational program of 2,500 year old Platonic-Aristotelian wisdom counseling subordination

---

3   Sarah Lyall, "Atheists Send a Message, on 800 British Buses." *The New York Times,* January 6, 2009.

4   Andrei I. Volkov, "Dostoevsky Did Say It: A Response to David E. Cortesi (2011)," https://infidels.org/library/modern/andrei_volkov/dostoevsky.html

of the passions to a will guided by a well-formed, rational intellect in favor of putting the passions in the driver's seat, passions which should they be found to be destructive will be claimed to be all the more useful. Speaking of useful, as in idiots, those of the general masses, us, you and me, duped into accepting naked will to power as a "scientifically accurate" model for life, we should not complain about the spilled milk later when those who pushed acceptance of such behaviors as some kind of norms exploited the new norms, and us most of all, assured that we would have no recourse to anything when awaking from our stupor to protest. Protest against what (?), you puppet-morons have long agreed with us that there is no God, no morality, no universal standards, no truth outside grabbing what you can grab on greasy ladders via greasier consciences in an ant farm of human meaningless. "Evil" is nothing but a hollow defense mechanism in a ruthless will to power world where, as the overused adage goes, the strong take what they like and the weak suffer what they must. If there is no God, never stop worrying and forget about enjoyment in life. I wonder what the bus people would say about putting that message on their vessels?

But let's put this aside and pretend Dawkins' advice is feasible, that one can ignore God and just get on with life. What general observations do we have concerning the last half-century since the publication of *The Moviegoer*? Have 98% of Americans already found what is to be found and so are happy, fulfilled, and for our specific interest as Catholics, practicing members of the faith fully alive in loving relationships with God and neighbor? No, it seems. Percy, many years ago, astutely diagnosed a very 2019 problem, a disease of the soul manifesting symptoms of a lukewarm, apathetic detachment from everything and everyone that the historian Brad Gregory terms "The Kingdom of Whatever."[5]

Does God exist or not? Who cares? Is there absolute truth? Impossible to say. Is there an overarching moral code, a standard of behavior all people in every place are bound to follow? Yes.

---

5   Brad Gregory, *The Unintended Reformation: How a Religious Revolution Secularized Society* (Cambridge, MA: Belknap Press, an imprint of Harvard University Press; reprint, 2015).

No. I don't know. Whatever. Maybe it was Pope Pius XII who beat Gregory to the punch when saying, in 1946, "the greatest sin in the world today is that men have begun to lose the sense of sin."[6] That "greatest sin" can today be termed hyper-apathy, special variant of chronic spiritual sloth syndrome. For what do the visible realties around us proclaim? What is the balance sheet of the Kingdom of Whatever? Drug abuse is rampant, evidenced by the conspicuous attention daily heaped on the opioid epidemic, significant abasements in acceptable public behavior and basic standards of public morality have long decimated that most important social unit, the nuclear family, and this marches lockstep with the desensitization surrounding violence, alarming rates of suicide, the ongoing abortion holocaust, and the growing normalization of the "death with dignity" movement putting the finishing touches on a full bore "culture of death."

What of religion in America, the Catholic Church in America, and the current state of the Catholic Church worldwide? Between the sexual abuse scandals, the across the board mass exoduses from religious orders, some experiencing a near 99% decrease in vocations over the past century, social issues statistics showing Catholics have stopped being the salt of the earth and are almost indistinguishable from secular society on moral questions, and the embarrassing state of former Catholic bastions like Ireland and France, it is better not to dwell too long on these realities lest one risk falling into despair.

If you're wondering what exactly this has to do with Catholic art and literature let me assure you, a lot. A society that reads good books, consumes good art, understands the objective reality of truth and falsehood, the fall and redemption, salvation and damnation, this type of society does not act like our society acts today. This type of society understands that knowing the truth—above all the Personified, Incarnate Truth Himself, He who is also the Way and the Life—is not the end but the beginning. Then it's time to start acting, start living, properly orientated towards the fixed eternal goal. This type of society, fortified by good books and good art,

---

6 Pope Pius XII, *Radio Message of His Holiness Pius XII to Participants in the National Catechetical Congress of the United States in* Boston, October 26, 1946.

does not pretend God doesn't exist so as to justify their favorite sins, does not deny sin, period, and does not live in the Kingdom of Whatever but, instead, seeks citizenship in the Kingdom of Heaven.

It's not like we arrived here overnight. Descartes' 1639 cogito, "I think therefore I am," turned orthodox theology—"I am, therefore I think"—on its head, transferring the start point of ontological reality from the Creator to His creation, severing the *res cogitans* from the *res extensa* and finishing the attack on universals, knowable absolute truth, and free will. (Work which began with William of Ockham, but was "perfected" by Martin Luther and John Calvin). The Enlightenment rationalism that followed Descartes and the deterministic scientism that followed that and all the secular religions of the 19th century downstream still, from nationalism to socialism to positivism, worked in tandem with an artistic devolution from Catholic posters like Duccio's *Madonna and Child,* painted in the year 1300, whose logical message was as clear as it was beautiful to, slowly but surely, moving Christ off to the side of the frame, as in Ciseri's 1864 *Ecce Homo,* to not having Christ present at all as the canvas blurred unto incomprehensibility through the Impressionists, the Expressionists, Pablo Picasso and Jackson Pollock.[7]

It took men of faith and architectural genius nearly two centuries to build Notre Dame Cathedral in Paris convinced this work could save the world; a grand monument to a living faith, with the living God truly present within to be adored and consumed healing a broken humanity. Centuries later, in 1974, another artist also claimed his work could heal and save, America, actually. The German performance artist Joseph Beuys flew to New York and, dressed in a full length brown habit of sorts, spent three days locked in a room with a coyote; staring at it, pacing, poking the animal, prodding it, listening to it and trying to be listened to, learning, he said. Beuys claimed *I like America and America likes Me* might just be the balm a post-1960s broken and divided society was looking for. Hearing him explain the intent behind his work—"I wanted to isolate myself, insulate myself, see nothing of America other than

---

7   H. R. Rookmaaker, *Modern Art and the Death of a Culture* (London: Inter-Varsity Press, 1970), 12–13, 71, 108–149.

the coyote"—one can't help feeling perplexed as to why he failed. If truth and reality are solely what we make them, and make of them, the view that Notre Dame Cathedral is of a higher spiritual and sensual caliber than a guy in a room bothering a poor animal with a stick is nothing more than personal opinion, subjective belief. Because, look, who cares? As a master practitioner of relativism, Pontius Pilate, put it himself: *Quid est veritas*?[8]

So, no, to answer Walker Percy's question, no, it would seem things aren't going that well in society and within the Church today, AD 2019, and that most people haven't found what they're looking for. Catholic art, and Catholic literature, matters now more than ever because we are living in the midst of a significant moral and artistic problem-thicket. Whether or not things are worse in the fields of art and literature, and within society writ large, *than ever before* is a debatable proposition. But that things are "not going well" is self-evident. Furthermore, it is possible to say that maybe the only thing that matches our general lack of artistic imagination is an inverse, nearly endless reservoir of false confidence and arrogant assurance that we're doing just fine, thank you.

True Catholic art and literature matters because it can be one tool, and a powerful one, in a larger project of raising the consciousness of a society slumbering in sin to consider the source of our maladies and then search for a cure, a way out, a way back. What is "true" Catholic art and literature? It is nothing more or less than the truth. It is avoiding the false presumptions of Neo-Pelagianists that say nothing is wrong and sin isn't real and people are not only doing good but great so, like Richard Dawkins counsels us, just sit back and enjoy life, don't worry. Within yourself, and without the help of God or religion, you have all the necessary components to live a good life and be a "good person."

It is also avoiding the despair on the other extreme of the spectrum, populated by nihilists who, assured that life is nothing but

---

8   Shira Wolfe, "Stores of Iconic Artworks: Joseph Beuys' *I Like America and America Likes Me*," Artland Magazine, undated post: https://magazine.artland.com/stories-of-iconic-artworks-joseph-beuys-i-like-america-and-america-likes-me/; No author listed, "Joseph Beuys: Actions, Vitrines, Environments: Room 4," https://www.tate.org.uk/whats-on/tate-modern/exhibition/joseph-beuys-actions-vitrines-environments/joseph-beuys-actions-4; John 18:38.

senseless pain and suffering driven by random, chance chemical reactions of unconnected atoms bouncing about in a dark and meaningless universe, dive head long into sin not just accepting it but celebrating it. Like Dawkins, once again, they too tell us don't worry, get all the pleasure you can while you can, because you're going to die and then that's it. There is nothing more. There is nothing but the bottomless, eternal void.

True Catholic art and literature tells us a much different story, the only story worth telling: that God is all good and all loving, that life is worth living, as Fulton Sheen often reminded us, but that this value comes not from a denial of sin but because of redemption from it. "Oh happy fault that merited such and so great a Redeemer."9 *Felix culpa,* indeed. To show the world and sin in all its ugliness and horror without forgetting that love—divine love as Dante explained in *The Divine Comedy*, the glue binding all of existence harmoniously together10—triumphs in the end is to touch the very nerve center of what Catholic art and literature should and needs to be. Only then, once intact and sensibly structured, can this most pressing message be conveyed to a postmodern, post-Christian culture in a "sly like serpents" way; subtly, softly, and thus with devastating effect. Nothing can be a higher triumph in this initiative than for a reader to pick up a book confident in seeing support for and celebration of "postmodern secular values," the apathy and the sin and the meaningless sex plus more sex and the sleepy ambivalence to it all, only to find, more than halfway done and enjoying the book, that the evangelical wool has been pulled over his eyes. But now, it's too late. Once you know, you cannot not know, cannot un-know or non-know, cannot feign ignorance any longer.

The same secular reader who, like Binx, would never pick up anything remotely resembling a religious book—"My unbelief

---

9   The Exsultet: The Proclamation of Easter. http://www.usccb.org/prayer-and-worship/liturgical-year/easter/easter-proclamation-exsultet.cfm

10   ...A l'alta fantasia qui manco possa;
         ma gia volgeva il mio disio e 'l velle,
         si come rota ch'igualmente e mossa,
         l'amor che move il sole e l'altre stelle.
                 Paradisio, Canto XXXIII, 142–145.

was invincible from the beginning. I could never make head or tail of God. The proofs of God's existence may have been true for all I know, but it didn't make the slightest difference. If God had appeared to me, it would have changed nothing. In fact, I have only to hear the word God and a curtain comes down in my head"[11]—has found himself agreeing with the message, has found his false and foolish preconceptions about God and religion irrevocably smashed, and all because the Truth was presented in a familiar and disarming way. That set the dominos in motion, now the harvest can be reaped. That's true Catholic art and literature.

If you are a Catholic artist or writer wanting to participate in this mission then, first, tell the whole truth about sin and redemption. Secondly, do it slyly, gently enough to make your readers, your critics, think you're telling them the story they want to hear and then, when it's already too late, inundate them, bombard them, with Christian truth. Want to be a bad Catholic writer and artist? Deny original sin, tell people not to worry, bless their sins and tell them they're perfect as they are. Or, forget any nuance and go 100% devout Catholic from the starting blocks and see how many atheists, agnostics, and seekers make it past the first page and arrive in that middle section that just might lead to their conversion.

I will say it again: the whole truth but do it slyly. Create a story that shows the full reality of human weakness and sin but, unlike a secular culture which venerates perversion as virtues, leave room for that artistic turn where your story reveals these things for what they are and demonstrates how and why living in such a way betrays not just God but humanity, and that the deepest meanings and ultimate happiness all seek, the very thing Binx sets out to find on his search, Christ alone can give.

Fyodor Dostoevsky, a Russian Orthodox Christian, was a master of this genre. Consider his novel *Crime and Punishment*. The protagonist, a young, brilliant and handsome man named Raskolnikov, thinks he is smarter than God, that he doesn't need God, that like Nietzsche's *uberman* his greatness sets him above, beyond, good and evil. (Not without reason did John Paul II say that man, on the

---

11   Percy, *The Moviegoer*, 145.

spiritual battlefield of existence, could never be *beyond* good and evil but only *between* it.[12]) The rules do not apply to him. God does not exist. Original sin does not exist. If this sounds a little like "God knows well that the moment you eat of it your eyes will be opened and you will be like gods knowing good and evil," you're on the right track.[13]

Raskolnikov murders a pawnshop owner because he's convinced morality is a fiction and, being a superior being, his psyche can handle what lesser men's cannot. Dostoevsky shows us what nonsense this is, that denying God and sin in no way make these realities less real. In a work of tortuous beauty, Raskolnikov only, and finally, escapes the living hell *he has created* by confessing his crime and accepting punishment for his actions. Dostoevsky could have tried to bring his readers to Christ by telling them not to worry, just be happy, that all God wants is for you to find your own, personal truths and passions, that dogma and rules are irrelevant, just "love," be "nice." Perhaps he knew people who hear such messages soon lose their supernatural faith. So instead he told us a horrifying story about the darkness of sin, a story about a man who thought he was above God but soon found out he was nothing without God. Maybe he knew these are the kind of stories that lead to conversions, that these are the ones worth telling.[14]

Flannery O'Connor was the same way. The protagonist of *Wiseblood* is a man named Hazel Motes, a non-believer who founds an atheist "church," the "Holy Church of Christ Without Christ." Motes' visceral hatred of Christianity leads him to, near the end of the novel, murder an itinerant preacher with his car, running over the man multiple times in rage. His car was supposed to mark his liberation from God and morality, a Raskolnikov-like "beyond good and evil" quality that would allow him speedy trips from town to town preaching his anti-gospel. Instead, the car becomes the instrument and symbol of his downfall, the literal tool with

---

12   Pope John Paul II, *The Way to Christ: Spiritual Exercises* (New York: HarperOne, 1994), 49.

13   Genesis 3:5.

14   Fyodor Dostoevsky, *Crime and Punishment*, trans. Richard Pevear and Larissa Volokhonsky (New York: Vintage Classics, 1993).

which he performs his horrendous crime and, soon thereafter, is brought to ruin when a police officer, following a routine traffic stop, kicks the vehicle over a cliff simply because he finds Motes' appearance displeasing.

Motes has failed. Now what? You guessed it, redemption. Motes finally surrenders to God and starts doing penance, filling his rocks with shoes and sleeping with barbed wire across his chest in the fashion of Middle Age ascetics, hoping that somehow he can expiate the wrongs of his troubled life. And all this after beginning the road to redemption by blinding himself with acid, so strongly had his conscience, that aboriginal Vicar of Christ as John Henry Newman termed it, revolted against his behavior.[15] Maybe O'Connor could have told us a "nice story"[16] instead of this disturbing one. But maybe it's disturbing stories that properly show sin for what it is and give us the greatest chance to seek redemption and salvation.[17]

If there is one Catholic artist who does the *showing sin in all its ugliness for the purpose of bringing people to God* genre best, it is Walker Percy. "Your Catholic imagination sees in the Incarnate Spirit a sacramental meaning. The imaginative artist is the custodian of our language and you have fashioned it to uses beyond the ordinary. Like Kierkegaard, you have been a spy in the service of the Almighty, casting a rye eye on the current state of Christendom and you have looked with care on a sadly secularized society and have seen a death wish in the assertion of a right to decide when human life is worthwhile and when it is not. Your writings explore from within the flaws in our nature, our sense of alienation from our true selves, but always with that unforced note of hope."[18]

---

15   Roy Huesel, "Conscience—the Aboriginal Vicar of Christ," *OnePeterFive*, February 24, 2017.

16   Speaking of "not nice stories," of books showing unchecked sin in all its horrible effects, original sin and Promethean pride let loose without brakes, please see: Stanisław Ignacy Witkiewicz, *Insatiability*, trans. Louis Iribarne (Evanston, IL: Northwestern University Press, 1996; org. 1930).

17   Flannery O'Connor, *Wiseblood: A Novel* (New York: FSG Classics, 2007).

18   "Walker Percy at Notre Dame." Presentation of the Laetare Medal from the University of Notre Dame, Commencement, 1989. https://www.youtube.com/watch?v=T6jaJy3gL2I

Such was the citation given at Walker Percy's 1989 Laetare Medal reception ceremony at the University of Notre Dame, the oldest and most prestigious award given to American Catholics in recognition of outstanding service to the Church and society. Percy, God's spy, did indeed, and brilliantly, speak of our post-fall sense of alienation from our true selves. He did so through characters like Binx and the physician Thomas More—star of *Love in the Ruins* and *The Thanatos Syndrome*[19]—a self-professed bad Catholic lapsed into alcoholism, misogyny, maybe even polygamy who cannot, despite himself, escape that which Flannery O'Connor called "the God-haunted state." Try as he might, he cannot escape God, cannot escape the unforced note of hope God offers to each one of us should we just repent and set out seeking salvation.

The depth of Percy's Catholic espionage quality was on full display in his 1983 book *Lost in the Cosmos,* a humorous if not hilarious parody of New Age self-help literature clearly showing that man's sin-induced alienation cannot be escaped or remedied but by Christ. If novels are not your thing, I encourage you to read two books, and as soon as possible: G. K. Chesterton's *Orthodoxy* and this book, *Lost in the Cosmos.* Although written fairly far apart in time—1908 and 1983, respectively—and by different authors, the two read like a series, as if *Lost in the Cosmos* is the sequel to *Orthodoxy.*

Chesterton begins *Orthodoxy* by showcasing original sin, calling it the most obvious and provable aspect of human nature. And when he concludes that utopias never work because the world cannot be perfected by fallen man, the reader has long slipped into a state of pleasurable mental exhaustion, verifiably battered by polemic after polemic denunciations of so many heresies one cannot believe that, in fact, so much error abounds. Chesterton is funny, witty, he might be a genius, but he does not sugarcoat. Catholic writers on the make take note: just tell it like it is. And because, not despite, his directness in treating sin and redemption he has been long regarded as one of the most successful apologists

---

19   Walker Percy, *Love in the Ruins: The Adventures of a Bad Catholic at a Time Near the End of the World* (New York: FSG, 1971); Walker Percy, *The Thanatos Syndrome* (New York: Picador, reprint, 1999).

of modern times. *Lost in the Cosmos* builds off *Orthodoxy* in treating the roots of modern depression, the neo-gnostic splitting of man's inherent body-soul unity, the false, "sophomoric" as Percy calls it, debates between faith and reason, and the crushing alienation and sense of loss all people experience, a disjunction that can be repaired, healed, either by the Cross and Redemption of Christ or not at all.[20]

Catholic art and literature matter because they are in short supply today, and therefore in need of replenishment, but not enough people *know how* to present this message, and not knowing how means not doing means not helping means, tragically, not giving something that to someone might just be the one thing they need to repent, to try to start again. Allow me to return to Binx one final time. He spends the entirety of *The Moviegoer* trying to fill his God-shaped hole with everything but God. He is promiscuous, he loves making money, and while he feels the interior push to start out on the search, to get serious and start seeking the truth, he just can't do it, can't find the catalyst to finally get going. And so he confesses, near the very end of the book, that the mammon worshipping, post truth, post-Christian society of scientific positivism has left him cold.

> Today is my thirtieth birthday and I sit … and think of nothing. Now in the thirty-first year of my dark pilgrimage on this earth and knowing less than I ever knew before, having learned only to recognize merde when I see it, having inherited no more from my father than a good nose for merde, for every species of shit that flies … living in fact in the very century of merde, the great shithouse of scientific humanism where needs are satisfied, everyone becomes an anyone, a warm and creative person, and prospers like a dung beetle, and one hundred percent of people are humanists and ninety-eight percent believe in God, and men are dead, dead, dead; and the malaise has settled like a fall-out and what people really fear is

---

20   G. K. Chesterton, *Orthodoxy* (New York: Dodd and Mead, 1908), 23, 51–73, 85–97, 137–186, 261–99; Walker Percy, *Lost in the Cosmos* (New York: FSG, 1983) 156–180, 201, 110–120.

> not that the bomb will fall but that the bomb will not
> fall—on this my thirtieth birthday, I know nothing and
> there is nothing to do but fall prey to desire.[21]

"Nothing to do but fall prey to desire"; how sad, and sadder still how true that attitude often is. Do we understand Percy's point here? Do we? We should, we need to if we want to both understand and appreciate Catholic literature and, far more importantly, be able to apply the lessons therein. God is Logos. From God flows all order, logic, right reason and rightly ordered behavior. Cling to Him, remain in a state of grace, i.e., avoid the forbidden fruit in favor of humble obedience—*God knows best, not me.* I don't know how to explain this concept more simply—and we will thrive, we will flourish in the full spectrum of our lived experience, relationships included.

But be like Binx, ignore God in favor of "doing it my way" and see how long it takes you to conclude that life is worthless, meaningless, merde capital M. But hey, consolation prize here I come, at least I can give into all my desires. Even if life is meaningless and I hope the bomb soon falls directly on my head, at least I can drown in a pool of meaningless sex day after day until I die. Because, what else is there? And that's precisely *it.* That's where the enemies of the faith and family want us all to arrive: life is nothing, I am nothing, there is nothing, but at least I can do this. And this same *it* is what makes Percy an all-time great Catholic artist. He beats them to the punch, he, our Virgil-like guide emerging out of the dark wood of modernity now post-modernity, he takes us there before they or we ourselves do; to warn us. Are we heeding the warning? Do we even perceive the ever-present danger around us? What are you going to do about it, now that you know?

Binx is surely down in the dumps and about to be down for the count. But then, because the book is not yet fully over, and perhaps like those beautiful deathbed conversions where decades of sin are melted by an instant flash of grace induced repentance, Binx has a moment. Maybe now he will be able to finally begin

---

21   Percy, *The Moviegoer,* 228.

the search, at last quit all his depressed idleness and start the journey towards redemption. For just as he is done feeling sorry for himself, done pondering the terrifying potentiality that contemporary life is so insufferable better an atomic bomb fall on us than continue on living such a horrid existence, he sees a man emerge from a Catholic church across the street, ashes fresh on his forehead, and realizes that today, this day, is Ash Wednesday.

> I watch him closely in the rear-view mirror. It is impossible to say why he is here. Is it part and parcel of the complex business of coming up in the world? Or is it because he believes God himself is present here at the corner of Elysian Fields and Bons Enfants? Or is he here for both reasons: through some dazzling trick of grace, coming for one and receiving the other as God's own importunate bonus? It is impossible to say.[22]

The word importunate means "persistent to the point of annoyance." You want to write good Catholic fiction, be good Catholic artists? Be importunate yourselves, showing sin in all its awful reality, indefatigably, showing the disaster and self-destruction of men and women who try to make their own earthly utopias without God. Be annoying about it, bring your readers to see these same men and women reduced to nothing, ready for the bomb to fall on them rather than continue on as they have only to, at the last possible moment, stumbling into safe harbors, finally back home where they belong by, and in, God's importunate grace.

---

22   Percy, *The Moviegoer*, 235.

Faith & Athletics

CHASING IMPOSSIBLE PERFECTION AS PREPARATION FOR THE ONLY PERFECTION THAT MATTERS[1]

THE IDAHO VANDALS ARE NOT GOOD AT football. So say the ignorant anyways, those who claim that while yes, needles are sometimes found in the haystack, broken clocks are right twice a day, even a blind squirrel, well, you get the point. The triumphant moments of the 2009 Humanitarian Bowl victory over Bowling Green, or the halcyon days of the 1990s—with the Vandals reaching the #1 national ranking for Division I-AA in October 1993 and winning the "Battle of the Palouse" against the Washington State Cougars in back to back years at the end of the decade—have, unfortunately, often come too far and few between, buried in a twice burnt over dumpster fire of failure punctuated by three consecutive one win seasons between 2012–2014, with scores such as 66–0, 56–6, and 79–7 all too painfully common. When the Vandals were demoted back to the b-level of Division I following the 2017 season and still lose 24–0 to their FCS compatriots, as was the case this past Saturday in Portland, one is tempted to conclude: the Idaho Vandals are simply not good at football.

Alas, I'm here to tell you a different story, a different story about Vandal football and a different story about the relationship between Catholicism and athletics[2], to talk about point of view, something I call "dual perspective point zero appreciation." If you're thinking I chose this name for its extreme pretension and an ambiguity that might get mistaken for genius by some

---

1   This article was published in August 2022 on the *Dappled Things Blog as a guest post.*

2   Please note that the words "athletics" and "sports" are used interchangeably within this essay.

non-geniuses, you're right. (At least I didn't make an acronym out of it though; DuPPZA; sounds too close to the Polish word *dupa* anyways). But what does it mean? Focus on "point zero," the active ingredient differentiating the dual perspectives leading to the hoped appreciation. St. Francis of Assisi is the beau ideal of point zero appreciation, what can be called full dependence on God, realization that even our next breath is a gift not a guarantee. St. Francis could truly appreciate the radical beauty of all of God's creation by assuming this point zero stance, aware that when one considers that even the most mundane realities come from the hand of the Divine Designer how new and lovely they appear.

Fine, "dual perspective," but what's then the opposite of point zero? A "point one-hundred" perspective would be unrealistic expectations, petulance, seeing life not as gift but flawed burden because things are supposed to be perfect, all the time, but they happen not to be; starting at and demanding the utmost best all the time, entitlement, pure and simple. A 100 point perspective is why people conclude the Idaho Vandals are not good at football. How dare they not win ten games every season, not win every game? The 100 point perspective expecting everything to be good all the time and immediately is why some, including Mother Teresa, have concluded that the depressed and hyper-medicated Western World's number one emotion is disappointment.[3] But apply point zero appreciation to the Vandals and maybe you'll be able to enjoy each game for the gift it is, independent of the score, and appreciate the players themselves for who they really are, phenomenal athletes, who, in making it to Division I are playing on the third best level in the world, behind only the NFL and CFL (my sincere apologies, Arena football fans) and what a truly remarkable accomplishment that is.

I want to challenge all types of 100 point perspectives concerning athletics in this talk simply because we live in such a sports-obsessed culture. Yet please note, this talk is not about how sports build the values of teamwork and camaraderie; not about how sports help you deal with the ups and downs, the "wins and

---

3 Walker Percy, *Lost in the Cosmos* (New York: FSG, 1983), 19, 80.

losses," of life; not about how sports keep kids away from drugs and bad decisions; not about how exercise is good for your health. It is neither a jeremiad against the sad state of America where sports have become a pseudoreligion taking up the time owed to God on Sunday mornings nor a polemic against a financial reality where teachers and bakers and candlestick makers struggle to make ends meet while the guy wearing a costume carrying an inflated pigskin who can outrun other costume wearing men trying to tackle him to the ground makes enough money to buy a few personal airplanes, summer homes in Europe, and a yacht.

No, this talk about athletics and faith is something truly original, something brand new, never heard of before tonight. Well, actually, Saint Paul kind of said it 2,000 years ago. "Do you not know that the runners in the stadium all run in the race, but only one wins the prize? Run so as to win. Every athlete exercises discipline in every way. They do it to win a perishable crown, but we an imperishable one."[4] My talk tonight is subtitled: *chasing impossible perfection as preparation for the only perfection that matters.* Extrapolating from this and the above scriptural passage it's obvious I'm arguing that athletics give one the tools necessary for ultimate victory in the spiritual realm. Okay, and true. But even further, I believe athletics, and really athletic training, is *uniquely* effective in assisting us Catholics in life's only goal: becoming spiritual athletes for Christ and His Kingdom.

Why uniquely, why more so, than other things? Because the times we live in today are plagued by many maladies, chief among them relativism, disdain for tradition, and an aversion to suffering. To become saints we must conquer these three. We must become convinced of the absolute Truth concerning who Christ is, who the Church, His Mystical Bride, is, and how we are therefore to live, and relativism just won't do. Neither can we advance in the spiritual life if we disdain all that came before us, if we stand aloof from the treasure trove of wisdom in our capital T tradition, our sacred Deposit of Faith. And, of course, what more can be said concerning suffering than from the lips of the Master himself.

---

4 1 Corinthians 9:24–25.

"Whoever wishes to come after me must deny himself, take up his cross, and follow me."[5]

Athletics are an excellent means for combatting relativism, disdain for tradition, and an aversion to suffering. Let's investigate these three in order. A lot of fields square nicely with relativism. If there are no objective standards to art and poetry today one may indeed rise to the top of his profession undeservedly, faking his way there, and should criticism come he can always respond, "well, that's your truth. And what is truth, anyways? Some collector paid me $20 million for the painting you're claiming is nonsense. Looks like I am a genius after all." But tell someone you can dunk a basketball and then it turns out you cannot dunk a basketball the response "well, it's your truth that I can't dunk, I believe I can" is immediately and unquenchably burned like chaff in the face of a cold, hard, and scientifically measurable reality. You can throw a football 60 yards in the air, or you cannot; your team either won the game or they lost the game. Sports often clearly presents life's ultimate black and white realities, *within the confines of a game,* that we lack in our gray, lukewarm *real life experience.* Would that we could apply the lessons learned in the "virtual reality" of the sporting arena to our daily existence.

Any athlete who has ever attempted to become a serious athlete, to become at least half-good in the sport of their choice, knows you cannot become even a little bit good without embracing the time-tested techniques and methods of the masters who proceeded you. Ever seen an Olympic lifter with bad technique? Ever seen an elite marathoner who ran with her arms flailing about wildly, one who didn't understand each and every mechanical tick for shaving off even a few seconds over the 26-mile course? Why do all major league pitchers and hitters arrive at the identical power position before throwing or swinging, regardless of the unique personal set-up beforehand? Is it because all world-class athletes are unimaginative conformists, or worse, communists, bent on stamping out individual expression at every turn? Or, is it because they value the timeless truths of tradition, of the

---

5   Matthew 16:24.

so-called "right way" to do something, knowing novelties and fads will only hurt their performance, and this after wasting their time first?

To speak again on suffering is to, once again, speak briefly. Anyone who honestly doesn't think that becoming an Olympic athlete or an NFL player or an Alpine Ski World Cup class skier or a PGA Tour golfer—and, I know, golf; is it a sport, is it not?—is extremely demanding and involves daily physical, emotional, and psychological suffering in the form of intense workouts and constantly saying no, to various foods, social experiences, and even sleep schedules, should be accused not simply of misunderstanding sports but life itself. Athletics are indeed an excellent school for overcoming relativism with absolute realities, overcoming disdain for tradition with reverence for the right way to do something, and evolving from a position of once seeing suffering as an uncomfortable obstacle to understanding it as the only path to true happiness and authentic success. And the whole point is this: wouldn't it be splendid if the tens of millions of young athletes in America who learned these lessons applied them to the higher things of life? Wouldn't it be great if young athletes understood that the absolutism, traditionalism, and suffering character of their preferred disciplines were but a faint intimation of these holy values as they pertain to the Faith, to the spiritual realities around which hang the questions of their eternal salvation?

The Catholic Church has produced ample commentary supporting the lofty ideal of sports as a way to glorify God and cultivate the necessary discipline so as to advance towards holiness and sainthood. No shortage, unlike us here, tonight, short on time, and so if you'll allow to me cite examples solely from one source—the late and beloved pontiff St. John Paul the Great, avid lover of, and commentator on, sports—I hope it might serve as an invitation for you to dive deeper into a consideration of this perennially fascinating topic.

Athletics, John Paul told his audience during the 2000 Jubilee of Sports People, "is a fitting occasion to *give thanks to God for the gift of sport,* in which the human person exercises his body, intellect and will, recognizing these abilities as so many gifts of his

Creator."[6] Furthermore, the practitioner of sports is ultimately "God's true athlete," using the springboard of athletic discipline and achievement to become a "strong *athlete of Christ*, that is, a faithful and courageous witness to his Gospel. But to succeed in this, he must persevere in prayer, be trained in virtue and follow the divine Master in everything."[7]

That which John Paul II said in October of 2000, less than five years before his death, he had been saying from the earliest years of his pontificate. In May of 1979 he told soccer players in Milan that athletic competition fosters, "many spiritual goods ... offering to society the precious contribution of a healthy morality."[8] Whereas the fallen world so often finds itself torn apart by war and strife, athletes, he told an audience of water-skiers that same year, "rend the tissue of social solidarity ... bearing a luminous witness of cohesion, peace and union."[9] This because, as his talk was entitled, sport is "a school of human virtue." The Church has always been interested in sport he told the Italian Sports Federation in December 1979 because "she prizes everything that contributes constructively to the harmonious and complete development of man, body and soul."[10] "Certainly, the value of the body must be supported and pursued in respect of the hierarchy of the higher moral and spiritual values," he continued, affirming "the absolute

---

6   Pope John Paul II, "Jubilee of Sports People," October 2000. Sourced online at: http://w2.vatican.va/content/john-paul-ii/en/homilies/2000/documents/hf_jp-ii_hom_20001029_jubilee-sport.html

7   Ibid.

8   Pope John Paul II, "Address to the Doctors and Players of The Italian Soccer Team Milan," May 12, 1979 in "Blessed John Paul II Speaks to Athletes: Homilies, Messages and Speeches on Sport." Kevin Lixey, Norbert Muller, Cornelius Schafer, eds, 10.

9   Pope John Paul II, "Sport: A School of Human Virtue" Address to the 23rd Water-Skiing Championship of Europe, Africa and the Mediterranean," August 31, 1979 in "Blessed John Paul II Speaks to Athletes: Homilies, Messages and Speeches on Sport." Kevin Lixey, Norbert Muller, Cornelius Schafer, eds, 12.

10   Pope John Paul II, "Sport as Training Ground for Virtue and Instrument of Union Among People: Address to the presidents of the Italian Sports Federation," December 20, 1979 in "Blessed John Paul II Speaks to Athletes: Homilies, Messages and Speeches on Sport." Kevin Lixey, Norbert Muller, Cornelius Schafer, eds, 13–14

primacy of the spirit, of the soul, created in the likeness of God, reborn to new life by the sacrifice of Jesus Christ, the Incarnate Word, and called to the imperishable wreath, after the happy accomplishment of the earthly competition."[11]

When we think of Christianity and athletics what often comes to mind is Tim Tebow and thanking God for championships claimed; sometimes these two together. These are good things, and there are plenty of Catholic athlete exemplars around us today. Like former Major League Baseball player Mike Sweeney who now runs Catholic baseball camps for kids that include recitation of the rosary, Eucharist adoration, and confession.[12] Or current Los Angeles Chargers quarterback Phillip Rivers, a Catholic from Bible Belt Alabama who has appeared on the popular EWTN show *Life on the Rock* and who has nine children with his wife, Tiffany. Or Olympic, multiple gold medal winning gymnast Simone Biles, who always makes sure to have a rosary packed in her gym bag whenever an opportunity for prayer might arise.

Or, Father Chase Hilgenbrinck, who, prior to his ordination, was a professional soccer player in South America and reached the pinnacle of the sport in the U.S., Major League Soccer, before retiring at the apex of his career, at twenty-six years old, to follow a higher calling. One can infer the divine providence at work in Hilgenbrinck answering his vocation to the priesthood while a member of the New England Revolution. Here was a young and successful athlete thriving in Boston, the very epicenter of the clergy sex abuse scandal, and he's going to leave all the glamour behind to become a Catholic priest; now? Here?[13]

---

11   Ibid.

12   Dan Lee, "People of Faith-Mike Sweeney Steps up to the Plate for His Faith," *Northwest Catholic*, June 9, 2014.

13   Mary Rezac, "Olympic Star Simone Biles Carries a White Rosary in Her Gym Bag," *Orange County Catholic*, August 9, 2016. https://occatholic. com/olympic-star-simome-biles-carries-a-white-rosary-in-her-gym-bag/; "Life on the Rock The 3Fs Fr Mark and Br Paschal with Philip Rivers 07-14-2011," https://www.youtube.com/watch?v=xR_Vxz5nqVw; Kathy Orton, "Whatever Happened to … the pro soccer played [sic] who left to become a priest," *The Washington Post*, July 15, 2011; Nuestra Fe en Vivo—16 de julio 2012—Pepe Alonso con Chase Hilgenbrinck. https://www.youtube.com/ watch?v=ZQ3v9u1F97k

It might be fine, permissible, to end the talk here. Perhaps I've convinced you that sports are something more than scantly-clad women shilling lite beer to face-painted men with single digit IQs shouting to their ex-wife elects to bring out a new round of nachos before halftime. Perhaps I haven't convinced you and, if so, that's okay, I'm sure it's not the first time you've been wrong about something. Nonetheless, allow me to return to the earlier *point zero versus point one-hundred appreciation perspective* paradigm in a consideration of another virtue of athletics: beauty. Does not our favorite online apologist-evangelist—His Excellency the Auxiliary Bishop of Los Angeles, California, USA, Robert Barron—says that's what *it's* all about, beauty?[14]

Athletics can be a form of high art dedicated to the cultivation and display of beauty. Put me against a wall and force me to define what I believe is the singular, ultimate meaning of sports in a Catholic context and here's what I'd say: *that people will see something beautiful and good in flawed man and in turn glorify Him who is Beauty and Goodness itself.* Who doesn't see the beauty in sports? The 100 point perspective, entitled crowd who thinks the Idaho Vandals are a terrible football team. To them, sports, in their artistic essence, are banal, even boring. Good for being put to pragmatic uses, like winning a long shot bet on the Super Bowl, or as a bludgeon to crush your hated rival into the dust, or for translating 10–2 and a New Year's Day Bowl into personal, self-esteem index capital because you happen to attend *that school*; but anything more than this? No.

The Saint Francis, everything is a gift, point zero appreciative people understand the beauty in sports. They marvel at major league pitchers who can throw a baseball more than one-hundred miles per hour (that velocity covers half a football field in one second) and perhaps marvel more at opposing hitters who, but sixty feet away, have two tenths of a second to see and process the ball coming towards them before using another 0.2 seconds to attempt hitting it with a round, wooden bat. They are in awe of decathletes like 2004 Olympic gold medalist Roman Šebrle who has

---

14 "Bishop Barron on Evangelizing Through Beauty." February 19, 2013. https://www.youtube.com/watch?v=bBMOwZFpZXo

the plyometric explosiveness to jump across a two-lane highway; are amazed by the Kenyan distance runner Eliud Kipoche, the first man to clock a sub two hour marathon, and are impressed to learn an NFL quarterback must mentally process an equivalent amount of information to a wannabe medical school student studying for their MCATs. Now, I don't want to offend any doctors by implying that NFL quarterbacks have the same mental capacity as orthopedic surgeons, podiatrists and neurologists. Don't want to offend them because doctors are very important people. And if you don't believe me, ask any doctor, and they'll tell you themselves how important they are.[15]

Sports, once more and for the last time, can help a person overcome relativism, disdain for tradition, and an aversion to suffering. And in being fundamentally about beauty, sports can point us in the direction of the God who is Beauty Himself and whose creation reflects this reality even in the smallest details, available to anyone willing to see all of life as a gift from the point zero appreciation vantage point. But let's return to "against relativism" one more time and conclude with a reflection on how sports training in light of absolute, inarguable results can help one progress in the spiritual life.

Let's use the deadlift as an example. Deadlifting is a popular, and according to many, preeminently important strength training exercise. Recently a man named Cailer Woolam—who goes by the YouTube moniker "Dr. Deadlift"; I'm completely serious[16]—set the world record in this exercise for someone 225 pounds or lighter with a 950 pound lift. Weightlifting fans and experts alike believe he'll be the first such "smaller person" to deadlift one-thousand pounds, half a ton. Imagine your deadlift is two hundred twenty-five pounds; two plates on each side. That's great, good work. But knowing what a true elite deadlift is, having no relativistic misconceptions that your 225 is something special, you can grow in strength with your eyes fixed on 950 lbs. as a standard of

---

15   Reed Albergotti, "The World's Greatest Athlete?" *The Wall Street Journal.* June 20, 2008.
16   Cailer Woolam, 'Dr. Deadlift,' YouTube Channel. https://www.youtube.com/channel/UCM3hG9mDDKH-TkvkJgybwug

greatness and perhaps one day get to four, five, even six hundred pounds yourself. And if progressing from a two hundred twenty five pound deadlift to, let's say, six hundred seventy-five pounds isn't beauty and progress harmoniously synchronized, I don't know what more I can say. Nonetheless, I'll say this: maybe you're a two hundred twenty five pound deadlifter in your Catholic spirituality but mistakenly think you're really something. I challenge you to find and learn from the 950 lb. Cailer Woolam Catholics, the great men and women of our Faith tradition like John of the Cross or Teresa of Avila and, doing this, perhaps you'll triple your "spiritual deadlift" in time as well, progressing on the only path worth trodding, the path of the spiritual athlete for Christ, with happiness and holiness, now and forever, the singular goal.

Should American Catholics Demand a True Third Party Political Option?[1]

DON'T DO IT. PLEASE, DON'T EVEN TRY it. Don't even think about thinking about trying it. It won't work, it can't work, no one wants a third party and certainly not a religious, let alone Catholic, political entity. Better toe the two-party line, choose the lesser of two evils, and pretend like that D or that R actually represent the RCC values that frame your everyday existence. ~~Because~~ it's about pragmatism, right? Put aside your pie in the sky utopianism, stop trying to actually change the world, stop attempting to resurrect all that "prejudiced," "hateful," "bigoted" Christendom of years gone by; it's gone, long gone, okay? The funny thing is, it seems the same people who want you to never inject Catholic values into our comedy of errors cesspool political system also want you to stop having children, eat bugs not beef, worship the environment, and live atomized, dying of loneliness in a "pod" in San Francisco paying some Silicon Valley oligarch $2,000 per month to rent the spandrel beneath the stairs.

But is politics really only about compromise, about settling, selling out a better option for the lowest common denominator palatable to all? That's not what Aristotle said about the polis. "Every State is a community of some kind, and every community is established with a view to some good ... But, if all communities aim at some good, the state or political community, which is the highest of all, and which embraces all the rest, aims at good in a greater degree than any other, and at the highest

---

1   This article was published in the March 2022 issue of *Catholic Journal.* "Should American Catholics Demand a True Third Party Political Option?" *Catholic Journal,* March, 2022.

good."[2] Is that what Saint Augustine had in mind when he claimed that a healthy, unified and prosperous society could only function via a "transcendent principle," namely God's law and the Catholic faith?[3] What did Pope St. Pius X mean, in his 1906 encyclical *Vehementer Nos*, written in direct response to the 1905 French law mandating a strict separation of Church and State, when he said, "That the State must be separated from the Church is a thesis absolutely false, a most pernicious error. Based, as it is, on the principle that the State must not recognize any religious cult, it is in the first place guilty of a great injustice to God; for the Creator of man is also the Founder of human societies, and preserves their existence as He preserves our own. We owe Him, therefore, not only a private cult, but a public and social worship to honor Him."[4]

Secular society—not to mention the innate hardwiring of Thomas Jefferson's 1802 letter to the Danbury Baptists into our American sensibilities, wherein the president translated the First Amendment's prohibition on the establishment of an official state religion to mean "a wall of separation between Church & State,"[5]—tells us politics and religion should and must be kept apart, that one only poisons the other, and the gulf of separation is so wide one soon thinks such ironclad presuppositions find their identical twin in the juvenile if not infantile "debates" concerning faith and science; that since faith and reason are supposed mortal arch-enemies, and one must keep them apart and choose sides, the only two acceptable exit points become ether claiming that dinosaurs are a conspiracy theory and the world is six thousand years old or that intelligent life evolved on the backs of "clay crystals"[6] or even though something cannot come from nothing,

---

2   Aristotle, "The Polis," from *Politics*. Internet Ancient History Sourcebook, Fordham University. Sourced at: https://sourcebooks.fordham.edu/ancient/Aristotle-politics-polis.asp

3   St. Augustine, *City of God* (New York: Doubleday, 1958), 34–35.

4   Pope Pius X, Encyclical Letter *Vehementer Nos*, On the French Law of Separation, February 11, 1906.

5   Thomas Jefferson, "Letter to the Danbury Baptists." January 1, 1802, Library of Congress. https://www.loc.gov/loc/lcib/9806/danpre.html

6   Martha Henriques, "The idea that life began as Clay Crystals is 50 years old." BBC, August 24, 2016.

it did, you know, just this one time; infinite regresses be damned, it's turtles all the way down, brother.

If you think believing in a few millennia old Earth, maybe a flat one ringed round by an Antarctic ice shelf separating We the People from Atlantis, or First Cause Crystals is absurd, well, that's basically our American political system today from the Catholic point of view. Recall a few minutes back what three people—two Catholics and an antiquarian philosopher—had to say concerning a "Catholic outlook" towards politics. To summarize: (1) the separation of Church and State is a direct assault on Catholic social theory and an offense to God's created order; (2) not only are religious values helpful to a society's wellbeing, they are essential to it; (3) far from being the domain of swamp-dwelling, duplicitous, dishonest and corrupt politicians seeking personal gain above all, and far from the place where compromise and capitulation are the watchwords for getting anything done, the political community, in its ideal manifestation, is the highest social good. Logos-soaked Greek political philosophy, Catholic theology, and, I dare say, common sense, offer us loaves of bread. Our two party system offers us snakes.

List me the three best qualities of the Democratic Party and I'll retort that it is an organization that doesn't just lack respect for the family but often actively seeks to destroy it, seeks to immediately squash any so called "traditional values" without the slightest reflection or nuance, supports socialist leaning if not outright communist money grabbing schemes based on interpersonal jealously and hatred, and is a party whose members must promote the pro-abortion line without the slightest dissent.

List me the three best qualities of the Republican Party and I'll retort that it is an entity that while usually defending the unborn—and praise God for that, that's no small thing—often has outright contempt for the living, too often sending young men and women to bleed on foreign sands for oil or obscure geopolitical schemas and who employ "capitalism" as code for usury and exploitive economics that place the American youth in the aforementioned two-grand a month water closet pods eating bugs and despairing for the future. One can imagine some conservative senator mounting a passionate defense arguing that the Second Amendment allows private citizens to own bazookas, inter-continental ballistic missiles, and fabricate DIY hydrogen bombs in one's backyard fallout shelter, you know, the one where you keep all your hard currency and gold bullion stored in empty Cougar Gold cheese tins.

Now, wait a second though, just relax, you very American, stars and stripes latticed apple pie American Catholics. Am I suggesting a Catholic theocracy? No, I am not suggesting a Catholic theocracy for America.

Taylor Marshall, in a 2012 article entitled "If America were a fully Catholic country, here is what it might look like…," imagines a presidential inauguration taking place within the Shrine of the Immaculate Conception, the anniversary of Roe v. Wade a "perennial day of penance," Holy Days of Obligation being federal holidays, crucifixes and the Ten Commandments prominently displayed in courtrooms, and the Blessed Mother's image emblazoned on both the national seal and legal tender of the land.[7]

As a practicing Catholic, I find no theoretical fault with the above suggestions. As a practicing Catholic happy to live in a country where he is free to practice his faith, and who prefers not to invite new Diocletian-style Christian persecutions like those that rocked the Church in the 4th century A. D. right up to Constantine's *in hoc signo vinces* revelation at Milvian Bridge, I find Dr. Marshall's theocratic speculations problematic. Because let's be clear, that's precisely the blueprint he's giving us, not an America guided by slyly disseminated Catholic values, as was the realty in immediate post-war America, a nightmare for the old guard WASP ruling class who viewed with dread growing Catholic demographic power[8] being coupled to old-fashioned

---

7   Taylor Marshall, "If America were a fully Catholic country, here is what it might look like…." https://taylormarshall.com/2012/03/if-america-were-fully-catholic-country.html

8   If you don't yet understand the push for contraception legalization and dissemination as the tip of the spear to smash Catholic demographic growth, to convince Catholics to undermine their own fertility and large families—and to undermine in such a disarming way, by promoting "choice" and "freedom" and me being "in charge" of "my life," for this is freedom,

evangelical genius, perhaps best exemplified in Bishop Fulton Sheen winning two Emmy awards for his program *Life is Worth Living*[9], which did to the multitude of his Episcopalian, Presbyterian, Methodist, and Baptist viewership what Alexander Fleming found penicillin did to bacteria: apply this here, problem solved, no more Protestantism.

There and then one could see the tender shoot of a fully Catholic America growing up out of previously dry ground, trying to break through sidewalk cracks in our concrete jungle of pluralism, accommodation and compromise. Alas, this *élan* fizzled out. Far too many Catholics, on both the institutional and individual level, allowed Protestants and secularists to water down the frothy espresso of Catholic traditionalism—the Gothic architecture, the Gregorian chants, the Latin, sweet honey basting the eardrums Latin—until one could hardly call it "coffee" anymore. A sad story, sure, but that Fulton Sheen methodology, non-coercive appeals to the American mind and soul with all the multifaceted beauty and rationality of the Catholic faith, was a good attempt to create the "authentically Catholic" America Marshall pines for. Who knows? Maybe had enough Americans become good and practicing Catholics our political landscape would look different, maybe not. What I do know is that in your face theocracies seem more of an invitation to violent backlash than genuine societal conversion.

American freedom and the American dream, less and then lesser kids so I can have more and more time to myself to sit out in my shop tinkering while the very people whose time to rule had been eclipsed by the most tranquil and natural transition of power, more people being born then bred to be proud Americans and proud Catholics, maybe even some of them intellectually equipped to make America more Catholic in the most beneficially *catholic,* i.e., universal, way for all Americans, Catholics or not, well, these people have retained power, and good for them, convincing us to be less like us and more like them; that Paul VI and his *Humanae Vitae,* what a bunch of . . . what a mean, mean, man! Telling us what to do with our freedoms and whatnot, like he speaks for Jesus or something—for many Catholics in the crib would later on mean many Catholics at the ballot box then in the seats of power, contraception *the singular* issue of the sexual revolution for it was and is the hinge upon which turns the "meaning of sexuality," then you, if you do not understand or want to attempt to understand this, then you understand nothing, nothing whatsoever.

9   "Life is Worth Living," Bishop Fulton J. Sheen (All Episodes on YouTube).

Therefore, no, once again, I am not suggesting anything resembling a Catholic, over even a cross-confessional Christian, theocracy. But, yes, to finally answer this essay's foundational question, yes, Catholics in America should demand a legitimate third party option that actually reflects the values they hold dear. And just what might this look like? First, the non-coercive principal. The Catholic truth, the truth about God and man, must be proposed in love, never jammed down throats or delivered in firm smacks atop the head. St. Thomas More said this in his seminal work, *Utopia*. St. John Paul II counseled professing and proposing the truth in love. Strong enough though these recommendations may be, it is God Himself who shows us the non-coercive principle right at the beginning in the Garden of Eden. God respects our free will. He clearly explains what is good and what is evil, he commands following the good and avoiding evil, he makes clear the stark consequences of following evil, but then, in his divine love and goodness, allows his creatures to act freely.[10]

This third option must be constructed upon a platform in accord with Catholic principles and morality, and explained in clear and unambiguous language, then dropped off at the doorstep of American democracy. You don't like these values, this platform, don't vote for it; like it, vote for it. But if power is attained here, it would be done the proper way, neither through some military fatigues coup nor lesser devious methods, but at the ballot box. Okay, but then what, exactly, would this platform look like?

Let's keep it as simple as possible. Catholic social teaching, both the dual umbrella values of solidarity and subsidiarity, meaning, respectively, advocacy for the common good flowing from the only unifying equality in existence, being made in the image and likeness of God, and, secondly, keeping it mind that that which can be done at the local level should be, so as to avoid a bloated and bureaucratic central leviathan in favor of decentralized modes of governance. For more specific guideposts, consider the following seven, more finely focused, planks of Catholic social teaching—

---

10   Sanford Kessler, "Religious Freedom in Thomas More's 'Utopia,'" *The Review of Politics*, Vol 64. No. 2 (Spring 2002), 207–229; John Paul II, *Veritatis Splendor* (1993), No. 110; Genesis 3:3

1. The life and dignity of the human person
2. Call to family, community, and participation
3. Rights and responsibilities
4. The preferential option for the poor
5. The dignity of work and the rights of workers
6. Solidarity
7. Care for God's creation

— and how an authentically Catholic third party option might implement them, why these ideas would offend both Democrats and Republicans, and why that is a good thing. Only by presenting a non-binary, third way would anyone in either the D or R, left or right, camp be tempted, more hopefully persuaded, to join this new movement.

First, *the life and dignity of the human person*: an unabashed commitment to life in the womb (no abortion), at death (no euthanasia), and in between; yes to the "seamless garment," as such perhaps this party would follow John Paul II's recommendation to oppose the death penalty, a recommendation which many Republicans would denounce, while, in this organic life ethic first rung would belong to pro-life advocacy, nothing being more important than defending the unborn, and, simultaneously, advocating for the family, one based on sacramentally unitive/procreative marriage, as society's integral and foundational unit, always be to prioritized over any and all state actors trying to "re-educate our children" according to the latest fad. If you don't understand why those things would anger your run of the mill Democrat, you don't understand current American politics. To continue further on this path, perhaps convince enough of the Protestants who would be in this party coalition (more on that soon) to join practicing Catholics in actually taking *Humanae Vitae* seriously, of seeing in contraception the root of so much sexual disorder today, as just commented upon a few lines ago below in the footnotes, and just watch heads on the right and left pop off, sky high, at the brazen, no, intolerant, no, insane suggestion of trying to return to the "dark ages" of pre-1965 America, pre-Griswold v. Connecticut, the Supreme Court decision that opened access to contraceptives, if not to the pre-1930 Anglican Lambeth Conference world before which every Christian on earth, at least theoretically and theologically, opposed contraception.[11]

Second, the *call to family, community, and participation*: just focus on the first word here, family, and see how easy it is to drive the left and right away. Family, I can imagine a Democrat asking, your party wants to encourage men and women to have larger families? Are you a fascist? You want to enslave women in the home? Give them medals for having kids like Mussolini did?[12] Don't you know how irresponsible having kids today is? Look, abortion and forced sterilization initiatives are good, responsible reproductive health at its finest, because it's helping save the planet, we're going to be running out of resources and practicing cannibalism soon, don't you know? Die so the planet can live! Tell a Republican a secondary idea to encouraging larger families that will avoid demographic winters and replenish the coming generation's economic output potential, ides he likes, is state-subsidized childcare, so Catholic mothers having these three, four, five kids can continue on with the jobs they like and are good at, and see how fast he starts agreeing with his Democratic opponent that maybe one or no kids isn't such a bad idea, not if we're going to be implementing "communist" policies like free childcare.

Thirdly, *rights and responsibilities,* can be seen as an excellent connector between that which comes before, namely the fundamental right to life and the upholding of human dignity and the family, and that which comes after. Because when else in American history has there been such a blatant disregard, and contemptuous ignorance, for a citizen's rights and responsibilities as today? Such as the fourth plank, the *preferential option for the poor*. You're

---

11 Pope Paul VI, Encyclical Letter *Humanae Vitae,* July 25, 1968; Estelle T. Griswold et al. Appellants, v. STATE OF CONNECTICUT (1965) https://www.law.cornell.edu/supremecourt/text/381/479; The Lambeth Conference, Resolutions Archive from 1930, *Index of Resolutions from 1930,* Anglican Communion Office, Anglican Consultative Council (2005), http://www.anglican-communion.org/media/127734/1930.pdf?year=1930

12 No author listed. "WW2 Italian Fascist Mothers Medal." https://www.armymuseum.co.nz/artefact-of-the-month-ww2-italian-fascist-mothers-medal/#:~:text=The%20World%20War%20II%20Italian,every%20extra%20child%20she%20had.

saying maybe after we've won the pro-life fight and encouraged more and more single mothers, or crisis pregnancy mothers, to have their children we might, as this most perfect Aristotelian collective community, really help them provide for their family until they can do it for themselves? Well, a Republican might say, depends what you mean; you talking about welfare?; more commy, big Daddy state-help nonsense?

And see what the Democrat thinks when you tell him that preferential option for the poor does not mean stirring up hatred of the rich for revolutionary gains, or enacting insane taxes on the rich that amounts to little more than stealing the fruits of their labor, and therefore hamstringing any initiative for our best and brightest to keep pushing forward, nor does this plan entail giving people money for nothing, legalizing every drug—because if you can't actually help the poor you can anesthetize them—nor, finally, is it aimed at anything else than helping people while they need help until they can help themselves. Because those who work hard and receive a due reward,[13] who see plans imagined become goals realized, live with an inherent dignity no one can take away.

To conclude, numbers five, six, and seven are, respectively, the dignity of work and the rights of workers, solidarity, and care for God's creation. I'll skip over number six, solidarity, because I spoke of that theme's importance above, of its umbrella, overall foundational significance in Catholic social ethics alongside the principle of subsidiarity. So regarding number five, *the dignity of work and the rights of workers,* see what happens when you tell both parties no, no you cannot lure poor men and women from foreign lands with empty promises dipped in fake compassion to make them scrub your Beverly Hills pool bottoms and pick fruits and vegetables in the scorching Central Valley sun for a fraction of minimum wage and no statutory protections, by the way, and that's the whole sinister point, by the way, so as to better boot them out without a moment's notice when the time arrives. I'm a huge fan of immigration. Cliché though it may be, we are a nation of immigrants, and our Blessed Lord Himself makes clear what the

---

13 The last words of the Book of Sirach (51:30): "Work at your tasks in due season, and in his own time God will give you your reward."

penalty for not "welcoming the stranger is" in that apocalyptic "Judgment of the Nations" section in Matthew 25.[14]

But try to explain to a Democrat that you're all for reasonable and legal immigration that actually puts the immigrant first and see how far you get, especially when you have the gall to suggest Americans should have first crack at American jobs. Oh, I see, you're one of those MAGA hat, America First, hyper-nationalist racists. See how far you get telling a Republican that a CEO making hundreds, even thousands, times more than his workers doesn't square so well with the common good. That "well, that's capitalism" is not an adequate act of contrition to expiate the manifold sins of avarice in you, Mr. CEO, having two, six, eleven jets and yachts while some of your workers live in squalid, slum like conditions having to practically beg for their daily bread. See how long Republicans put up with your advocacy for unions, or how long Democrats tolerate the claim that "rights of workers" might protect workers' freedom of conscience, too.

Finally, an authentic praxis surrounding *care for God's creation* would please neither liberals nor conservatives, not even the tree-hugging, granola crunching, let's go barefoot everywhere, whale venerating, Green Party. For this third party option would say to the right: every piece of untouched American soil is not an oil field that just doesn't know it yet. Protected wilderness, being shielded especially from questions of profit and development, is an intrinsically good, and quintessentially American, thing, and seeking alternative sources to pollutants like coal does not mean selling out middle America. It really just might be about cleaner air and water, and who doesn't want that?

This party would likewise say to the left and the Greens: no, we are not going to make environmentalism the new religion, not going to blindly follow the updated and repackaged Paul Ehrlich *Population Bomb*[15] doomsday proclamations of Extinction Rebellion or Mademoiselle Green New Deal AOC who tell us we have twelve years—or is it twelve weeks, twelve days, twelve minutes, twelve seconds?—before climate change destroys life as we know it and

---

14   Matthew 25:31–46.
15   Paul Ehrlich, *The Population Bomb* (New York: Ballantine Books, 1968).

we're scrounging for scraps in a dystopian wasteland devoid of potable water and hope. Or, perhaps climate change means a new ice age[16]; a melt age?; tons and tons of snow in east Alabama?; no winters in Iceland? Look, whatever actually happens just know *it's happening,* so stop flying planes and driving cars, but please ignore that we, the leaders of this movement, take carbon-bomb international flights like they're going out of style, it's okay, we're only doing it to warn humanity, and, above all, fork over every last possible human and political and social right to us, this globalist elite, because, you know, it's for your own good. Plus, if you don't, the sun is going to boomerang crash off Jupiter before both slam into the earth and make things, uh, not good. I'm only telling you what *the science*™ says.

Before we conclude and you conclude that a return to that beginning is called for—don't do it; third party, no; Catholic, Christian party, please, no—consider two things.

a. This hypothetical third party is not a "Catholic party."

Yes, yes, yes again, a hoped home for American Catholics for sure, and a party openly and unabashedly driven by Catholic principles, but a party open to all men and women willing to attempt to put this blueprint into action. There is bad ecumenism. I don't want Lutherans advising Catholics on church architecture (on second thought, I mean, looking at the post Vatican II Catholic churchscape…) and I don't think Mormons or Mennonites should be leading lights in the New Evangelization. But having Mormons and Mennonites along with all and every sort of Protestant denomination, even non-believers like the group "Secular Pro-Life"[17] as part of the above third-party experiment? That's the whole point. This is good ecumenism, putting aside confessional differences to work in tandem to create a better society by way of promoting better values.

---

16   Peter Gwynne, "The Cooling World," *Newsweek,* April 28, 1975. Gwynne's later on clarification/regret regarding this can be found here: Jack El-Hai, "In 1975, *Newsweek* Predicted a New Ice Age. We're still living with the Consequences," *Longreads,* April 2017. https://longreads.com/2017/04/13/in-1975-newsweek-predicted-a-new-ice-age-were-still-living-with-the-consequences/
17   Secular Pro-Life, Website. https://www.secularprolife.org

And before you once again say "no, it just wouldn't work" consider point

b. Demographics is power.

Christians represent nearly three-fourths, seventy-five percent, of the total U. S. population. I'm not suggesting implementing a Catholic social teaching, Christian Democratic party in a country predominantly Muslim, Hindu, or Buddhist; agreed, not going to work. But in America, of the three hundred and twenty-something million general population, almost two-hundred and fifty million come from some Christian background, a massive bloc where, perhaps just enough of a portion could be persuaded to take a chance on a third way, of taking a fresh look at what is, and how we can arrive at, a politics of the common good.

Frozen Music

HOW THE ARCHITECTURE WE BUILD EXPLAINS WHAT WE BELIEVE[1]

"I LOOK AT A LOT OF BUILDINGS AND CONsider them ugly. Most of them, in fact," Frank Gehry, one of modern America's most famous architects, opined in 1999, "so I figure this one building isn't going to wreck Seattle." *This one building* was his Paul Allen funded MoPOP, the Museum of Pop Culture, a place formerly known as the Experience Music Project, or, more precisely still, the Experience Music Project and Science Fiction Museum and Hall of Fame; that acronym's EMP-SFM, by the way. Maybe all the letters are there to distract you from this structure being arguably the ugliest building ever built. Maybe you've seen it before, it's not hard to find, close to the Space Needle and Key Arena, former home of the NBA's Supersonics. While Gehry claimed the melting in on itself metallic brown, red, and pink-silver structure was meant to resemble a "smashed electric guitar" others compared it to a "blob," "hemorrhoids," or that it looked like "something that had crawled out of the sea, rolled over, and died." Perhaps it's fitting that the MoPOP collaborates on an annual Science Fiction and Fantasy Short Film Festival with the Seattle International Film Festival whose own SIFF acronym sounds like a venereal disease well complementing the hemorrhoid afflicted Experience Music Project. Or, just maybe, it's a warning. They're being helpful, telling us to avoid post-modernity at all costs, stay away if you don't want to catch some nasty STIs of the mind and soul rendering whatever intrinsic artistic talent you possess immediately and irrevocably sterile.[2]

---

1   This article was published in the June 2022 issue of *Catholic Journal.* "Frozen Music: How Architecture Explains What We Believe."
2   Devin Alesso, "These are the Ten Ugliest Buildings in the World." *Elle Décor.* September 16, 2016. https://www.elledecor.com/celebrity-style/

Is that really the standard today? *It's not going to wreck Seattle.* Not, how beautiful can it be?; how can we convey this or that important message?; but, rather, in effect, *yeah, we know this is awful but not awful enough to mess up the entire cityscape. Right? Okay. Good enough for me, fellas. Let's build it.* The implications of Gehry's statement are:

my building is unbelievably ugly but

so is Seattle and

so is the entirety of our depressed, meaningless state of being and, so,

Seattle's citizens will surely offer little resistance because

d.1 they're idiots who don't know better or
d.2 they're stoned 24/7 so they don't know what's good or bad, up or down anyways or,
d.3 they're that special type of contemporary art critic who likes something all the more the more obscure, senseless, repulsive it is;   but, if d.3,

then this is only a return to

d.1 we designers think they're idiots, so,

e. build it.

If there's one thing true about buildings, about anything in the built environment, it is the concept of "frozen music." What we believe gets put into what we build and, conversely, one can extrapolate our beliefs from our buildings. There are no neutral buildings. All of them are signposts and symbols, meaning something or pointing to meaning elsewhere. And the interesting thing about the placement of Gehry's design is that it is in a very beautiful spot in one of the most beautiful cities in America. The Queen Anne neighborhood has a lot of what many would claim

luxury-real-estate/g3276/carbuncle-cup/; Erica C. Barnett, "EMPty: The Experience Music Project is a flop on all fronts—financial, musical, and intellectual." *The Stranger,* June 17, 2004; Lawrence W. Cheek, "On Architecture: Corrugated Steel is Nice Wrinkle," *Seattle Post-Intelligencer,* September 26, 2006; Jonathan Raban, "Deference to Nature keeps Seattle from becoming World-Class City," *The Seattle Times,* April 4, 2004.

is having it all, not just the Seattle Center and its component parts—McCaw Hall and the Seattle Repertory Theatre of first rate note—but turn of the century houses tucked in snug one next to another, burrowed into the elevated sides of sloping grades, markets and coffee aplenty, five minutes to Elliot Bay, and Kerry Park from which one can look back down into the Space Needle dominated skyline and out unto Mount Rainer beyond, framing the distant horizon in a picture perfect stereotype of come here, see this, snap the photo.

All of these realities, on the neighborhood and individual structure level, tell us a story, construct for us a picture of values and of value itself. This is why architecture is so important and why Gehry's seemingly intentionally ugly creation is more troubling than humorous. What is he, via his building, saying about the values contemporary Americans hold? Are such buildings actually built so as to poison our minds and hearts, to corrupt us intentionally? Is there are an f. component past the *e. build it* which might read:

f. and so we'll finally kill off the stupid fantasies about transcendent beauty, meaning and purpose. Just give'em nasty buildings and they'll become nasty themselves, vulgar, stupid, addicted to everything, exactly the kind of mindless wage sex slave robots we want to keep our wallets fat and our gnawing consciences at bay.

Yes?
No?
What if the question is refocused?
What if the obvious architectural malaise we've been suffering under for the past fifty, sixty, even one hundred years, perhaps dating back to the Great War era, is really a product of something larger? What if it's the age-old yet ever changing, in vicissitudes and vehicles employed, foundational and fundamentally simple choice between logos and chaos? The one and same question our first parents confronted in the Garden of Eden. Either Logos, order, and rational harmony within God's divine design or the haphazard mess and subjective missing of the mark, every mark, for the goal's existence is itself called into question when following our self-designed chaotic call to be like gods ourselves, knowing

what is good and evil. Christ, Logos; not Christ, chaos; peace and prosperity via logical restraint, penniless paupery, material and moral, when letting all those lower appetites loose over our communities, canvases, cityscapes, and churches.

Churches, especially. One can look around the post-Vatican II American churchscape and *hear* composed in stone and steel—frozen music, remember—chaotic anti-values of disbelief, an absent God not present in an imaginary heaven, empty pews, organ-less choirs unable to send unwritten, unsung notes upwards to the God not there for the flat roofs aggressively horizontal in their complete disdain for the vertical dimension are but ten feet above us. They're blank, the walls, the ceilings, the churches. They're blank like our minds, our hearts, our souls. Many of our churches and buildings today are ugly and ugliness in sacred space is the most appalling ugliness of all.

But it's really all around us, everywhere. And indeed, we need less structures like the J. Edgar Hoover FBI headquarters which the American Institute of Architects described as a "swaggering bully of the neighborhood . . . Ungainly and ill-mannered"; less of the Morris A. Mechanic Theatre in Baltimore, thankfully demolished after more than a decade of abandonment, which looked like a five year old slapped it together from collapsed *Jenga* blocks and pieces of cardboard; less buildings like the Aoyama Technical College in Tokyo, at first glance resembling a Transformer robot being eaten by a metallic arachnid, described as representing "a new order, not achieved through simplistic control from above, but through tolerance of chaos."[3]

They're not even being sly anymore. *Ah, no, ma'am, you see there is a kind of beauty here, it just might be hard to see at first;* that's at least trying. Now they just come right out with it. Tolerance for chaos? No. No tolerance for chaos, not if we ultimately care about our centers of worship, our houses of God, the very places men and women come to the fork in the road, come to take in the frozen music about them that will, in mutually exclusive fashion, either rise their hearts and minds into closer union with God or, too

---

3   Alesso, "These are the Ten Ugliest Buildings in the World."

often and quite tragically, drive them further and further melting away until nothing remains but a puddle of disconnected doubts. It wasn't always this way.

Take heart, I'm here to tell you something hopeful, something positive after too many minutes lamenting our current artistic state of confusion and meaninglessness. It was not always this way. People, Catholics more specifically, us, we used to compose different types of frozen music. We used to build churches whose architecture declared that God exists, that God is good and logical, that God loves you. Look and behold that stained glass, smell that incense and hear that polyphony honey-smacking the hundred-foot roof above you, pause and take it all in and know, without a single word being spoken, that God is love, God is good, God is beauty.

Know that you too are beautiful, that all of life is beautiful and but that you rest here, that you come to this place and keep God's law and trust in his divine mercy, you can someday possess a beauty beyond description for all eternity. That is what our church architecture used to tell us. And because it wasn't always the way it is now it need not be like this anymore. Even around us today there are hopeful examples that we can look to in building the more beautiful churches of our future. I'm going to speak briefly on four examples of beautiful frozen music, after which I will conclude with that which all of you have come here for: *so, what do we do then? What next?*

The first example I present to you is arguably the most famous: Notre Dame de Paris. More than four hundred feet long and half a football field wide, with ten bells, two towers and a now destroyed spire three hundred feet tall, Notre Dame was built over the course of two centuries, with the groundbreaking in 1163 to the final completion in 1345. This because people used to understand that some things, in order to be done properly, have to be done with meticulous attention to detail, without rushing, without the breakneck haste that defines our society today.[4]

---

4   The Editors of Encyclopedia Britannica, "Notre Dame de Paris." *Encyclopedia Britannica.* https://www.britannica.com/topic/Notre-Dame-de-Paris; No author listed, "Notre Dame de Paris." General Information site (in French) https://www.notredamedeparis.fr/

Maybe we can begin here. That if dioceses didn't hope the construction of a new church could be done within a year, or eight months, or eight weeks, or 3 shifts of eight hours if we want to go on those TV shows where they build a house from scratch in 24 hours, then maybe, relegating this attitude to the trash bin, we might make some progress. It is an uphill battle, one can imagine a church community going to their bishop and explaining that they have the blueprints to create a truly beautiful, authentically worthy, house of God ... and it looks like it'll take about 200 years to complete. No, no, no, we *don't do things that way anymore.* That's true; but is that good? That it is an uphill battle does not mean it is not one worth fighting.

Notre Dame de Paris was built over 200 years not just because of technological limitations or the fighting of the Crusades or any other wrench in the mix. It took that long primarily because people cared. They actually believed the faith they professed and would rather die trying to make God's house perfect than live to see the slightest imperfection. Would that we had some of that latter attitude today. Today it's about getting it done as fast as possible, period. In sacred and secular spheres alike nothing seems to matter more than the bottom line, the quickest turnarounds unto the next project, the cheapest materials, the most unjust wages, who cares? And so the built environment around us today, its frozen music so aggressively discordant and off-key, proclaims those philosophical principles precisely. You people are nothing but mammon worshipping, talent squandering, pseudoreligious imbeciles. The joke's on you, by the way, and future generations will surely condemn you thanks to us, the "monuments," you'll leave to posterity.

But it wasn't always this way. This can be easily deduced from the western façade of Notre Dame, its circular window within a square outer border verifiability living the maxim that a picture is worth a thousand words. Here is beautiful frozen music 101. The square symbolizing limited created space, the world, now holding the transcended circle representing infinity, representing God. In one glance at just one piece of this architectural marvel one comes to know exactly what this space is about: Christ's Incarnation, the infinite Word made flesh come to dwell within space and time, the circle within the square, entering the square so as to redeem it, elevate it, perfect it, perfecting us and this fallen world. And that rose window circular in its infinite reach? Rose for a reason, for the rose is the symbol of Notre Dame herself, the Blessed Mother, whose long ago fiat[5] to the angel Gabriel made it possible for the circle to dwell within the square, for the infinite God to so love the world that he could send his only begotten son into the square[6], into the very heart of our time-bound, temporal quotidian vale of tears. Right behind this striking symbol is the circle and the square theme raised to the loftiest heights. God Himself truly present in the Holy Eucharist, the circle and square on the façade an invitation to step inside this time bound sacred space to feed on the Bread of Angels, the very Infinite God's infinite gift of his body, blood, soul and divinity, just waiting for us poor sinners to repent, to turn to him, and begin to eat and drink our salvation.[7]

Now that's good architecture. But, as you know, that's but one percent of a beautiful cathedral called the *liber pauperum*—"poor people's book"—and if there's one litmus test for good church architecture it might just be this: can you build something magnificently grand and elaborate yet simultaneously readily understandable to the most rude, uneducated, and illiterate peasant, that such a person could come and read his faith in stone and so begin to trod the path towards salvation? Notre Dame de Paris is indeed a *liber pauperum,* with the Last Judgment tympanum over the central portal of the already mentioned western façade, a sculpture showing the coronation of the Blessed Mother as Queen of Heaven, another of Saint Anne, rose windows embellished with medallions, segmented into, themselves, narrative pieces from the Book of Genesis, the Gospels, the Passion and Resurrection of Christ, the Saints Peter and Paul. The list is practically endless, the architectural riches impossible to exhaust,

---

5   Luke 1:38.
6   John 3:16; John 1:14.
7   John 6, "The Bread of Life Discourse." Encyclopedia Britannica, "Notre Dame de Paris"; No author listed, "Notre Dame de Paris." General Information site.

even the demon-like gargoyles, grotesques, and monsters of the most imaginative nightmares are there for a theological reason, in support of "orthodox" frozen music, to remind the faithful of the battle for our souls raging ever fiercely from cradle to grave. This is good church design, good architecture, period.[8]

So are the following three churches that I would like to speak to you about tonight. Each of them offering something instructive without words, speaking from the silence of their constructed Logos. Kościół Mariacki (St. Mary's Basilica) on Krakow's Main Square, a 13th century Gothic church like Notre Dame, has the architectural bones to make sinners strivers and searchers soon unto saints. Go ahead, walk into that church, your eyes having to rise up and up and up to the 260 foot ceiling above, take in all the iconography and smell the dampness and the musk of wooden columns half a millennium old and soon your ears are enveloped in auditory assaults by the organ music itself going up and up and up and then back down, back down to you and, I promise you, you just "get it." You understand, even if you couldn't name the most basic facet of Catholic theology, that this building is silently telling you: God exists. God is all-powerful and all-good, beautiful too. All this before you even reach the forty foot high Veit Stoss altarpiece, the largest Gothic altarpiece in the world, illustrating the Assumption of the Blessed Mother unto her coronation, a veritable national and worldwide treasure completed three years before Christopher Columbus set sail for America.[9]

But you don't have to go that far, neither geographically to Europe nor into the past so many years ago, to find examples of nice, theologically stimulating, architecture here on the Palouse. Anyone here been to Saint Boniface in Uniontown? It is the first Catholic church consecrated in the state of Washington, built by German immigrants beginning at the end of the nineteenth century. This strikingly red brick neo-Gothic church has towers, real wooden floors and pews, a communion rail not ripped out but handsomely preserved, statues and iconography and columns breaking upwards

---

8   Ibid.
9   No author listed, "Historia Bazyliki." General Information site (in Polish). http://mariacki.com/bazylika/historia-bazyliki/

onto a vaulted roof within. There is even a rose window at Saint Boniface and it, like the church in sum, is beautiful. My wife and I have taken our two young boys to many Masses in modern and postmodern churches, some with the most spacious and toy-filled cry rooms, and yet still, chaos eventually ensues.[10]

At Saint Boniface there is no cry room, no toys, only the statues, stained glass, columns and a communion rail. More than enough for any kids, even the rowdiest, to sit still and look around, to keep quiet, for beauty is real and it matters. Saint Boniface, it's like this: You're in the back of the church, left side last pew, the church about 30% full, Saturday 4:00 p.m. Mass, late summer, early fall, the sun sets now at about quarter to eight but it's a warm sun and the temperature as you walk through the door is still about 80, and you walk in the wooden floor creaking beneath your feet, the smells so sweet, that old wood, those cold, stone walls, the stained glass allowing that late summer sun to stream in slowly and so the interior of the church, you taking it in left side in the back last pew, is aglow in a buttery yellow light, something like buttermilk and full fat whipped cream and sometime during the signing of a Marian hymn, your head resting against the cold wall under a stained glass window you want to turn and just put your face into the wall, rub your nose into the wall, later on smell the wooden door on the way out, man, it just all smells and looks so good and the singing is good and even the homily was good today and you think to yourself, this is the "New Evangelization" most especially because it's not old but timeless, this is the "I left the world, I stepped across supernatural boundaries for an hour traversing into something heavenly," and, sure, it's a pale foretaste, because ear has not heard and eye has not seen but, I'm telling you, the beauty I see and hear in this space, this place, the holy palace is enough to make it all make sense no matter how much sense you might have abandoned, first time visitor, but long detained pilgrim in our vale of tears, may God have mercy.

---

10   Robert M. Lambeth, "Saint Boniface in Uniontown." *Spokane Historical.* https://spokanehistorical.org/items/show/425; No author listed. "St. Boniface Catholic Church." Uniontown, Washington Information Site. https://uniontownwa.org/service/st-boniface-catholic-church/; No author listed, St. Boniface and St. Gall Parish information site. https://www.saintbonifaceandsaintgall.org/

We even have our very own Notre Dame de Moscow right here in town, St. Mary's in the Fort Russell district on East 1st street between Polk and Howard, a Tudor inspired English Gothic church, with a parish establishment dating to the 1880s and Ursuline Sisters as the founding, spiritual active ingredient, has much to recommend it. One doesn't have to cross oceans to find good church architecture. And once we know what good frozen music is, we can start making more of it for the generations to come.[11]

Okay, so then what do we do, where do we go from here, how do we do *that,* make more "sacred" sacred spaces for our children and grandchildren? What are the solutions, the prescriptions? Are there any solutions and prescriptions? Hearing me I'd imagine you might guess I'm advocating for a strictly pre-Vatican II church architecture and simply, simplistically, taking the proverbial time machine back some eight centuries. *He just said all these nice things about the Gothic style. So I think that's his advice: just start building churches in that exact same style, just do that.* I can imagine you sense the previous phraseology is a set-up. Yes, it is, and no, in fact, no I am not in any way suggesting an attempted return to the 13th century and assuming an ahistorical, imaginative posture that nothing has changed since then.

The answer comes from combing the wisdom of two books I assigned for my UI-Augustine's architecture class this spring: Michael Rose's *Ugly as Sin* and James Howard Kuntsler's *The Geography of Nowhere.* Rose claims all good church architecture has three features—permanence, verticality, and iconography—while to mine the most important takeaway from the Kunstler's book just substitute "somewhere" for "nowhere" in the title. Kunstler argues that one of the most depressing features of the contemporary built environment and landscape is that in every place looking like any other place—the strip malls, the fast food joints, the outlet stores, etc.—any real sense of place, and therefore meaning, has been lost.[12]

---

11 No author listed. "History of St. Mary's Moscow." St. Mary's Moscow Parish Information Site. https://stmarysparishmoscow.org/history-of-st-marys-moscow/

12 Michael S. Rose, *Ugly as Sin: Why They Changed Our Churches from Sacred Places to Meeting Spaces and how We Can Change Them Back Again* (Bedford, NH: Sophia Institute Press, 2009); James Howard Kunstler, *The Geography of Nowhere: The Rise and Decline of America's Man-Made Landscape* (New York: Free Press, 1994).

So instead of geography of nowhere churches that look like they were purchased from a pre-made kit at Home Depot how about we take seriously the timeless *geography of somewhere* approach, putting in the time and requisite effort to create something unique and thought out, something original and teeming with a sense of place and rootedness. If we want good frozen music, well-built Catholic churches today, no need to return to the 13th century or whine about today's art and architecture scene, distasteful though it might be, just follow, or at least begin with, these four principles. Make sure to build *permanent* structures under the philosophy of *geography of somewhere* that will stand the test of time, quality structures whose *verticality* directs one's mind, heart, and worship up to where it belongs, to the heavens to God, and, like that famous western façade at Notre Dame, or the Veit Stoss Altarpiece at Kościół Mariacki, eschew the white-washed and blank walls of a blank faith for vivid *iconography* that can still today, for the literate and illiterate alike, be a true *liber pauperum* once more.

Stupid, Silly Superheroes

WHY COMIC BOOK HEROES AND SILVER SCREEN STRONGMEN ARE WOEFULLY INADEQUATE SUBSTITUTES FOR MEN AND WOMEN OF HEROIC VIRTUE...THE SAINTS.[1]

I WAS HOPING TO GIVE THIS TALK UNDER different circumstances tonight and that the COVID containment measures might be lifted so we might, once again, meet in our common home, St. Augustine's. I planned on wearing a *Spiderman* onesie (ironically and mockingly, but nonetheless in keeping with tonight's theme) and jokingly comment in my opening, "It's been a long time since we've been able to gather here, and I'd like to say it's really nice to see you all again in person, but that would be a lie." Something funny and clever and witty and unexpected and hilarious and obnoxious and overdone and overkill and just plain old stupid like that.

Alas, all my plans in this regard have come to naught, gone to pot. But, a silver lining remains. We still get to do the exact same talk despite the distance; a talk where I will compare and contrast superheroes and saints and hope to convince you to do that thing everyone secretly lives for... the drag and drop into the desktop trash bin followed by a click on "empty trash" so as to hear, but for a fleeting moment, that peevishly pleasant crinkle and crunch of files formerly filed away now gone; to the superheroes, if you needed me to specify.

---

1   Lecture given via online streaming due to the COVID-19 pandemic on April 22, 2020

In this talk I'm going to list a few well-known superheroes, diss track roast them, and then explain that, since saints have "better powers" than superheroes, you should like saints more. The saint is a real person (emphasis on real) who, by the grace of God, lived a life of heroic virtue and now intercedes on our behalf in Heaven while beholding, in perpetuity, the Beatific vision. The superhero is a fake, caricaturized, literary device (emphasis on fake) for whom even the upfront, advertised artificially of the comic book/action flick universe does not adequately function to high-pressure hose off the gallons of cringe-queasiness and general free-floating, crowbar-me-in-the-throat distaste and nausea-bubbling-up-from-the-stomach sentiments and sensations. That too, I guess, is why I think you might consider liking saints more than superheroes and, better still, might consider learning something about these exceptional men and women.

Look, if you want to like superheroes, go ahead. Father Mike Schmitz likes them enough to have done multiple YouTube videos about them. A couple named Jackie and Bobby have an article on their blog entitled "The Catholicity of Captain America." There are articles online entitled "5 Catholic Superheroes in Comic Books," "Superhero Catholics," "The Catholic Nerd's Guide to Superheroes," and "I know everything about DC and Marvel but am still afraid to talk to women." That last article is fictitious, but it sounds believable, right?[2]

The serious Catholic and cultural problem here can be understood by referencing the dichotomy Christ presents us in the Sermon on the Mount: that you cannot serve God and mammon. James Papandrea's book, *From Star Wars to Superman: Christ Figures in Science Fiction and Superhero Films*, implies as much. It's bad when science fiction is so nearly biblical it can, rather than point to God, distract people from real salvation history in favor of the saccharinely confectioned pseudo story. Wait, wait, wait, you protest, Papandrea's probably saying, "Look, this genre is art done right. It leads people to faith." Fair argument, but allow me to pose a few counter questions. Do you think your average 16-year-old kid

---

2   Even a hastily typed, grossly misspelled search engine entry, "Fater ike Schmtz superheroes," produces a rich harvest.

would rather an all-expenses paid trip for a pilgrimage to Rome or another type of "pilgrimage" to Comic-Con? Do you think it's more likely this same kid has read all of Stan Lee's comics or all of the Bible? Do you think it's more likely he can name and describe 25 superheroes or 25 saints? Are we winning the culture war? Just how is that New Evangelization going?[3]

You cannot serve God and mammon.

Perhaps you cannot have as role models both superheroes *and* saints.

You might find yourself devoted to one and despising the other. But where to place that devotion and derision, if we must? Ernest Hemingway once described another author's work as non-alcoholic beer, "better to drink water."[4] Saints are beer (they are real) whereas superheroes are near beer—a gross and insulting half-facsimile of culinary art that tastes best poured down the drain. Near beer: so close to beer, yet so far away. Superheroes: so much like Christ, so much like the saints, and yet, upon further investigation, often not at all.

Allow me to return to beer to introduce our first saint of the night, Brigid of Ireland. She's one of the country's patrons, along with all the limelight Saint Patrick. (And, just to be clear, pursuant to the identified problem of knowledge deficiencies concerning saints, yes, Saint Patrick was a real person. No, "Saint Patrick" is not some kind of collective identifier for green clad lads vomiting onto New York City streets during the early morning hours of March 18 following the previous night's festivities.) Saint Brigid, born two decades after the death of Saint Augustine of Hippo, imagined Heaven as a lake of beer. Her reputed "superpower," if you will? Turning water into beer.[5]

Being able to turn water into beer might seem like the ultimate superpower, and maybe it is. Who am I to say it's not? But this essay will proceed beyond liquid alchemy in presenting the findings of a four-section study:

---

3   Matthew 6:24; James Papandrea, *From Star Wars to Superman: Christ Figures in Science Fiction and Superhero Films* (Sophia Institute Press, 2017).
4   Ernest Hemingway, *A Moveable Feast* (New York: Scribner, 1964, 1992), 133.
5   No author listed. "Lake of Beer in Heaven?" https://catholicdrinkie. com/lakeofbeer/

1. Healing powers
2. Wealth put at the service of the common and greater good
3. Intelligence and/or mental powers
4. Overall "superheroeness," the *you know it when you see it* factor

These are the analytical categories framing this essay.

I will first list the relevant superheroes, then the complimentary and, ultimately, more impressive—have I already mentioned more real, too, have I said that already?—saints. We will compare and contrast and see what can be learned, what can be of intellectual and spiritual benefit, if anything.

Therefore, let us consider our first category, healing powers. Wolverine, a diminutive X-men mutant with a nasty disposition and nose for the fight, who, I kid you not, is Canadian (the "kid you not" referring to my initial surprise that *really, other countries also traffic in this sh-...*) and has this thing called a "healing factor" which enables him to recover from injuries with lightening speed and resist poisons along with bacterial infections and viruses. The healing factor's anti-aging quality helps keeps his supercentenarian body looking in prime physical shape. That the healing factor does not suppress the pain he feels from being injured is a consolation. Can't someone make another movie where Wolverine is in that honey badger clip and the honey badger kills him like it does to all the other poor creatures therein? Asking for a friend.[6]

Wolverine's healing powers are noteworthy but how do they stack up compared to Christina the Astonishing? She died of a seizure during her 20s only to resurrect from the dead during her own funeral. First impression: Christina > Wolverine. Second take: Wolverine owned, the impressiveness of his healing factor, destroyed. Like all good saints, filled to the brim with love of God and neighbor, Christina told people God had brought her back to life solely to suffer for souls detained in purgatory and for the conversion of poor sinners on Earth. Suffer she did, this indestructible, invincible saint, forthwith throwing herself into burning furnaces, staying submerged in icy waters for days on end,

---

6 Original Narration by Randall. "The Crazy Nastyass Honey Badger." *YouTube.* https://www.youtube.com/watch?v=4r7wHMg5Yjg

running full speed through thorns, all in reparatory mortification which, needless to say, she added to her daily, more normal deprivations and penances simply so more souls might be saved, the most real of all real things. Her healing factor was so powerful she passed unscathed through these trials.[7]

St. Vincent Ferrer was also reputed to be blessed with the most healthy healing gift of all, bringing people back from the dead. The story goes that Saint Vincent once appeared at a hanging to plead for clemency for the condemned. A stretcher happened to pass by upon which lay a corpse. "Is this man guilty?" Saint Vincent asked the corpse. "He is not!" was the response from the formerly dead body now flush with life. Vincent offered the just dead, now alive, man a reward for cracking this case. *No, thanks*, he replied. Whilst dead he had learned of his salvation and so, presumably, was content—no, rapturously happy in an eye has not seen, ear has not heard way—to return to his true home, and so lied back down and died, again.[8]

Onto comparison number two, wealth put to the service of others. Example A, Batman, or, perhaps I should say, Bruce Wayne. Wayne is an oligarchic industrialist and owner of the philanthropic Wayne Enterprises, Inc., possessor of a vast personal fortune enabling him to purchase and fine-tune the most cutting-edge equipment in his nighttime Batman role ridding Gotham city of crime and corruption. The formula here is simple. I use my money to buy things that help "the people" against bad guys who want to hurt them; "the people." This is money well spent. My question is, if Bruce Wayne is so rich he can afford anything, why does he buy things that make him look like such a massive, insufferable tool? If his outfit is trying to say, "I have no fashion sense whatsoever, my MO is to disable my adversaries with laughter, them laughing at me, then I strike," mission accomplished.

One does not have to dress like Batman to put material blessings to good use. The 11th century Queen, Saint Margaret, the "Pearl of Scotland," was widely noted for her tireless devotion to the poor, especially orphans, even washing the feet of society's most neglected

---

7   ChurchPOP Editor, "5 Saints Who Totally Had Superpowers," *ChurchPOP*
8   Ibid.

in imitation of Christ. Margaret's constant charity, both of spiritual and material variants, probably staved off one-thousand fold more "bad guys," who often infest kingdoms like locust in times of corrupt and selfish rulers, in real Scotland than Batman did putting his money towards gadgets fighting comic book characters in fictional Gotham City. One of our very own Americans, Saint Katharine Drexel, heiress to what in today's money would be a near half-billion dollar fortune, left it all behind to follow God, providing a truly superhero testament to what matters in this life and the next, what is the real, bottom line balance sheet between God and mammon. Tony Stark uses hundreds of millions to produce the latest weapons technology and transform himself into a fighting machine. Saint Katherine Drexel refused use of hundreds of millions of dollars to become a spiritual fighting machine in the Army of Christ. Iron Man, owned. Blessed Pier Giorgio Frassati, scion of a wealthy family (his father was founder of the internationally known Turin based newspaper *La Stampa*) noted for his good looks, athleticism, and religious devotion—upon seeing him with a rosary in hand a man reportedly exclaimed, "Pier Giorgio, you've become a fanatic!" "No," he replied. "I've remained a Christian"[9]—so prodigiously helped the poor and downtrodden of his native Turin with food, medicine, anything they needed, that at his funeral thousands upon thousands lined the street to pay their respects, as if some great father of the nation political figure had passed. Pier Giorgio was but 25 years old.[10]

Finally, one must not forget the great Bishop of Myra, upon whom the legend of Santa Claus is based. Saint Nicholas gave freely of his material blessings to help the poor, and in keeping with Christ's instructions in the Sermon on the Mount did so in secret, not letting his left hand know what his right was doing, most famously when he anonymously left sacks of money

9   No author listed, Bl. Pier Giorgio Information Site. "Blessed Are you When They Revile you and Persecute You," July 3, 2013. https://frassatiusa. org/blog/blessed-are-you

10   No author listed, St. Margaret of Scotland RC Church Information Site. "Saint Margaret Queen of Scotland." http://saintmargaret.com/saint-margaret-queen-of-scotland/; No author listed. "Saint Katherine Drexel, Saint of the Day for March 3," *Franciscan Media*. https://www.franciscanmedia. org/saint-katharine-drexel/

outside the door of a man with three daughters to help pay their dowry and so save them from destitution and, more tragically still, prostitution. Presents delivered to those in need under the cover of night, thus the legend of Santa Claus was born. St. Nicholas' hands were good for fighting, too. Whereas Batman and Ironman beat people up over trivial matters, St. Nicholas right hooked the heretic Arius at the Council of Nicaea, his act of force defending the sacred doctrine of Christ's Divine Nature, Jesus indeed consubstantial with the Father, True God, True Man. So even as far as punching power goes, advantage, Nicholas.[11]

Onto number three, super intelligence. Professor X, Charles Francis Xavier, the founder of the X-men, world authority in genetic theory, inventor of the mutant gene identifying device named Cerebro, a telepath who, in addition to reading, can *control* the minds of others. Professor X seems to be smart. But, I have to admit losing some sleep over this one question. If he's really so smart, why does he spend so much time hanging out with the X-men? While I'm confident that there is much to be learned, philosophically, psychoanalytically, and sarcastically from profound and solemn investigations of Professor X's writings it's worth remembering that our vaunted tradition lacks for intellectual superstars like a beach lacks for grains of sand.

Why not consider first the man who, in his magisterial *Summa*, rather than reconciling Christ to Aristotle, reconciled Aristotle to Christ, for as Our Lord Himself said, "before Abraham was born, I am."[12] This same man who memorized and could perfectly recall all of Sacred Scripture and the whole corpus of the Church fathers yet was so humble, so seemingly "dumb ox," that he tolerated being tutored by someone of lesser knowledge without comment or complaint until, one day, his tutor made a mistake, our man explained it perfectly, and the tutor fell to his knees begging for a reversal of roles. The man who, at the close of his life, was told by Christ Himself, "you have written well of me."[13]

---

11 No author listed, St. Nicholas Center: Discovering the Truth About Santa Claus. "Bishop Nicholas Loses His Cool (At the Council of Nicaea)."
12 John 8:58.
13 Raissa Maritain, JMC (Jacques Maritain Center at the University of Notre Dame): Saint Thomas Aquinas "XXI Divine Favours." https://

This man, Aquinas, is an intellectual giant of all times and places, but if you prefer someone more X than Professor X himself, check out Padre Pio, for whom mind reading was basic and perhaps boring so he took up bilocation, or 3rd century Egyptian princess Saint Catherine who put mind control to evangelical ends. A convert herself, she won an audience with the Roman Emperor Maxentius to try and convince him, using reason and logic alone, to stop persecuting Christians. The trap the Emperor had set, having all of his domain's most renown philosophers, rhetoricians, and scholars present to debate her failed. Catherine won every debate, dispensed with each opponent on every question posed. Many of these men converted to the faith. The emperor put her in prison. This was another mistake, for she converted the whole prison. The Emperor was now so angry, especially because she refused, under torture, to renounce her faith, that he made his boldest move yet, the one sure to shut her up. He proposed marriage. She turned him down and so he cut off her head, this after the first attempt to kill her via a spike breaking wheel proved insufficient when the saint touched it, shattering the device immediately. She died, by the way, following beheading, something I feel must be mentioned within the context of this essay. She died. God, it would seem, had decided she had done enough and so called her home to her eternal reward.[14]

Finally, we arrive at the final category, general "superheroeness." Here I'm thinking about figures so famous they hardly need any supplementary biographical information. Spiderman, Wonder Woman, Captain America, the Flash, the Hulk; no doubt the Man of Steel himself too, and at the top of the ledger, alien invader sporting impossibly tight tights with weak spots for vapid clichés and kryptonite. If there's one thing this collection of heroes has in common—whether by super strength or super speed, sometimes airborne—it's an uncanny knack for finding the bad guys and defeating them whilst, and this is all-important, being able to do

---

maritain.nd.edu/jmc/etext/sta21.htm; "Dio o Niente: parla il cardinale Robert Sarah." Talk posted to YouTube December 17, 2015. https://www.youtube.com/watch?v=omw2yTUiu1w

14   ChurchPOP Editor, "5 Saints Who Totally Had Superpowers," *ChurchPOP*

and withstand practically anything in the performance of their duties. In other words, they're super, and all around.

Well, have you ever heard of the following saints, all of whom possessed a similar propensity for supernatural exploits? Like Saint Joseph Cupertino, nicknamed the "flying saint," because, you'll never guess it, he could. He would levitate and keep levitating, I mean, wouldn't you if you could? The superiors of his order deemed this phenomenon disruptive and eventually kept him in cells by himself. Perhaps the final words on super St. Joseph Cupertino have been penned by authors Richy Craven, Dustin Koski, and Dagmaer Baer in an article entitled "6 Saints with Superpowers Straight from the Marvel Universe." I'm quoting directly now, "Most saints used their miraculous powers to help their fellow man: healing the sick, feeding the hungry or something equally altruistic. As far as we know, there was only one saint who used his miraculous powers just to look really, really badass."[15]

How about St. Thomas More—patron of politicians and states-man, honored even in the USSR for the ideas found in his magis-terial classic *Utopia*; martyr as well—so perfectly trusting in God, so super in his faith, that he joked with his executioners on the way to decapitation? Or Saint Lawrence, who while being grilled alive quipped, "turn me over, I'm done." Or St. Denis, the first bishop of Paris, who like More and Catherine of Egypt, lost his head, except that even this did not prevent him from preaching. Legend has it that after the incident he simply picked up his now severed head and set out for a six kilometer walk, only then did he expire. Or, reportedly eighteen foot tall St. Christopher, patron of travelers, who's insatiable quest for power (because, we can assume, his one ton deadlift, 1,000 pound bench press, and arm strength that enabled him to throw a football 200 yards and touch 130 mph when pitching a baseball was not enough) manifested in an uncompromising commitment to serve the most powerful Lord in existence. Ferrying people across a dangerous river he almost drown with a tiny child on his shoulders who

---

15 Richy Craven, Dustin Koski, and Dagmaer Baer, "6 Saints with Super-powers Straight from the Marvel Universe." https://www.cracked.com/article_19948_6-saints-with-superpowers-straight-from-marvel-%20universe.html

got heavier and heavier by the step. If you're guessing that this child was probably the Divine Child Himself, because you know this saint's name means "Christ-Bearer," and so it was probably at this moment that he first encountered the most powerful Lord he wished to serve then . . . right, that's correct.[16]

Or, finally, how about Saint Moses the Black? A guy who, like St. Christopher, liked to ford rivers, expect that Moses preferred doing this with a knife in his mouth, all the better to engage in hand to hand combat upon reaching the other side of the shore. St. Moses was a bandit, a brawler, a bad guy too intimidating to define. But, these people being precisely God's people, for where sin is found grace abounds all the more, Moses converted after seeking refuge at a monastery and being won over by the monks' way of life. Sometime afterwards, Moses, at this time a monk himself, went full Chuck Norris in singlehandedly wrecking a crew of robbers with his bare hands. He brought them to the abbot who forgave them on the spot and ordered them released. These men, shocked by the abbot's gratuitous show of mercy, like the former bad guy Moses himself, also converted and joined the monastic community. Like all good superhero slash Norris slash Terminator type figures, St. Moses the Black died in battle at the hands of another band of bad guys, this time professional warriors, later in life. But only after he helped his brothers escape to freedom by volunteering to stay behind with a few other monks to fight, King Leonidas at Thermopylae style, the entire invading horde. That St. Moses the Black was at this time more than seventy years old does not seem to be a trivial detail.[17]

If you want to like superheroes, go ahead, keep on liking them. It's fun to joke, but I honestly don't believe there's anything wrong with the genre and, in fact, find the movies quite fun and the special effects great. Certainly it's a nice way to spend a few hours on a lazy summer afternoon with family. Perhaps we can even hope

---

16   Craven, et al. "6 Saints with Superpowers Straight from the Marvel Universe"; No author listed, Saint Lawrence Catholic Church Information site. "About Saint Lawrence the Martyr." https://www.saintlawrencewr.org/about-saint-lawrence-the-martyr.html

17   Jamie Frater, "Top 10 Truly Badass Saints." Religion, *Listverse.* January 30, 2011. https://listverse.com/2011/01/30/top-10-truly-badass-saints/

that superheroes *can* serve as an evangelical tool, the themes of good triumphing over evil, of helping those who need it most, pointing, in the end, to the God who is goodness itself, pointing towards the ultimate triumph of good over evil in our own existence.

But one should not be confused for a moment that any super-hero can hold the dimmest candle to saints, to the real men and women whose examples don't just point to God but are infused by God's Real Presence and plan. And while you can like Superman and Wonder Woman do not forget the everlasting importance of the only woman worthy of being called wonderful, the majestic Queen of Heaven and Earth, mother to us all and mother to the right and just singular Superman, the God-man, Jesus Christ.

The Church and the Environment(alism)

OR, IDAHO HOT SPRINGS
AS HEAVEN ON EARTH[1]

"IN THE BEGINNING, WHEN GOD CREATED the heavens and earth, the earth was a formless wasteland... then God said, 'let there be light,' and there was light. God saw how good the light was...God looked at everything he had made, and he found it very good." Forget all the politics, the politicians, the posters, posers, polydactyly, pterodactyl-like postulations, intellectual positions stretched so thin to fit they require extra fingers and freedom from close inspection. Head in the clouds, they fly high in flight from reason, not unto things more sublime. So come back down, plant them one, two, firmly the left and the right, muddy boots the better, for if the Earth is steadily warming melting permafrost into puddles to stand in one is to be the most fun and the most far-sighted too. Like right now you are here, not there, because here, you, in the puddle, here, the slush and the pulpy-sluice but a few drops deliquesced past edible, you see the problem over there and over there it's ice-shelf phantasmagoria, just one stray ray of sunshine enough to split the glacial sheet in two, four, eight, sixteen; the ice as flaccid as saran wrap pulled tight, see through gelatinous illusion, even the snows and the bears have left. If it breaks and by if when then...[2]

Since pondering environmentalism, any variants, activism especially, can quickly lead one deep into the dreamworld of dark, deforested tundras peopled by radioactive coyotes, plumbers named

---

1 This article was published on the *Dappled Things* Blog. "The Church and the Environment(alism); or, Idaho Hot Springs as Heaven on Earth."
2 *The Holy Bible* ('New American Bible: For Catholics') published for Catholic Extension by the American Bible Society, New York: 1970/1991. Gen. 1:1–31, 2:15.

"Colin," ants who breed with ever disappearing bees, and the collected works of Al Gore translated into Finnish, best begin, as Catholics, with the aforementioned first chapter in the first book of the Bible; best begin with straightforward common sense, something lately uncommon in our commonly upside down, down is the new up world. God is good. God is the author of all things. And since God made the environment and himself specified its goodness we, ourselves God's creatures, should, as a healthy starting point, look at the environment as "good" and as something to be respected and cherished and grateful for, for we, humanity, were at first, before the original transgression, set ourselves in the lush garden of life to cultivate and care for it.

I've titled this essay "The Church and the Environment." I plan on taking you on a brief survey of this topic from the Genesis springboard through the experiences of varied saints and luminaries such as Ketari Tekakwitha, Benedict of Nursia, Dorothy Day and Francis of Assisi, without taking our eyes off that foreboding iceshelf in the distance, those albatrosses environmentalists hang around necks their own the most popular choice, assuring us that if we but for one moment forget about the problem that will be the surefire last straw sending us into alternating cracked earth desert utopias and flood lands filled brim high from formerly hardened Artic ice like our very own example A; blue like the precise colors Alaskan blue, (or) like Arctic blue, (ibid … and henceforth, ibid) like blue chalk, bubbles, buoyant blue, fish pond and fluorescent turquoise. The thing is, our iceshelf, that one and same stretched thin thing primed like two brushstrokes three for tapdancing on thin ice musicals, it's clear too, translucent and as seemingly sweet as, and no less inviting than, heat wrought crystalized sugar glass. You can bet your bottom dollar we'll be keeping tabs on, and a thorough record of, freeze, creak, freeze, crack, crunch. Paraphrasing Leon Trotsky, you may not be interested in climate change, but climate change is interested in you.

A thorough record (kept, by us) too in the mainframe discussion at hand as we proceed, certainly as gingerly as those walking if not dancing if not dancing while singing on thin ice the eyes darting down below every now and then, from one Francis to the next, a discussion of the Pope's recent encyclical *Laudato si'* rounding out our analysis. (Did he really have to lowercase the second part of the title, though? Like, for real, like, why?). What have Catholics said and continue to say about the environment? What are the important takeaways, the overarching themes, the rules and responsibilities for us living in the 21st century?

Then, following this, then, then, then, listen up, then we will look at how Idaho hot springs can serve as a concentrated distillation of our thematic principles put into action. And if you don't know about Idaho, and about the Idaho wilderness, and about natural hot springs found in the Idaho wilderness, and about the way in which people can go into the Idaho wilderness in search of these hot springs, yes, these the one and same ones indeed, and then get into them and then soak and soak and stay and look and listen at/to all that nature so vast and remote and sometimes even silent then, suffice to say, you have lived an impoverished life, one that will hopefully be a few ticks enriched at the close of this essay.

Catholics have long been concerned with environmental issues. Ketari Tekakwitha, the 17th century "Lily of the Mohawks," survived smallpox as a child and converted to Catholicism at 19 years old, thereafter taking a vow of perpetual virginity. She was renowned for the many strict mortifications and penances she subjected her body to. She was also deeply in tune with her surrounding environment. Environmental scientist Bill Jacobs claims her natural, lived experience, knowledge of flora and fauna would make any contemporary biologist and botanist "envious." Green with envy to the point of self-inflicted poison ivy rubs to the face is taking it a bit far, but, you get it, she knew her stuff, and effortlessly too. Raised in the Iroquois nation, daughter of a people who "carefully managed the fields, forests, and wildlife of their homeland," Kateri's life is additionally a testament to the virtue of humility, of understanding one's place in the larger world—as a steward and servant, not exploitative consumer—and how to thrive in harmony with the surrounding ecosystem.[3]

---

3   Fr. Michael Rennier, "5 Saints to Inspire us to take care of our Planet," June 18, 2017. https://aleteia.org/2017/06/18/5-saints-to-inspire-us-to-take-care-of-our-planet/; No author Listed, "Reflecting on Blessed Kateri Takakwitha,"

In this harmonious balance, Kateri, who "often went to the woods alone to speak to God and listen to Him in her heart," has come down to our age as a patroness of the environment, environmentalists, and, perhaps unsurprisingly, of exiles, too, she showing us how to live well in our temporal, temporary home on Earth while we await the perfection of God's glory in Heaven. The fist Native American to be canonized, she bequeaths her name and legacy to the former Catholic Conservation Center, a "Catholic faith-based, non profit organization," whose goals include "protect[ing] clean air and water, conserv[ing] energy and limit[ing] climate change." Furthermore, in keeping with her personal example reconciling care for the Earth with care for our souls and a focus on salvation, the Saint Kateri Conservation Center also strives to "increase faith and rebuild the Church ... restor[ing] our relationships with God, each other, and nature."[4]

Next, we jump forward approximately three centuries into a consideration of Dorothy Day, flying south over our iceshelf leaving it, fingers crossed and hoping for the best, unto destination: 20th century; destination: New York City; destination: not to that guy on the corner of 5th avenue and East 81st shilling unsolicited advice about "world's best, yeah top grade museums" in South Orange, NJ, "not Newark, not none any but right smack dab on the campus of Seton Hall University, you see; go there and don't never leave" without the slightest recognition, even when pointed out to him point blank, of that gargantuan see: leviathan-like memory and memorabilia structure directly behind him and his soapbox; no, destination not even Brooklyn Heights, her place of birth, nor her place of work on Manhattan's Lower East Side, rather we journey into the mind of this woman who happened to exist in 20th century New York City by accident, so too we all of us each to his own circumstances, she part journalist, social activist, bohemian and political radical as a young woman, now and maybe forever best known for founding the *Catholic Worker Movement.*

July 13, 2011 https://catholicecology.net/blog/reflecting-blessed-kateri-tekak-witha; Saint Kateri Conservation Center, "Mission and Vision." https://www.kateri.org/mission-and-vision/

4   Ibid.

Environmentalism, harmony with nature specifically, was part of that sociopolitical philosophy. Day's time at the communal co-op Maryfarm certainly fit with Saint Kateri's aim to strike an organic balance between people and nature under the auspices of a loving God, sovereign creator of all, but it was even more in tune with the next saint we will investigate, Benedict of Nursia, for no one better embodies the idea of rootedness than Benedict, the concept of living in a place and drawing sustenance from that place.[5]

This is precisely what Day and her compatriots did at Maryfarm, a communal farm in Williams Township near Easton, Pennsylvania. Far from the communist implications such a designation might imply, Maryfarm can be more precisely explained as Catholic co-operative tilling the land so as to bring forth fruit to feed the poor. And how beautiful a Catholic environmentalism this was. As Day noted in 1954, "there were not many guests" during the harsh winter months of January and February, and yet still days were spent chopping wood, cooking, washing and cleaning, organizing concerts and maintaining a full daily schedule of spiritual reading—the Bible at breakfast and the Seven Story Mountain during the day—planning retreats, and praying at a makeshift Grotto dedicated to the Blessed Virgin Mary. "Life is a night spent in an uncomfortable inn," Day noted St. Teresa of Avila saying yet she, Day, in living in harmony with the surrounding environment and drawing sustenance from it to feed her less fortunate brothers and sisters, "try to make it as comfortable as possible at Maryfarm."[6]

While Maryfarm aimed to combine fruitful farming with the spiritual fruits of prayer, no one did this better than Saint Benedict and his compatriots, founders of Western monasticism, for while the Roman Empire lay in tattered ruins, its scattered embers smoldering from a century of barbarian invasions, Benedict and his community occupied themselves with the heavy lifting saving then

---

5   Daniel Patrick Sheehan, "Dorothy Day's roots to Sainthood run to Communal Farm in Williams Township," August 14, 2012. https://www.mcall.com/news/local/mc-xpm-2012-08-14-mc-maryfarm-dorothy-day-burbs-20120814-story.html; Dorothy Day, "Maryfarm," *The Catholic Worker*, March 1954, 3.
6   Dorothy Day, "Maryfarm," *The Catholic Worker*, March 1954, 3.

pushing forward Western Civilization. The ancient philosophical texts invaders preferred to burn and trample, they transcribed and stored away safe. So too the architectural and artistic forms and formulas of antiquity, many of which were lost in the chaos following 476, the monks preserved, they themselves serving as the link between ancient Rome and the New Rome of Christendom which rose phoenix-like from the ashes of the "Dark Ages" in AD 800 when Charlemagne was crowned Holy Roman Emperor.

One of the Benedictines greatest contributions is an environmental one. It is the colligation of their motto, "prayer and work," to the concept of "rootedness." We hear often in environmental circles that we must care for our common home, Earth. To do this we must love the Earth, love the land, love a real place. That is rootedness, loving the dirt beneath your feet, not some abstract idea, and that is precisely what the Benedictines can teach us. Agricultural life was a huge, dominant, feature of the monks' daily life. Within St. Benedict's guiding *Rule* one can find instructions that since "idleness is the enemy of the soul" it was incumbent upon brothers and sisters to "be occupied at certain times in manual labor." Monks were commanded to fast often, naturally, but the intensity of a fast could be lessened if "the monks have work in the fields." Work in the fields they did have, lots of it, and in tending to it they gave a forceful testament to the relationship between human labor and the environment. If people approach nature, and her gifts, with humility, not avarice, being committed to being rooted in a singular place so as to make the most of that place, in prayer as well as work, great fruit will come. For not only will the community and those who come to this place find themselves well fed, they might just become holy along the way, too. For if idle hands are the devil's plaything, what can be said about hands ceaselessly at work, in equal measure on rosary beads and on the plow? If "they themselves do the work of gathering the harvest," the Rule of Saint Benedict stipulates, "then are they truly monastics when they live by the labor of their hands, as did our Fathers and the Apostles."[7]

---

7   *Rule of Saint Benedict*, chapters 41 and 48.

Finally (oh, no, it might be happening, *it,* our iceshelf, soon liquefying down into the puddles too?), it is true that little can be said about St. Francis of Assisi that has not already been said; stigmatic, reformer, filled to the brim with such an evangelical zeal it bordered on holy insanity, as when he went to Egypt during the Crusades and practically begged the Sultan to martyr him. Francis was a man of impetuous, rash promises, stripping naked before his father in a renouncement of everything, only to rush off into the forest following the guidance of a voice counseling him to "rebuild my Church." Rash indeed, but, as Chesterton pointed out, "never was a man so little afraid of his own promises. His life was one riot of rash vows; of rash vows turned out right." And if a more grandiose claim that Chesterton makes is also true—that the imitation of Christ can be said to begin with St. Francis—then his most famous patronage, of animals, and nature more broadly construed, takes on an even greater importance. Because with St. Francis we have not just rash passion proved true, a full dedication fulfilled not burned out, we also have a living example of that modern maxim, "what would Jesus do?" Considering environmental questions, we can look to St. Francis of Assisi with confidence.[8]

In his famous poem, the *Canticle of the Sun,* from which Pope Francis took the title for the encyclical we will soon investigate, we see Saint Francis' most important contribution to a Catholic environmentalism: seeing all of nature, along with humanity, as *part of God's creation* not, as a multitude of modern environmentalists will mistakenly claim, some pantheistic divine force *unto itself.* This contribution, although easily missed, is enormously important. For in a modern environmentalist scene that wishes to return to paganism, to nature as divine, it was Francis who returned the "flowers and stars" to "their first innocence. Fire and water are felt worthy to be the brother and sister of a saint. The purge of paganism is complete." "Brother Sun, Sister Moon," St. Francis declares, "Brother Wind . . . the air cloudy and serene . . . Sister Mother Earth who sustains us and governs us and who produces varied fruits with coloured flowers and herbs." Brothers and sisters,

---

8   G. K. Chesterton, *St Francis of Assisi* (New York: Image Books, 1957 Org. 1928), 42, 59.

Sister Mother Earth, for we are all of us kin, all of creation, adoring in unison the "Most High, all powerful, good Lord, Yours are the praises, the glory, the honour, and all blessing. To You alone, Most High, do they belong, and no man is worthy to mention Your name. Be praised, my Lord, through all your creatures."[9]

And so, in no particular order, from the previous four saints we can deduce the following bullet points of an approach to a Catholic environmentalism.

1. Harmony and humility, that we are part of something larger than ourselves and although the crown of creation, we are stewards not exploiters.
2. That when respected the earth can be fruitful, literally, in serving the needs of our own, rooted community, one driven by the ideals of prayer and work along with the needs of the less fortunate. And, finally,
3. God alone is God. Correctly esteeming the environment as a brother or sister, as another part of God's sovereign realm, leads us to properly worship God in all his majesty.

What lessons can we therefore take from a brief look at Pope Francis' Encyclical *Laudato si'* in order to add to our above, synthesized themes? Ecological reflections are nothing new for church leaders, Francis begins, quoting Paul VI's 1971 apostolic letter *Octogesima Adveniens.* "Due to an ill-considered exploitation of nature, humanity runs the risk of destroying it and becoming in turn a victim of this degradation."[10] Little has changed today as

> This sister now cries out to us because of the harm we have inflicted on her by our irresponsible use and abuse of the goods with which God has endowed her. We have come to see ourselves as her lords and masters, entitled to plunder her at will. We have forgotten that we ourselves are dust of the earth (cf. *Gen* 2:7); our very bodies are made up of her elements, we breathe her air and we receive life and refreshment from her waters.[11]

---

9   Chesterton, *St Francis of Assisi*, 36; St. Francis of Assisi, *Canticle of the Sun.*
10   Pope Paul VI, Apostolic Letter *Octogesima Adveniens*, On the Occasion of the Eightieth Anniversary of the Encyclical "Rerum Novarum," May 14, 1971.
11   Pope Francis, Encyclical Letter *Laudato Si'*, On Care for Our Common Home, May 25, 2015.

That humans often see "no other meaning in their natural environment than what serves for immediate use and consumption," as John Paul II noted in his 1979 Encyclical *Redemptor Hominis* has led the current pontiff to denounce myriad problems that betray the original, Book of Genesis balance between man and nature in God's creative plan.[12] "Obstructionist attitudes," non-biodegradable electronic and industrial waste, the lack of access to fresh, potable water, "short-sighted approaches to the economy, commerce and production," (what has been captioned today as *profit over people*), crowded cities, and the "way that humanity has taken up technology and its development *according to an undifferentiated and one-dimensional paradigm*," are just a few of the many problems Pope Francis faults for creating what he sees as an improper and unjust perspective on the environment prevalent today. And these injustices have, are, and will continue to affect "the most vulnerable people on the planet," namely the poor, the least, the afterthought if thought of at all.[13]

We are not God. The earth was here before us and it has been given to us. This allows us to respond to the charge that Judeo-Christian thinking, on the basis of the Genesis account which grants man "dominion" over the earth (cf. *Gen* 1:28), has encouraged the unbridled exploitation of nature by painting him as domineering and destructive by nature. This is not a correct interpretation of the Bible as understood by the Church.[14]

To view the planet, its goods and its inhabitants, organically connected "one and indivisible" within *The Gospel of Creation,* the "theology of creation" that is found in the first chapter of Genesis when "God saw everything that he had made, and behold it was *very good,*" is for Pope Francis perhaps not the privileged but rather the sole proper perspective. Despite the manifold problems we face today, and there is an endless stream of critiques throughout *Laudato si',* the above with which we barely scratched the surface, we need not despair for, as the pope reminds us "...we know that things can change. The Creator does not abandon us; he never forsakes

---

12   Pope John Paul II, Encyclical Letter, *Redemptor Hominis,* March 4, 1979.
13   Pope Francis, *Laudato Si.*
14   Ibid.

his loving plan or repents of having created us. Humanity still has the ability to work together in building our common home."[15]

So, it seems we've come full circle. I began this essay with a reflection on the first chapter of Genesis and it can be argued that *Laudato si's* thesis is precisely that, recapturing the authentic meaning of Genesis 1, even more so employing it as a guide in restoring the proper man-nature environmental balance. But so what does this have to do with hot springs? How are hot springs, more specifically Idaho hot springs, good examples of all these Genesis 1 plus themes lived out fully?

Imagine yourself driving on US-55, north out of Boise up through Horseshoe Bend past Smiths Ferry, Donnelly, and Cascade en route to McCall; the deep forests on your right, so thoroughly green they're almost black and the Payette River rushing and churning and frothing down on your left, you're already at this point, this trace on the way, in a complex nexus of environmental harmony. You, the solitary dot in the small car on the narrow road, aware of the grandeur of God's large, overwhelmingly, even terrifyingly beautiful creation all about you—not bad for a prayer of thanksgiving either, that thought; there's some Franciscan natural spirituality for you—juxtaposed against your corresponding smallness, dotspeck insignificance. And yet as you drive and drive on, preferably sometime near sunrise or sunset so those variegated colors can fall down from above, accentuating everything, you realize that while you are a speck, God loves the speck. God died for you, for all of us dotspecks so small in such a created space so vast.

You get to McCall but McCall's not where you want to be. Burgdorf, the town and its hot springs[16], is your destination. Leaving McCall headed northwest into the heart of the Boise National Forest you bump along a road more desolate than 55 and therefore more reflective and more real. The dust, the squeak break turns at less than 20mph, the 100 foot plus trees packed together tighter than grains of sand on the shore, the road more

---

15   Ibid.
16   Burgdorf Hot Springs—"The Official Site." https://www.burgdorf-hotsprings.com/

like dirt untouched, now paved but soon just pebbles, then potholes, then slog forcing you to drive so slow it's like a water tap trickle. What doesn't change is the silence about you; 45 minutes of silence and staring.

You arrive at Burgdorf but you have not returned to civilization. Burgdorf is neither a civilized place nor one for polite conversations about 5-star getaway resorts and teatime in the countryside manor. There is no running water, there is no electricity, there are no mattresses and no TVs, there is no internet, no cellphone towers, not even a credit card machine. These barbarians don't accept anything but cash; animals. What is at Burgdorf is a handsome spread of wooden cabins varied in size and style, places to set recently chopped wood on fire so as to burn things before placing them in your mouth and chomping down, and, ringing the place on all sides, forest, forest, forest, trees and so many trees so deep and so thick it appears to stretch on forever, even back in time.

All of this highlights the main attraction at the heart of the place. From first foot gingerly dropped into the 100 degree main soaking pool, you get it, instantaneously, finger snap immediacy from no to yes, behold, environmentalism, no, rather a complete environmentalistic practical philosophy come to life, hot springs, as close to heaven on earth as it gets. That testing foot now two feet firm on the pleasurably pebbled, turquoise and orange colored mineral bottom of the large pool, the calciums and magnesiums, the lithium and silica too, mixed and smash strewn together to form the foundation for a water now up past your waist, autotoning those abs you've long neglected, the steam rising up from the water entering your nostrils then plunging down into your lungs, cleaning, cleaning, oh, you're breathing now, brother; breathe, deep, up from the diaphragm and exhale slowly, it's a team effort here, the rocky pool bottom prune-exfoliating your well-worn feet, the warm water now up to your neck, the crisp mountain air and the foggy steam rising up from the water not for one moment, not for even a falting second, restricting your view of the surrounding mountains, some of them snowcapped, and just for you, you enjoy yourself here, okay (?), and those rows of trees, trees, trees, forest and fall foliage, looks sweet enough to eat.

This is Catholic environmentalism, the closest glimpse at Eden before the Fall, the simultaneous living out of our main three themes from above and the entire sapsticking umbrella of Genesis 1, umbrella and underpinning undercurrent, gulfstream lodestar, true guiding light for all conversations concerning this topic. Here, you, this hot spring, any hot spring—not just Burgdorf but, maybe, Atlanta Hot Springs near a mile high ghost town in the Boise National Forest, or Sheepeater Hot Springs in the River of No Return Wilderness requiring a six mile, one-way hike to reach, or one of those closest to us here on the Palouse, Stanley Hot Springs on US-12 out towards Missoula[17] —in a hot spring, should so you be, should you find yourself thus, you, witness consciousness of harmony and humility between man and nature, the appreciation that God loves us and made this for us but for us to care for it and enjoy it, not exploit it, as you are doing exactly right now, properly enjoying this, savoring it, right at this moment waist deep in warm water nearly hot almost too hot but still not quite therefore perfect, this reflection leading to point number three, that God as Creator is worshipped all the more gloriously when we properly honor his handiwork, we, this being point number two, being placed here, on this Earth, in this environment, to by prayer and work till the land, steward creation, and ultimately, reap its benefits; benefits open for all people, for anyone with a map, a free weekend, a bathing suit, and the will to walk, ride, or drive deep into the Idaho wilderness in search of dark forests and hot water.

No one who would find themselves in a hot spring surrounded by mountains and forest with steam cutting through crisp air up to their windswept face feet squishing through mineral deposits below would think, even consider, doing anything on the prohibitive laundry list Pope Francis mentions in *Laudato si'*. No thoughts of profit or city planning, no smog or sub-prime mortgage shilling, no time for simple, mind-numbing consumerism, complex corporate scheming, roidrage hyper-capitalism, avaricious communism, Keynesianism, the invisible hand, visible pollution, urban sprawl, or global market trends.

---

17   Evie Litton, *The Hiker's Guide to Hot Springs in the Pacific Northwest* (Falcon Press: Helena, MT, 1993), 222, 217-18, 155.

No spare thoughts for pandemics, vaccines, social distancing or social sardining. No Bill Gates, no George Soros, no Georges Stephanopoulos, Bush, Clooney or King (as in III, where the ****** is Patrick Henry when we need him?), no time even for a passing thought for Curious George, now think about that. The ice-shelf? Yes, it has finally melted and is *en train de* flooding the earth; chain reaction, domino theory type stuff; abrupt rising of sea levels, abolished coastlines, sinking cities, et cetera. But here, in an Idaho hot spring, no worries, for here, in an Idaho hot spring, one is on high ground, geographically and as pertaining to the spirit; and for good, happily ever after, "yeah freaking buddy!" you scream at the top of your lungs, beer in hand, body in hot spring, your exclamation broken by raucous laugher, your own and that of your companions, they themselves in that same blissful aquatic headspace you are.

Now I'm not saying that all the world's problems, especially those related to the environment, would be solved if people visited hot springs on a bi-monthly basis, came to places in the middle of nowhere to be immersed physically and mentally in natural states too often uncommon in our busy, out of joint world. I'm not saying this would solve all the world's problems.

I'm also not saying that it would not.

On Beer

LOVE AND RESPONSIBILITY[1]

"FROM MAN'S SWEAT AND GOD'S LOVE, beer came into the world," St. Arnulf of Metz. "Beer makes you sleep easy. Easy sleep makes you not sin. Not sinning gets you into heaven," an anonymous German monk. "It is my design to die in the brew house; let ale be placed to my mouth when I am expiring so that when the choir of angels come they may say: 'Be God propitious to this drinker.'" It's not only Catholic saints who have sung the praises of this gold and foamy drink. "Beer is proof that God loves us and wants us to be happy," Ben Franklin supposedly, debatably, probably did not say. But the sentiment's nice, right? Just like this tweet sent by *@Woke Rhinoceros* at 2:20 a.m. in July 2020, that reads, verbatim, "no time read, no time write, I don't love or fight, beer tho be right, yo." Ah, maybe best to return to the reputable source of a Catholic saint, here St. Brigid of Ireland. "I would like a great lake of beer for the King of Kings. I would like to be watching Heaven's family drinking it through all eternity."[2]

Catholics like beer. Supreme Court Justice Brett Kavanaugh succinctly explained this at his Senate Judiciary hearings. "We drank beer. I liked beer. I still like beer."[3] This is true down to the truest declaration of truth, jokes. Where did the Irish family go on vacation? To a different bar. Beer is hardwired into the tradition of Christendom, present at the very origins of monastic life and

---

1   This article was published on *The Catholic Gentleman* Blog. "On Beer: Love and Responsibility. The Catholic Gentleman," November 30, 2021.
2   Xavier Mora, "The Beautiful History of Catholicism and Beer," October 16, 2016; ChurchPop Editor, "6 Catholic Quotes on that Great Merrymaking Gift from God: Beer," February 21, 2016.; Anchor Brewing, "Say What? Says Who? Benjamin Franklin on Beer—or not," February 29, 2012.
3   https://www.youtube.com/watch?v=GdTTjY8soVc

lived practice. More on that soon. First, some disclaimers. This talk is subtitled *Love and Responsibility* as an intentional homage to John Paul II's book on the Catholic sexual ethic. More on *that* next month, that's my next talk. Wow, so many previews here pretty soon you'll hear me say something like "on October 32nd, 2051 extraterrestrials will return to the pyramids and repossess their millennia old handiwork," but, trust me, that's not going to happen.

Beer is a love story, one whose thoroughgoing underpinning must be responsibility. If a person is prone to alcoholism, teetotalism can be a Cross picked up and dutifully borne, following the Master himself all the way to Heaven. Here, abstinence becomes holy mortification, and who would doubt those poor souls in purgatory can ever have enough sacrifices made on their behalf by us? Forget legal limits, why not live by a rule that even a few sips makes you turn those car keys over to a drier friend ferrying you home safe and sound? And what Catholic would deny the Aquinian communitarian sense of the common good that beckons us gently to follow established societal norms? Not 21, don't drink, this because at sub-21 you most likely can't properly think, probably have rocks in your head or maybe nothing at all. Not airhead, antimatter empty head, you, so why add alcohol to the mix?

Those are your disclaimers, for this talk is not some frat boy's midsummer night's dream extolling the virtues of 40oz malt liquor, swimming goggles, funnels and duct tape, the tape to better affix 80oz total to five digits each, left and right, while your boys Tecate Tom and PBR Petey record the exploits for posterity. Catholics: beer, if it is to really be loved, properly loved, must be done so responsibility. Leave it to a man who looked like he was born in a pub, and whose mother tucked him into bed with the stories of Kegman and the Fairy Princess Frothsip, GK Chesterton, to pen the definitive words on this subject. "You thank God for the gift of beer by not drinking too much of it."[4]

So, I've told you what this talk is not about. How about some positive direction, though? You've heard some saints on the subject, I'll start by giving you some more, then some input from the Lord and Savior Himself, this before arriving at the beating heart of this

---

4   G. K. Chesterton, *Orthodoxy* (New York: Dodd and Mead, 1908), 117.

talk, a trip to Norcia, Italy, followed by a final brief stopover at Mt. Angel seminary in Oregon, this then being the final destination of this talk, should time, flight itineraries, and arbitrary perhaps purposely contradictory gubernatorial edicts concerning in-fight and inside/outside dining social distancing and/or face mask slash my Aunt Karen's unsolicited epidemiological opinions allow for it.

The relationship between alcohol and the Church is as old as the Church herself. Saint Paul counseled Saint Timothy to give up the habit of drinking water alone and to have some wine to settle his stomach and help with other illnesses. Earlier still, let's raise our pints in a toast to the Old Testament, the Psalmists rejoiced over God creating wine to "gladden the human heart" while, in the book of Proverbs, heavy-hearted depression is to be cured in similar fashion: with wine. For in drinking, the Scriptures tell us, people forget their poverty and remember misery no more. Alcohol only grew in importance as the young Church itself grew into the large seat of the former Roman Empire then laying in ashes. For as Christendom became the New Rome, with monastic life often the active, catalyzing ingredient, within the monastic walls it was often beer, the catalyst within the catalyst, that allowed monks to live the laborious requirement of Benedictine's rule that monks should provide for themselves. And, lucky us, lucky world, this self-sustaining goldfrothed yeah too sometimes amber and yeahtoo sometimes dark oatnutty if not beyond that unto molasses tinged if molasses tinged then darker and darker still, black like purple a starless summer night provision, provided for us art in liquid form, sips of sublime satisfaction, daily bread lowest common denominated down to watery essentials; all this but a pour and a few pulls away.[5]

Monasteries started brewing beer as early as the 5th century AD. A few centuries more and there were five hundred plus monastic breweries spread about the continent. The typical design of these included partitioning into three separate brewing areas, one producing beer for customers and travelers visiting the monastery, another area making beer that would be given as charity to the poor,

---

5 *The Holy Bible* (New American Bible: For Catholics) published for Catholic Extension by the American Bible Society, New York: 1970/1991. 1 Timothy 5:23; Psalm 104:14–15; Proverbs 31:6–7.

and a final, personal area if you will, where monks brewed beer for themselves. Medieval monks were reputed to drink up to four liters of ale per day—that's 135 ounces, or eleven "standard" beers—and during Lent some monks would actually drink more, not less, for this "liquid bread" was a form of nutritional sustenance to get them through long, one-meal days. And far from being restricted to the monastery, and from this wellspring spilling over to kings and commoners alike, the importance of beer to Middle Age society is brought into starker relief when seen under the guise of that long-repeated legend that beer was safer to drink than water, the boiling element of the preparatory process killing pathogens the scientists of that time did not know existed. "Let us make use of a healthy, natural drink which will sometimes be of benefit to both body and soul," the Abbot Lupus Servatus declared in the ninth century, specifying that it must be "drawn not from a muddy cistern but from a clear well or the current of a transparent brook." This timeless drink, brought forth from a labor of love, has come down to our time today, and makes use, still today, of our own transparent brooks and clear wells—and if you're looking for that here, near us, then nearer still geographically and of the spirit is that would be world famous if it were known at all River of No Return Wilderness with so much water so much of it so clear so much of it cold as cold gets, colder even perhaps and then colder still, and so I say why don't more people say, "why not?," why not venture there-yonder deep within and set up (even if it must be but a) portable shop next to so much of the potable pure by nature natural base ingredient and get to all the adding and fine-tuning and trying and sampling and sipping?—with the hope that it may still be, to those who can love it responsibly, a benefit to both our bodies and souls.[6]

It is therefore to our current times today that we now turn, readying the end of our very brief historical reflection as we board flight 1234567891011 to Norcia, Italy, the flight attendant right now, as I read you the forthcoming few sentences two, in fact, handing you beers, two, in fact, crème-foamed blonde in the left,

6   No Author Listed, "Oh, Brother! A Quick History of Monastic Brewing," no date listed. https://www.praguebeergarden.com/news/post/history-of-monastic-breweries-prague

an amber-auburn Chimay for the right, so as you sip you do know now that it really is all going to be, all of it, alright, your ears now ready to listen to the historical reflection's *denouement,* a return full circle, back to the beginning, back to the very beginning of Our Lord's public ministry, the strongest possible argument for alcoholic drink as a gift to be responsibly enjoyed.

The public ministry that was quite literally kicked off, and at a wedding to boot, with alcohol, a miracle, water into wine, wine, the pre-Transubstantiative foundational material for the arrival of Christ's real and true Body, Blood, Soul and Divinity, and the final instructive words from Our Blessed Mother in Scripture: "Do whatever he tells you." Her parting words in Scripture, given to us all as general instruction: just do what Jesus wants you to do, whereas, in that moment then, a command to a waiter to follow her son's guidance without hesitation as he, the Divine Son of God, began the road to Calvary by first gladdening the hearts of wedding guests shocked to learn post-sip that he had kept "the good wine until now."[7]

The flight has landed in Italy. But our Italian driver showed up fours late. Then our car broke down and had to be left, still smoking, by the side of the road. We took a taxi to the nearest train station but the train was itself a little bit tardy; three days late. When we finally made it to the penultimate train station we found it closed for business. This region in Italy, a local woman informed us, takes a daily siesta from 9am to 6:30 pm. No worries, though, she assured us, you can always take the bus to Norcia, the station's five minutes in that direction.... or, excuse me, no, it's behind us, in...wait, hold on, I think it's...When she finally asked an older gentleman in a plaid shirt and slacks smoking like a chimney slouched against the side of a newspaper kiosk "does this town have a bus station?" we knew this wasn't our lucky day.

Transportation problems notwithstanding, to arrive at Norcia, the birthplace of St. Benedict, Western Monasticism and really the West, "Western Culture" in sum, is to arrive at what seems like a slice of heaven on Earth, especially if you were lucky enough to go before the devastating 2016 earthquakes that destroyed and

---

7   *The Holy Bible* (New American Bible: For Catholics) published for Catholic Extension by the American Bible Society, New York: 1970/1991. John 2:5.

damaged much of the city and the monastery itself. Fear not, however, these men are monks, Catholic special forces, so I refuse to answer the question of whether they are rebuilding and building back stronger than ever. I will say that what the monastery once was, and soon will be once more, was a nuclear reactor of spiritual energy running on long hours of prayer, the full office chanted in Latin, prayer at daytime at during the wee hours, midnight, 3:00 and 6:00 a.m., and Gregorian chant so hauntingly pretty the fact the monks' recordings have topped Billboard charts seems more like an insult than recommendation.[8]

Their music, like the beer they brew, is better than awards, beer that comes in two varieties—a blonde and a dark beer—and is sold in cases and six-packs, the latter known to run you a cool 85 USD. The Benedictine monks in Norcia practice what they call "brew evangelization," a name which is cheesy but at the same time horribly cheesy, so there, that doesn't sound cool, c'mon, call a spade a spade, but the results of which appear to have marvelous effects. Trendy Atheist Italian guy number 005 visits the monastery along with his best friend, Obnoxious American Tourist #CiaoBella and these two long lapsed Catholics start sipping and speaking. Soon, maybe after beer number three, they are no longer offthecuffbreezeshoot speaking but speaking about serious things, scratching off old, hardened wounds of resentment and allowing the brew master Doctors of the Soul monks to have a look, and why not? It's not too long afterwards, and by this time beer number four has long been filed away safely in the stomach, that both of these men have made appointments for confession at the monastery; the first time in twenty-one and sixteen years, respectively. Yes, the beer is intrinsically good at Norcia, delicious even, but its true import lies in allowing the monks to, in their own words, "preach the Gospel without preaching the Gospel."[9]

---

8   Judith Valente, "Singing monks in Italian city of Norcia top the charts," *USA Today,* August 14, 2015.

9   No Author Listed (Loyola Press), "How Monks Revolutionized Beer and Evangelization," no date listed. https://www.loyolapress.com/catholic-resources/prayer/arts-and-faith/culinary-arts/how-monks-revolutionized-beer-and-evangelization/; Monastero di San Benedetto in Monte Norcia. https://en.nursia.org/.

One cannot leave Norcia without having a glass or two of the monk's beer. But if you can by virtue of the fact that you cannot, can leave without a beer because you cannot or will not drink beer, at least allow the descriptive words on the bottle's label to send you on your way. "In the birthplace of St. Benedict, set in the beautifully preserved nature of the Umbrian landscape, the monks of Norcia brew this beer with the finest ingredients, following the ancient monastic tradition. We invite you to enjoy Birra Nursia in the company of friends and family, "Ut Laetificet Cor," "that the heart may be gladdened."[10]

Want your heart gladdened somewhere closer to home? Well, I have two suggestions for you, one closer than the other, both closer than Italy. In fact, in our chartered direct flight from Norcia to Mount Angel Abbey, one of these two options, in, surprise, surprise, Saint Benedict, Oregon, our flight takes an unscheduled pit stop a stone's throw from the Palouse in Cottonwood at St. Gertrude's Monastery.[11] How did we end up here? To make a long story short a gentleman on the flight had to go to the bathroom and both "could not hold it" and was "unsure that the in-flight facilities would be up to the task of my personal challenge," whatever that meant. The plane rerouted and landed in a secret airport near Cottonwood. The passengers were none too happy, having their plans gashed mid-air and now having to wait patiently in place, TSA regulations requiring their seatbelts remained fastened, tray tables up, and their baggage stowed overhead while the man disembarked to answer nature's call. Returning two hours later he was met with jeers and boos from the still seatbelted passengers. One woman yelled, "you're probably a Trump supporter!" Turns out it was Donald Trump. Actually, it was Joe Biden pretending to be Donald Trump, MAGA hat and all. See, it turns out that Biden, while on the campaign trail . . . ah, never mind, long story, like I said before.

Long story, but one with a happy ending, here in Cottonwood, at Saint Gertrude's Monastery, a monastic community following the every inch and detail of Saint Benedict's rule, the motherhouse

10   Monastero di San Benedetto in Monte Norcia. https://en.nursia.org/
11   Monastery of Saint Gertrude (Cottonwood, Idaho)—official site. https://
stgertrudes.org

of which was founded in 1909 because of three sisters who had originally left a cloister in Sarnen, Switzerland right in the middle of *La Belle Époque-Fin de Siècle* Europe and came to New York and then onto Idaho, to become proprietors, Book of Genesis style 'man's dominion' over the surrounding greenspace, 1400 acres of pristine Idaho land, here, in Cottonwood, and if you want a beautiful church then see a chapel hewn from locally quarried blue porphyry, matching twin towers with candy apple red domes, the two them with golden crosses on top and inside a majestic, golden-hued altar and Tabernacle at the center of it all, the center of the universe. Saint Gertrude's sisters host a "Raspberry Festival Arts and Crafts Fair" where select items include raspberry shortcake, pancakes, and raspberry jam, a list, nonetheless still, remaining incomplete without the wine they make and sell. It's not beer, fine, but this Wedding of Cana Feast near the Palouse gives, each one of us, a very close "Norcia-like" experience where one can come and drink from the wellspring of integrated architecture and agriculture, holy hymns and homemade cuisine, while driving the experience, activating it, with the *do whatever He tells you* gift from God to us.

But if you're a purist, and a talk on beer should not veer from the beer, steering likewise clear of deer, assorted car gear and fear itself as you drive on the nexus of highways near us to that nearer to where we are not, and I mean St. Benedict, Oregon, one will soon find it crystal clear that there, after the trip here, at Mt. Angel Abbey, that there is beer here, plenty of it, three cheers for beer at the simply named "Benedictine Brewery," founded in 2018, the year, and it really is all about the beer here, "taste and believe" the brewery's slogan, the simplicity of that only outdone by the simplicity and simple beauty of the process behind the product, for, as their website declares, since Saint Benedict envisioned monasteries as self-sufficient communities, the monks of the here and now follow the example of the monks of days gone by, "striving for the same" the site says, meaning, as in such places such locales such gem-jewels such true like True communities as Norcia, that the monks do the brewing, the water comes from their own well, and the hops from their own land, an agricultural tradition on land owned since the 1880s. It may be hard for us to get to Norcia. But one can come to the Norcia in Oregon, can come to pray, can come to find peace, can come to taste and believe. This confirmed belief in the brewing brilliance of the Mt. Angel monks perhaps, just like their Benedictine brethren in Norcia believe, serving as a catalyst to belief in someone still more sublime, that arriving at the table of the monks brewery men and women might progress to one day coming to the table of the Lord's supper, to eat and drink their own salvation so gratuitously offered by a God who loves us so much.[12]

Okay, so I've given you a very brief, thinly superficial admittedly, history of the relationship between alcohol and the Church, have given you some introductory information on monasteries in Italy, Idaho, and Oregon, and began the talk with some notes on how a love for beer should always be connected to responsibility. Let's end here because this is the most important takeaway. That beer drinking can be harmful if abused is perhaps the whole point. Maybe God gives us beer as it is, healthy *and simultaneously* harmful depending upon context and contingencies, because he wants us to experience the full measure of our freedom. Maybe it all comes back to Genesis and our first parents. Beer is the Garden of Eden, glorious, golden liquid good for the heart and mind and better still for fellowship with friends, gateway, in thanksgiving to God for the taste and the theological implications behind it, to a deeper love of God and neighbor, a way to appreciate the good gifts of the Creator so to be moved to appreciate Him Himself in the fullest measure.

Brew evangelization, indeed.

But drunkenness, alcoholism, and worse still the decisions made while drunk, that's the forbidden fruit. Just as God told our first parents not to eat the forbidden fruit, and that there would consequences for doing do, we can be assured that we too are to avoid the forbidden fruits of alcohol abuse lest dire consequences fall upon us once more. Do not eat the forbidden fruit. Rather, in the full flush of responsibility, eat from the fruitful cornucopia of God's gift of beer with a joyful and mirthful heart, in moderation, with respect, and doing so you might just stumble upon a lesser type of love marking out the path to the God who is Love Himself.

---

12   Mount Angel Abbey, Benedictine Brewery—official site. https://www. mountangelabbey.org/benedictine-brewery/

Maybe, Probably, Definitely, Yes

THE TYRANNY OF RELATIVISM

I.

My friend claims nothing is real.

I say him saying nothing is real proves something is real, and if something is real we've already blown up his philosophy.

He asks me what I mean by "blown up."

I tell him it's been exposed, demolished, reduced, to dust. I tell him the very act of speaking, that is a real thing, and if there are real things there's a larger reality… probably.

—How sure are you, he asks.

—About the larger reality?

—Yes.

—100%.

—Then not "probably"; assuredly, for certain, that's what you should have said.

—You know, you're probably right.

—There you go again, "probably," take a stand, man.

A stand? A stand? A stand? You're here telling me nothing's real and you want me to take a stand?

II.

My friend says the only way out of the meaninglessness numb-pain of this no point world would be if God would actually show up on earth Himself and tell us what to do. And if he left some kind of instruction manual that clearly told us what to do, we'd know, we'd know what to do then. And then, if He would just do something, something like an act of love, or a sacrifice of some sort, something showing us, "hey, I do love you and I'm going to leave no doubt," then he's quite sure the world would be a much different and probably better place and probably filled with a bunch of stuff like hope, like joy, harmony between people.

He finishes saying this and then we both look at each other and say nothing for a few seconds.

"You wanna go to the casino or bet on greyhounds down at the track?" he asks me.

"We have that here?" I ask him.

"The dogs or the casino?"

"The dogs."

"Yeah, what?"

"Yeah."

"What are you saying?"

"What are you saying?"

"I don't know. But what do you wanna do?"

B. I

Albert called me and said he had just attended a Catholic Mass and it was the most beautiful thing he had ever seen in person, with his own eyes; there was music but it was very old, very subdued, but I liked it, he said, and there was tons of sweet smelling smoke and it was obvious the people there took it all very seriously and it made him want to act the same, to mimic them. And so he had done that. And he finished by saying he was pretty sure he would probably continue to do that going forward.

III.

My girlfriend Angie is probably going to break up with me because she told me the next time I take her to a fast food restaurant for a date, when it's my time to plan date night, it's not going to be good, a good choice by me, a good thing, that, I'm saying I'm assuming she won't be happy about that, because she's told me she would not like that the next time that happened or was about to happen like was being planned, by me. And so now I'm freaking out, now I'm stressin, my palms are sweating, I even forgot to put socks on and that's usually the anchor to my day, fresh socks, matching pair, no holes, no repeats until it's a different month but now, because it's date night and date night's on me tonight, I don't even have any socks on and my belt is upside down, forget just missing a few holes, yeah, that too, but man I gotta go to the bathroom, man drinking all that Mountain Dew, what a bad idea, what a terrible idea that was and then Angie walks in.

"Hey, babe," she says, smiling. "I was thinking: let's go to Chik-fil-A. What to do you say?"

IV.

My friend told me I should go see a therapist and I told him he should shut up and stay out of my life and mind his own business.

V.

Walked past a guy on the street today holding a sign that read *The Climate Crisis is Now: We've got Ten Years before the flood and the fire come.* The flood and the fire, I asked the guy. Yes, he said, and let me tell you I could tell he was none too pleased to be answering questions. But if you don't want to talk to people why are you standing outside in a very public place with a huge sign? Yes, flood and fire, he said, or flood or fire, look, at the rate we're going, especially with the disgusting carbon pollution everyone just carries on with without a second thought, it's going to be fifty feet underwater or 200 hundred degrees Fahrenheit soon. Do you, he said, accentuating *you* as he pointed at me, do you think that's okay? Do I think being underwater or on fire is ok, I said in reply. Now he seemed more angry than before because he scoffed, held his sign higher, and began chanting, "2, 4, 6, 8, Down with the humanity, bugs are great. 2, 4, 6, 8, Down with humanity, bugs are great." Excuse me, I said, so I take it you don't like that people aren't doing their part, right, not recycling, driving cars, eating meat, all this just adds to the collective carbon footprint? And he looked at me and said, Yes, you ignoramus! Yes, and that's just the tip of the iceberg. It's worse than anyone can even dream of. And especially all these, these 9-5 working stiff useless eaters who just drive the car, fill the tank, drive car, fill tank, car, tank, over and over again. How I wished they'd all just disappear, good riddance! But, I said, what about the fact that all the useless eaters like you call them, all of them and their carbon footprint put together are nothing compared to some of the important figures in your movement who, in just one flight, hurt the planet more, carbon bomb the atmosphere a million times over? Now the man had lost all patience with me. He was in no mood to answer my question let alone even think of answering. After three seconds of an icy stare he slowly pulled back his coat to reveal a gun holstered to his belt. I got a long enough look to see it was some kind of BB gun. Still, and now I'm the one thinking, and fast too, on my feet, still, that would probably leave some nice welts. And so I left, at a brisk pace.

VI.

My friend says he's looking for God in his life and I asked what he meant by that and he said that's why he was looking, that he didn't know, he didn't even know where to start and so how about me did I have an idea of what to do, where to begin, how to do this?

Me? I asked. Me? You're asking me? Me? You want advice from me? Me? Me? You're really asking me, of all people, you're asking me? You want—

By that time he had already left. He was gone. The thing is, I had been turned around, away from him, answering him with my back to him and kind of speaking into the corner of the room in which we were standing.

VII.

Angie called and asked me if we should get a pet together. I have to admit I didn't really care what she was calling about because I had written a rap song about her, about us, I mean, the background being I'm thinking we should start thinking about being more serious, her and me, because the date at Chick-fil-A went great, it was awesome, it was just so nice, she let me finish off her waffle fries and that was just great and so I had gone home that night and, boom, the words were writing themselves, therapist my butt, all's not just good upstairs it's clicking on all cylinders, and so she asked about getting a pet together and I said nothing and so she asked again and I just launched into it:

Angie, girl you on my A-list
Angie, cause you I deleted my bae list
Baby A, if I was a teacher I'd give you that, an A, an A grade, you so fine—

Then I stopped because she had hung up. I don't know if it was because I had ignored her question or because she didn't like the song. That's what I mean, it's hard to know things, get clear answers, find out why.

VII.

My friend said to me, "so, tell me why, exactly, a person can't marry a pillow or a tree or even the ocean if they want to?" And I started at an answer, I even licked my lips to chase away the cottonmouth and bring forth something but, nothing, I don't know, I thought, I didn't say that, rather, I said nothing. And then he left.

IX.

Walked past a guy on the street today, he was sitting down on the sidewalk, next to a box and a handwritten sign. It read "Not homeless, only a lonely artist looking for that priceless human touch." Below that, in a different font and different color, it said, "Leave a donation if you want to support my work. But, you give this guy a hug, and I'll give you 5 dollars. Love is priceless." And I just thought, nope, nope, nope, nope, no, and resumed walking.

X.

My friend told me he's been meditating, I asked him what that meant and he said it was hard to explain. Well, I said, if it's hard to explain, how can you be sure you're doing it? He said it was a feeling. What kind, I asked? He said it was hard to explain but, you just kind of got into position and did it. And that just sounded awful, the whole phraseology there, and so I told him that. Look, wait, he said, it's about getting into your zone, your vibes, your feel, even the deep feel sub-space place of bliss. Do you get it now, do you see what I mean? No, I said.

XI.

I called Angie and told her that I'd be totally up for getting a pet but so long as it was—Wait, she said, stopping me cold in my tracks. But didn't she want to hear my idea, I'm thinking. I'd been working on it for a while now. I think…wait, she said. Remember when we agreed to have an open relationship?

No, I said, what?

Look, she said, I'm sorry, I think I remember that maybe even you suggested it. I'm pretty certain that maybe you did, she tells me.

No, I didn't, I say. I know I didn't, I'm the one who told you my friend Albert told me about that Christian idea of marriage, the church wedding thing plus the gold rings and the commitment, especially that, you remember.

Remember what? she countered. That I laughed at you, laughed in your face. That I told you no one wants that or does that anymore.

And as she's speaking I'm thinking, no, I told you that because maybe I wanted that and so that's why I suggested it.

I'm sorry, she says, I have to go.

I think about trying to get her to listen to the idea I have about what pet we should get but—

Hey, listen, she says, I think we're, she hesitates, I think we're probably done.

Probably? I say. You think, probably, probably, probably?

XII.

I've made up my mind to go see that therapist. I don't know, it might be fun. Why not?

XIII.

My friend says he's a dyed-in-the-wool liberal. Okay, I say, cool. I'm not political at all, I tell him. He says he had to leave this really big city because, despite being a liberal, and he tells me he's liberal down to his core, despite being a liberal in a liberal big city the liberal policies of that city had ruined the city completely, made it dirty, and dangerous and just downright disgusting. He told me that when he was at his favorite wheatgrass organic vegan smoothie and voting rights tiny house coffeeshop and he looked outside and there was a guy relieving himself in plain daylight he knew it was time to leave. He said he picked a small town in the countryside, far away from the big city, because it seemed like it was a good place to live owing to it being generally clean, safe, orderly, basically not like a 24/7 post-rave recovery session plus bad indy music. So, he said to me, and now smiling, now that I'm here, in this new place, it really is a good life, I'm living the good life, but there's just one thing missing. Oh, what's that, I asked him. The politics, he tells me, everything here is just so backward, so bigoted and outdated. I'm telling you, as soon as me and my likeminded big city expats get a hold of the policies around this town we'll be making the proper changes and pronto, the revolution is coming, Wait, I said, and don't get me wrong, I hate the left, I hate the right, I hate everybody, so I'm not trying to be biased here, but, have you ever considered that the policies you like are the reason that the big city got so messed up that you had to leave and so, just maybe, don't do that here, don't try that here, or ever, again? What, he says, and I can tell he's genuinely perplexed, what, what do you mean, what, what are you talking about?

XIV.

My friend says he's kind of a Buddhist, kind of Hindu. He's kind of New Age and really into days spent strolling about on foot perusing through old bookstores and sitting on park benches doing what he calls "communing with the pigeons." He says this kinda earns him the title of First Consul of *avant gardia* in the coming pan-religion of the new and now. That's what he said. But he also said kinda, so I say probably, maybe just maybe though. Maybe he is all this, like he claims, what I do know for certain is that he's really into smoking weed.

XV.

First session with the therapist. It can't believe how cliché it was; satisfyingly so. The room was dark enough to make first impressions creepy, I'm immediately thinking, where are the exits, are they labeled, are the lighted? The therapist—Dr. Cowslappperrr, yep, C o w s l a p p p errr, 3 ps, 3 rs—had me lay down a couch. It was super moist, not like incidental sweat from before, no, it felt like he had lathered it with something. But it smelled good, really good. He had me lay down and then he said nothing for about ten minutes and so I said, "Hey-" but he immediately silenced me and then went back to that which was before: me laying there, looking at the wall, him over my right shoulder, looking at me. Fine. Is this how this is done, who am I to say this is weird? Do I have a degree in whatever it is he does? After eleven hours like this he told me session one was over. I stood up to leave and he offered me something that looked like a breath mint that he had just pulled out from his coat pocket. And me, who's thinking *no, no, no, no, I'm not eating, I'm not anything with that,* I declined, politely. He then tugged aggressively on his jacket and pointed at me. What? I'm thinking. He did it again and then a third time. I still didn't get it. "Suit yourself," he explained, unhappy I had not understood his meaning.

XVI.

Was talking to a friend today and she kept asking me what I'd do if I knew the world was coming to an end? If the world was ending today, now, she said, would you ... and she asked me about like 20 scenarios, posed 45 questions, and it was basically nonstop for at least half an hour. End of the world, I'm thinking, end of the world, end of the world? When will you stop talking?

XVII.

My friend says practicing mindfulness will increase your self-esteem and overall deep-feel connectivity with the universe's inner magmatic will-pulse. "Hey," I said, "did you ever consider just getting a dog?"

XVIII.

Walked past a woman on the street today and she stopped me and just blurted out, "I love your jacket!" Where do people get such confidence, to just stop and compliment strangers. But, okay, but, okay, and, look, Angie who?, this must be fate, because she stopped me, and, I mean, good looking, no, gorgeous, more than that, I mean this woman, well, she stopped me so I'm going tell her "I'd love to get your number" and so I resolved to do that but by that time she was long gone.

B. 2

Albert says I gotta go to Mass and that I should go with him. He tells me to read the Bible. Get a Bible, he says, and just get to it, get on with it, it's inevitable. About the Mass, he says, look, not that its peaceful or beautiful or serene or melodic or sweet on the ears, the eyes, not just, rather, not just peaceful, beautiful, serene, melodic and sweet because it is all these things, but that's it's something more, it's true, he says. True, I ask? True, he says. True for you, I ask. True, he says. But, me, I'm, I'm trying to, I ask him again, true, true like probably true in your opinion. No, he says, true, just true.

XIX.

Why do women love arrogant men? I ask my beer bottle. I mean, I was nothing but nice, but kind, verifiably sweet to Angie and she just walked all over me. Now she's probably with some guy who's head of a motorcycle gang, or a quarterback, or an accountant, something badass like that. I remember there was this girl who I had biology class with in high school and I would always tease her in the style of putting her down, not mean stuff, but just kind of always be trolling her. And then one day, during the Young Computer Scientists of Tomorrow after school program she confessed her like psycho-obsessed, I'm not just in love I want to like steal your old T-shirts and sniff them in fields of wildflowers with me. And I'm like, what? And she's like, do you love me? And I was like, no. And then she started crying and I did feel bad about that. I just don't get it. Is this what women want, secretly? Guys who treat them like dirt, like put them in their place, be all toxic around them and stuff. Really? But so how I do become that, how do I do that? Next time some woman stops me on the street to say something I'm gonna act super broodish, standoffish, something that says, and probably without words, "you think I care? You think I need your approval?"

XX.

Session number two. Dr. Cowslappperrr asked me about my personal philosophy. Could I sum up my personal philosophy, he asked. You, know, I just don't, I don't know, I said. See, he said, and that's exactly your problem.

XXI.

Angie called today and left a message, and I couldn't believe it, but she told me she wanted to get back together. I thought about calling her back but decided to start living my aloof towards women thing. Maybe that's what I'll tell my therapist next time he asks me about personal philosophy.

B.3

Albert says that people search the world over and do a bunch of crazy stuff like go on four day darkness retreats, and seek out mountain sages in Tibet, and get put in hyperbaric chambers, and do all kinds of drugs, and talk, take vows of silence, take walks, take more pills but, he claims, they never take the time to just walk into a Church and sit silently in front of the exposed Blessed Sacrament, doing what he says is called "Eucharistic Adoration," and realize that everything they're searching for is right there.

XXII.

My friend says I'm a bigot. I'm not a bigot so I tell him: I'm not a bigot. He says me denying I'm a bigot means I'm a bigot. I'm not a bigot, I say. That you say you're not a bigot, he says, means you're a bigot, probably a very extreme form of one. No, I'm not, I say. You saying you're not a bigot means you're a bigot, he says, again. Okay, so it's opposites I guess, I say to myself, fine.... okay, I'll admit it, I'm a bigot. See, you're a bigot, he says. No, I protest, it's opposites, when I come out and say I'm a bigot you come to the rescue and say, actually, well, I had you pegged all wrong, that's the game we're playing, right? No, he says, you're definitely a bigot. And how are you so sure, I ask. Because you just told me yourself, he says. You just said, I'm a bigot. I say nothing, but only momentarily. Okay, so let me get this straight: If I admit

I'm a bigot I'm a bigot because I admitted it but, if I deny I'm a bigot it means I'm actually, secretly, a bigot. Yes, he says, good, now we're getting somewhere.

XXIII.

Angie called again. She called me five times today, left five messages. Same message: Let's get back together. My message to her? Silence.

XXIV.

My friend, the New and Now New Age one, called me again; high. He said, giggling the whole time, "Hey, man. You know how at Coug football games they play that song and it's like Na, Na, Na Na Na, Na, Cougs always find their way home. You know? You know, you know?" After he had asked me "ya know" eight times, I finally said, "Yes." "Okay," he said, "well, what if, what if, listen, dude, what if, bro, listen, listen, wait, what if instead, okay, what instead they sang Na, Na, Na Na Na, Na, Cougs always find their way stoned."

XXV.

At my third therapy session today I asked Dr. Cowslappperrr if he had any leads as to why I could not and cannot still identify a personal philosophy. No, you know, I really, I really have no idea, he said, shaking his head the whole time. About what, I asked? Excuse me, he said, now looking intently at me. About what, I repeated. You have no idea about me not having an idea or about the lack of the idea altogether? And he just shook his head and said, no, I was thinking what I'd say to my wife later when she asked me what I'd like for dinner.

B. 4

I told Albert about everything. I told Albert especially that I've now been in therapy for a month and have gotten no answers and seem like I can't find answers anywhere anyways, like where would I even think to begin to look and so, I was saying to him, but do you like have any ideas? You should go to Mass, he said. You should read the Bible. Okay, I said, but you've said that before. Okay, he said, but have you tried that yet? No, I said, I had not and so I said, no, no.

XXVI.

Angie called again. I ignored her call again. This time her message included a whole laundry list of I'm sorrys, I messed up, boy did I have no idea how good I had it, how good we were, and then so many promises and just please give me a call. But I'm not going to.

But then she texted. Her text read: 'I'm calling you one minute from now. If we ever had anything real, if I ever meant anything to you, you'll pick up and hear me out.' Sounds fair, I thought. I put the phone down, five seconds later it's ringing, it's Angie, I put it to my ear.

Yes?

She clears her throat and jumps right into Mariah Carey's song *We Belong Together*.

. . . .

And I was so moved, so touched by that, that I thought it would be wrong, disrespectful even, not to respond in kind. But if was going to sing, I was going to pretend my phone was a mic, so I could really dig in with my voice and get that raspy, gravely rebound vocal thing a lot of people like. And I chose Edwin McCain's *I'll Be* because it makes sense.

. . . .

Dead air. Silence. Still silence and now it's been 10 seconds. I guess both of us are speechless. Also, back together. Definitely, I'm thinking, not probably, certainly back together and, I gotta say, when our kids one day ask, so tell us again how you guys met, how you fell in love, I'm going to—

"Hey," Angie says.

"Yeah?"

"I think," she says, "I think now I know, now, yeah, now I know that we should definitely never, ever get back together. Please don't contact me again."

"What," I say, taken aback. And it takes a lot to take me aback, to catch me by surprise.

"Yeah," she says, "I'm gonna hang up now. Bye."

XXVII.

My friend says he has this favorite fault, it's bad, oh, he's embarrassed, oh, please can we just, can we not talk about that not go into that? But so anyways, he says, it's habitual, this thing, I keep, I keep going back to it, again and again, time and again. I keep falling into it, this, can we just call it a sin, can we say sin, he asks me. Yeah, I say, I'm not sure what you mean, exactly, but yeah, do you, be you, do what you want. Name things with names you feel comfortable with, go for it. So I keep falling into this sin, he says, but, I mean, I'm saying there's hope for me. Okay, good, I say. What is that? Yeah, he says, I mean I, I hate it but I'm gonna keep doing it, that's for sure. But, here's my hope, here's the thing, each time I do this bad thing I do a good deed. Did the bad thing, gave a donation to my library. Did the bad thing, recycled extra carefully next trash day. Did the bad thing, mowed my neighbor's lawn for free, then watered it, with sandcastle buckets too, the hose was broken, got it all watered though. It's not perfect, he says, it just helps, a little, with the guilt, I don't know, but look, the guilt with this it's like crazy big and large. How do you expiate guilt, he asks? You're asking me? Yeah. Really? Yes, if you do something bad how do you get rid of all the bad doing the bad has done to you, how do you wash it off? Wash it off, I say, what are you washing, you mean like, showering? Sure, yeah, whatever, he says, how do you, can you, can you like, uh, can you take a spiritual shower?

XXVIII.

Saw on the news today that Dr. Cowslappperrr was arrested and his practice is definitely, well, at least probably going to be shut down so I'm now done with therapy.

B.5

And so what do I do now, I thought? Personal philosophy, I was thinking, nope, nowhere closer on that, I have no idea and so I called Albert and asked him what to do. He said I should go to Mass. He said I should read the Bible. Then he asked me if I had tried to go to Mass, even like thought about it, since we last spoke. No, I said: no to both, hadn't gone, hadn't thought about going. But why would I, I said, in my defense, you have to actually believe in what the Mass is, what Catholics do, what they're about, right? Yes, Albert said. But do you actually believe these things, I asked him. Yes, he said. But you're not, you're not even a Catholic yourself, are you, I said. No, he said, not yet. I made this grand discovery less than a month ago, he explained, and ever since that day I've been at Mass, daily Mass, they call it, even though I can't yet receive the Holy Eucharist, I can't yet do anything as I've just started this preparatory program they have. But when I get made official, I'm going to do it all and everyday and, even now, even now as I'm just entering the whole deal, I'm going to be here, at Mass, daily Mass, everyday, that's for sure.

Grand discovery, I ask him, grand discovery you said. What grand discovery?

That's it's all true.

What is?

Everything.

Everything?

Everything.

Everything?

Everything.

You mean...

Yes, Albert says, yes, it's all true. I couldn't believe it but, yeah, everything, it's all true, the Mass, the Eucharist, about the Blessed Mother, ecclesiology, Thomas Aquinas on kingship and the just political state, Augustine on just war theory, Padre Pio being able to bilocate, confessing your sins to a priest, Hildegard of Bingen's music, the Council of Trent, ad orientem, incense, ex cathedra proclamations,

You're saying...

Everything, Albert says, it's all true. But so, and I can feel him turning the tide of the conversation from Catholicism unto me, you wanna know your deal?

My deal, I say, you know my deal?

Yeah, he says, I think so.

You're gonna like, diagnose me, identify my malady?

Yeah, Albert says,

oh, yeah, see,
I think that beyond all the maybe,
the probably,
even the definitely
it's just let your yes mean yes
and your no mean no
clear, to me, that you're a relativist and that's your problem. And I used to be a relativist myself, believing nothing, supporting nothing, weathervane flip-flopping in the wind, milquetoast, weak-kneed, just kind of like a no-person.

"A no-person," I ask, confused.

Yes, Albert says, a no-person, an anti-person. You see, now putting his hand on my shoulder, it takes one to know one and like I said I was one but now I'm not one and the only reason I'm not one now is God, is my faith, that's it. I'm pretty sure everything does kind of suck and is bland and is basically anti-happiness otherwise outside of that, and so you gotta decide if you want the way out or if you want to keep stuck in that mud and muck.

I don't say anything.

Albert says my name and asks if I'm okay. He says my name again.

I nod.

You sure you're okay?

I don't know, I finally say, I don't know.

B. 6

Albert and I've have been hanging out a lot lately. He's a good guy. We keep discussing religion and philosophy and each time more deeply and it's just great. We don't agree, or at least he knows what he believes whereas I don't, but it's awesome. I love it and look froward to it. One time we were at a coffee shop and sitting and talking and I looked away, for what I thought was like a second, tops, and he was gone, like he'd vanished into thin air. He later told me he had vanished because he actually was an angel. After a few seconds of silence he burst into laughter and told me he was just messing with me but, he said, that is real though and it does happen.

What, I said.

Angels, he said.

They walk among us and you never know when that guy you thought was just some bum or some lady you dismissed as an airhead is actually an angel in disguise. So, he said, best to always be on your best interpersonal behavior and all that. And he said some more stuff but it basically boiled down to two important takeaways: angels were real and he was not an angel. I don't know about all that but we have been playing a lot of one on one basketball, Albert and me, and he's like 5′7″ and Irish and he can dunk so, I'm just saying that's not normal. If, instead of hiding at the coffeeshop, he had been like "I'm an angel, check this out" and proceeded to dunk, I'm saying I'd have a lot harder time dismissing it out of hand.

Walking downtown again, by myself. Parked the car on Main Street, got some ice cream, not a half bad day by my lights. Albert gave me some books to read by this guy named Saint Augustine who, prior to his conversion, apparently said, "Give me chastity, Lord, just not yet," and I'm thinking that if I ever start doubting my ironclad no-person relativism I might even say, pray, I guess, "Give me certainty, Lord, a compass, just not yet." But the thing is—

  —oh,

no,

no,

no,

no,

no,

no,

no

no

no

no

no

no

no

no

no

no

no

no

no

no

no

no

no

no

no

no

no

no

. . . . oh, no. No, this can't be happening. No, it can't be. I see it, I see it right there but, no, no this can't be real. I actually pinch myself. It hurts, I'm not dreaming, no. I've reached my car and I look down and there it is, there it is. Immediately I'm filled with regret. This is what I should have said to him, to Dr. Cowslappperr. My personal philosophy, now it all comes into focus, now it's all clear, now I know you don't really know, don't really appreciate what you have until its gone. Up to this very point in my life, I have never, ever received a citation of any sorts. "Perfect law abiding citizen," that's what I should have told him. That's me, I mean, that *was* me but now, finally picking up the ticket and holding it in my hand, each word like a firm slap across the face—parking without permit, $25, please pay online or by check, fine increases by $5 after 30 days—I understand what it means to really have one's philosophy blown up, to have it exposed, demolished, reduced, to dust.

I sit down on the sidewalk and begin to weep.

On Theology of
the Body and
the Sexual Ethic[1]

I PICKED TONIGHT'S TOPIC, THE FORTHCOM-
ing discourse titled "On Theology of the Body and the Sexual
Ethic," because I like a challenge. This topic is not interesting to many people. Few would say they have spent a significant
amount of time thinking about sex, some have never given it even
a passing thought. Now, a talk on industrial regulations regarding paper clips silver and blue, the most efficient way to watch
paint dry on a wall, whether or not armadillos can communicate
with sloths and anteaters, or is it better to vacation in southern
North Dakota or northern South Dakota, these are the types of
inquiries that promote themselves. They draw large crowds and
hold the audience on seat's edge from the first word to the last
reverberations of applause given from the standing posture. But
sex, announce you're giving a talk on sex, and prepare to speak
over the sounds of crickets, dead air, empty chairs, no one here
because no one cares.

But I like a challenge. So, tonight, I'll try to make what is a
very dry and boring topic as interesting as possible. As you incor-
rectly infer from the title, we will spend a fair amount of time
discussing the writing and input of Pope St. John Paul II on this
ever pressing, perennially curious issue. We will not be. What I
am going to present you with is a brief—and by brief I mean a
crash course emergency exercise in hyper-brevity, folks—reflection
on what the Bible and Catechism say about sex and then what
main points, in quick-shift summation, we can draw from John

---

1   This lecture was also presented (earlier and in a slightly abridged form)
at the St. Thomas More Catholic Student Center on the campus of Washington State University (Pullman, WA), October 15, 2020, as an invited talk
from the St. Thomas More Center

Paul II's *Theology of the Body,* better yet and by that I mean simpler still, some introductory points from an introduction to the topic itself, Christopher West's *Theology of the Body for Beginners,* because with such a topic as this best start at the very ground floor.[2]

Following the quick Scriptural, Catechetical and instructional reflections I will segue into that which you all came here for tonight, the real armadillo and anteater of the whole issue: my take on this subject. And what might that be? Three things, three frames through which to view sexuality in the light of Christian teaching that I hope will be helpful and hopeful.

First: Christian sexuality must always be a *both-yes* proposition if it is to be enjoyed in the fullest measure. Debating whether procreation, on one hand, or the mutual comfort slash enjoyment of the spouses' physical intimacy should have pride of place is a fool's errand.

The only answer is both-yes.

Both procreation, openness to life and the inestimable gift of children, along with the romantic expression of the act itself, meant to heatweld glue two soulmates into one flesh fully, are preeminently important, equally important; both-yes.

Secondly, I'll speak to you about a phenomenon known as *born again virgins.* You might surmise what this is about but, whether you do or don't, I do ask a small favor of you. Does that name "born again virgins," strike the ear as a bit cheesy, really overly cheesy as if your friend Chet "Giga-Chad" Fromage melted blocks and blocks of cheddar and gouda and swiss and poured that combined mixture down your ear canal while singing, *a capella,* Glenn Miller's classic Chattanooga Choo-Choo? Sure. And I agree. But fulfilling my favor consists in acknowledging that a Protestant is probably behind this term therefore one should not feel any cringetingles up the spine when considering that Protestants are born and bred to make everything as cheesy as it can possibly get and that for them there is neither a limit nor any acceptable threshold they will not attempt to cross in attaining their aims. Also, could Giga-Chad Fromage be any more based?

---

2   Christopher West, *Theology of the Body for Beginners: A Basic Introduction to Pope John Paul II's Sexual Revolution* (West Chester, PA: Ascension Press, 2004).

My third, and final point, brings us back to the driving thesis of my essay—a healthy sexual ethic is a both-yes proposition—and adds that one should possess, and failing that pray so as to try to possess, an attitude I term *devout levity* when it comes to all things concerning sex.

Before I jump into that I'm going to provide you with that tiny helpsheet of what has already been given and said, some foundational rooting, although being but 1% of 1% of the whole Catholic sexual ethic it might encourage you to read on, research more, learn more for yourselves, and in doing so you might find it to your benefit. For those of you not sure where to start, here you go, try this first, read here first, and soon you'll be on your way.

The idea that man and woman, made in God's image and likeness, have been made for one another and that by their coming together they may be "fruitful and multiply," as we read in the first chapter of the first book of the Bible, is found throughout Scripture. In fact, the very verbatim phrase found at the end of chapter two in Genesis—"they shall become one flesh"—is repeated in both St. Matthew and St. Mark's Gospels and in St. Paul's letter to the Ephesians.[3]

We hear the gift of sex extolled in the Old Testament—"may he kiss me with the kisses of his mouth, for your love is better than wine...your lips, my bride, drip honey, honey and milk are under your tongue...may my beloved come into his garden and eat its choice fruits," quoted directly from the Song of Songs[4] —as we hear it praised in the New Testament, too, as when St. Paul counsels periods of extended abstinence only "that you may devote yourselves to prayer" soon after "com[ing] together again" because husbands and wives should "not deprive one another."[5] Sex is good. Sex can be holy. And if you're still not convinced of the biblical blessing upon the conjugal act, let me give you one more citation from the inerrant Word of God, here from the Book of Proverbs: "Rejoice in the wife of your lovely youth, a lovely deer,

---

3   *The Holy Bible* (New American Bible: For Catholics) published for Catholic Extension by the American Bible Society, New York: 1970/1991. Genesis 1:28, 2:24; St. Matthew 19:5; St. Mark 10:8; Ephesians 5:31.
4   Song of Songs 1:2, 4:11–16
5   Corinthians 7:5

a graceful doe. Let her breasts fill you at all times with delight; be intoxicated always in her love."[6]

What then does our Catechism say about sex, and what conclusions can we draw from the aforementioned *Theology of the Body*? "Conjugal love involves a totality," we read in the Catechism, "in which all the elements of the person enter... it aims at a deeply personal unity, a unity that, beyond union in one flesh, leads to forming one heart and soul." Furthermore, this unity is to be ordered towards "procreation and education of the offspring and it is in them that it finds its crowning glory," children being, the Catechism declares, "the supreme gift of marriage." But lest anyone put too much emphasis on procreation, listen to the Catechism once final time. "The conjugal love of man and woman ... stands under the twofold obligation of fidelity and fecundity... these two meanings or values of marriage (the good of the spouses themselves and the transmission of life) cannot be separated."[7]

John Paul II, here via Christopher West's abridged introduction, confirms nothing less, that marriage is about a "sacramentality of the body" where husband and wife try to reclaim the original meaning of human sexuality, being "naked, but not ashamed," seeing sex as the good it is so as to "re-inflate their tires[8]"—being in proper relation with themselves, God, and God's original design for sex—and finish 'inebriated' in the love God has so gratuitously poured out for us in the gift of human sexuality." "Do you know what you really want here?" West asks near the close of his book, connecting the sacrament of marriage to the source, center and summit of our Faith, it too fleshy in the full incarnate glory of the God who gives it to us. "You want the Eucharist and marriage, and the Catholic Church has them in their fullness."[9]

---

6   Proverbs 5:18–19.
7   CCC, 1643, 165, 2363.
8   Giga-Chad Fromage is a big fan of Christopher West and has promoted *Theology of the Body* to many a frat brother and, post graduation, Wall Street co-worker. He brings up Christopher West randomly at Thursday night post work bar runs in lower Manhattan. But about this one particular phrase— re-inflate their tires—Giga-Chad opined the following: "Bruh, I mean, son. Cringe? Dawg, what the, bruh, are you for real, bruh? Re-in-'(expletive deleted)-flate their (expletive deleted) tires? What the, ... bruh ... "
9   West, *Theology of the Body for Beginners*, 4, 26, 85, 123.

There is of course more, so much more, but I'll leave it to you to explore those valuable sources further, the Bible and Catechism at the top of the list, as we now turn to my aforementioned three focal points I would like you to reflect further on, the very heart and catalyst of this essay: the both-yes proposition—which you've just heard about in a certain form, that catechetical two-fold obligation of fidelity and fecundity—born again virgins, and devout levity.

Sex is a both-yes proposition. With equal estimation, especially for the sake of equilibrium, we must understand that an openness to life along with the mutual comfort and pleasure of the spouses are the 'point' of sex. You may see no controversy here but there is a silent, sometimes open, philosophical war waged around these two poles. Taking one to the extreme always comes at the expense of the other, an unholy polarization that wreaks havoc within the marital union and beyond. So, let's begin there, the extremes.

Quite a few people hold that sex is solely about pleasure and that procreation need not factor into the equation at all. Rampant promiscuity, one that drives widespread acceptance of contraception, further seeds the rotten fruits of venereal disease, infidelity, and the ongoing abortion epidemic, the latter a necessary result of seeing sex as a common exchange of goods—as common as a handshake or kiss on the cheek—where should any member of the transactional party experience buyer's remorse, so to speak, the product can be painlessly and easily returned (see: removed and/by way of being destroyed) without question. No need to belabor these points here, piling euphemisms upon euphemisms, suffice to say the imbalanced mindset and behavioral patterns that emerge from seeing sex solely as a means to personal pleasure are openly acknowledged even by proponents of this position. There might be literally a thousand half-hour sitcom episodes dedicated to the after the fact depressed state of someone who finds their latest one-night stand not as fulfilling as was hoped.

But the other extreme—that sex is only about procreation—is destructive in its own way, too. Catholics, devout Catholics, often forget this. But tell me how it could not be for a woman who feels her husband only wants to be intimate with her so she can get pregnant with their next child, who feels her husband sees her as nothing more than a baby-making machine? How could a husband not feel wounded when ascertaining that the only time his wife plans a romantic evening together is when it coincides with her peak fertility? Is she still madly in love with him, he the person, or is she only after the biological matter he can provide her in the fulfillment of her lifelong motherhood goals (?), he now in the role of the baby-making machine spouse.

Sex is, sex must be, if you want to be both holy and happy, the two of you, a both-yes proposition. Be open to life, always. Have as many children as God is calling you to for parenthood is a holy vocation and children are one of the most precious gifts we can receive. Give the population control freaks posing as climate change alarmists posing as *authentic* posers, for some of them are so fake they make other fakes look real, the same friendly advice Mother Angelica gave the then Archbishop of Milwaukee in the wake of World Youth Day-Denver (1993): "he can put his head in the back toilet as far as I am concerned."[10]

Have as much kids as you want, let the people who have five kids themselves while telling you to have none—because, now, this is going to be shocking, you ready?, can you handle the truth?, because they think you're nothing but feudal serf peasant useless eater worm-level scum so *of course,* you *shouldn't be having kids! Here's your pill, your condom, your abortion clinic, your sterilization shot right up the spine, like the firm kick in the ass you deserve from us, your oligarchic duke-lords, lest you be getting uppity about places and ranks and freedoms and such poppycock, but we, well, someone needs to be here to inherit the riches of the vastly depopulated earth, right?, and shouldn't it be humanity's best and brightest?*—find clean toilets for their brilliant, handsome, so much better than you and me and he and she too heads. Let these people sleep in the demographic winter bed they made for themselves, and for us, too, that's the sad part, that.

Have as much kids as you want because yes, the Catholic sexual ethic is about procreation, but too as in also as in do not under any circumstances forget that *in the same measure* it is about the mutual

---

10   Jacqueline L. Salmon, "Mother Angelica, founder of Catholic TV and radio empire, dies at 92." *The Washington Post,* March 27, 2016.

comfort spouses offer one another as well—both-yes, always—the spouses offering their most intimate selves to one another freely, no strings attached, not even holy strings, rather enjoying the marital act because they're supposed to, they are free too, and realize few joys can match a mutual appreciation that that person right there, with me now, with me forever, loves me and only me in this way and I them the same. We are supposed to be in alignment with the Church's sexual ethic. I mentioned that before and I'll say it again because it's true. And while demanding, it is like all the aspects of our religion, something to be embraced not feared, for in living in accord with the Church's teaching on sex we'll soon find ourselves truly free and ready to give and receive love, not bound in a prison of archaic rules aimed at sapping our joy as the world tells as.

This brings me to my second point, "born-again virgins." If you are still waiting for marriage, wait for marriage. It is worth it. But, if you have fallen in some way, maybe fallen far and many times, I'll ask you this: so what? You're claiming to be a Catholic and yet you seem to know so little about your faith. The Catholic Church counts amongst its greatest saints the greatest sinners beforehand, great saints who some of them were formerly hardened sinners, licentious profligates, even out and out bad, immoral, if not wholly amoral, people. For to be Catholic is to be lukewarm to the lukewarm, being hot or cold, never in between, and some of the coldest frozen in sin men and women became, by the grace of God, hot flares of heavenly fire. Saint Paul held the robes of people murdering a man by whipping stones off his face from close proximity; Saint Stephen, the Church's first martyr. Saint Augustine lived a life of prodigious lust prior to his conversion, famously quipping, when already on the path to repentance, "grant me chastity, Lord. Just not yet."[11]

If you've fallen into sexual sin of whatever stripe, so what? Listen to the words of the Lord Himself when counseling another sexual sinner, the woman caught in adultery, she too, like St. Stephen, about to be stoned to death. "But Jesus bent down and started to

---

11   St. Augustine, *Confessions,* Book VIII.

write on the ground with his finger... 'Let anyone of you who is without sin be the first to throw a stone at her'... they slipped away one by one... until Jesus was left in the middle of the crowd with the woman. 'Woman, where are your accusers? Has no one condemned you?' 'No one.' 'Neither do I, go and sin no more.'"[12]

That's it.

It's that simple.

You've fallen into sexual sin?

So what? Many, most, have.

Who then can condemn you?

Not even Christ condemns you.

But, but, but...

but, the key is in the parting words:

go and sin no more. Repent. Resolve to commit these sins no more. Be made new, by God's grace.

And that's precisely what this second point, 'born again virgins' is all about. You can be clean again, whole again, regain your purity, and in full, once more. If you've fallen in the past, no matter how many times, resolve to stop today. Repent, be forgiven, by God, then forgive yourself, and move forward. And what a gift that would be to give your spouse on your wedding night: your reclaimed virginity. That while you had once fallen you made amends and since making amends you have been kept whole, remained pure, and, as we Catholics all know, what God has made clean no one can render impure.

My third and final point in is the vein of that which I am often wont to do in these talks, return to the start, but here the half-start, not to the opening of the essay but to the opening of my three points, the both-yes proposition. Just as a healthy Catholic sexual ethic entails an openness to life and the gift of children alongside the romantic flame for one's spouse kept burning bright in mutual comfort, so too is this final point, "devout levity," a both-yes-like, simultaneous proposition and invitation.

"Devout levity"; Catholics should approach sex with the highest devoutness, meaning seriousness and respect, while, at the same

---

12   John 8:1–11.

time, not taking it or themselves too seriously. Paradoxical? Sure, but ours is the faith of paradoxes proved true, the reconciliation of seemingly incompatible principles that upon further review cannot henceforth be imagined separated.

Devout levity. Sex is a serious thing, the most serious thing, maybe, for as the singular action by which new life is brought into the world, along with the mechanics of the act itself guaranteeing that two persons who engage in it together will find their relationship forever changed, in ways good or bad, means we should always have the highest respect for sex and fight for its proper expression and our own holy purity. Sex is not a joke, it is not a game, an adventure, a recreational activity, a mechanism for revenge or something to pass the time when bored. Sex is not "not a big deal," and only a devout approach to sex, living out all Holy Mother Church asks us to do in this domain, can give us the hope to be men and women with relationships fulfilled, not broken, by sex.

Allow me to end on a lighter note with levity itself and I'll start in the negative. People who don't understand the necessary levity needed for a healthy sexual ethic cause themselves much self-inflicted suffering. Putting sex on a pedestal, as if it's the end all be all, is anti-levity. It creates false expectations for both spouses, leading to night after night of disappointment and sometimes resentments, and can lead, in malignant cases, to the traps of infidelity and pornography, the poor sufferers here chasing imagined ideals of sex that do not exist. Similarly, expecting marital intimacy to be the magic pill that cures all other ailments is as naïve and stupid as it is offensive.

Sex is not a substitute for the other myriad aspects of a healthy marriage built around the deepest friendship—the authentic 'soulmate' thing—profound mutual respect, the helpmate equality quality of the "lived everyday," for hand in hand walks in the park, meals together, raising children together, growing, laughing, and suffering together. Sex, while incredibly important, is not the whole of marriage but rather one aspect of it, no matter how interesting and exciting it may be.

Levity, holy lightheartedness, will make one's sexual ethic the best it can be. That, having been found in accord with the devout part of devout levity, the openness to life of the both-yes proposition and the waiting for marriage, perhaps the perseverance in starting over and now staying chaste as a born again virgin if one has fallen, once all this devout stuff has been taken care of, now is the time to truly enjoy the exhilarating fun of the second part of the both-yes, the mutual comfort of marriage built fundamentally around the realization that I love this person and they love me and it's just us, just the two of us in this way, and all the world could fall away but our love would be enough for it's built on the love of God. And however this part of marriage is going, it's best taken, the good times and the bad, with a light heart, with levity, with the knowledge that it's neither the salvation nor the end of the world; sex. It's but one part of one of the greatest gifts God has bestowed upon men and women, a most special and exclusive partnership where it can be declared with the joy of an intimate love sought and fulfilled, "this now is bone of my bones, and flesh of my flesh."[13]

---

13   Genesis 2:23.

Logos and Human History

CHRISTMASTIME IS ABOUT SOMEONE NOT something. This person, this God-Man, is Logos Incarnate, God Incarnate, the Second Person of the Holy Trinity, consubstantial with the Father, and through this singular Logos, the only begotten not made, light from light, true God from true God, Son of God all things were made, for as the Second Genesis proclaims:

> *In principio erat Verbum et Verbum erat apud Deum et Deus erat Verbum. Hoc erat in principio apud Deum. Omnia per ipsum facta sunt et sine ipso factum nihil quod factum est. In ipso vita erat et vita erat lux hominum, et lux in tenebris lucet et tenebrae eam non comprehenderunt,* [this soon culminating] *in et Verbum caro factum est et habitavit in nobis et vidimus gloriam eius gloriam quasi unigeniti a Patre plenum gratiae et veritas,* [so therefore] *laeti triumphantes, Deum de Deo, Lumen de lumine, genitum non factum, Regem Angelorum, in Bethlehem natus est; venite, venite, fidelis, venite adoremus.*

Understanding this we understand not much but all, and how very artistic this really, profoundly, is. God, the Unmoved Mover; God, the unique non-contingent Being; God, divine, but his creation not for there is a distinction on a different level of being between God, essence itself, and everything else, non-contingent human beings, nature, animals, all, and so you have the scientific gift of secondary causality, that because God created everything by His Logos, we, humans, one of these created things, can ourselves create in an independent fashion via our free will. Precisely because God loves us, we are free agents who can use our reason to study and discover things that in themselves play according to the divine rules God established *au commencement et pour tous les temps,* and, you already know, here, finally, is the possibility and very seedbed of scientific inquiry, something like the intellectual ferment of Middle Age Europe at its philosophical and theological peak, and something like all that good and well-laded 'science' snapping off shocks of electrical ingenuity later on and on, we assured that all the universe makes sense because God exists and God is good and his creation is intelligible, to be studied and understood by creatures created by Him, themselves endowed with this λόγος σπερματικός, we, all of us, having been made in the Image and Likeness of God.

Rejoice, then, you, me, we, let us sing in exultation this Christmas, alongside the countless choirs of angels, in thanksgiving for the moment when God himself left heaven to win our salvation spurning not the lowest and humblest beginnings in completing the only work that has ever mattered. Amen, you may say, but how do we arrive at this central point of our story, and how do we trace the movement of Logos alongside its aping and profaning anti-Logos imitation, throughout history, all of history, from the beginning until now?

A dark cave, sometime after Eden; cold outside but warm within, a dying fire's last embers shine a faint light emanating from a fading last gasp spittle juxtaposed against firmer crackles from the lightening outside cutting swaths of brightness through the downpour and the darkness. A man and woman, nearly naked, shivering, take turns ripping through the carcass of the afternoon's kill not quite cooked through. The mother drops a few pieces into a child's mouth. And then, a miracle, evidence that man is made in the Image and Likeness of the Logos Himself, a miracle, foil to all blind chance postulations, unexplainable by the many-millennia long durée of evolutionary necessity but easily comprehended as gift of God. "Can I have that?" he asks. "Yes," she replies, giving him precisely what he asked for, for when one spoke the other understood.

Quitting the cave these our early ancestors walked out into the light of a pristine religion, as translucent as a snowmelt fed Idaho mountain brook. Rudimentary and roughed up by the Fall though it was, it was clean, clear in stating that the sky god above in whom they believed was great and all powerful but good, omnipotent but benevolent, a father, in short. Tales of the two-thirds god Gilgamesh slaying forest monsters and bedding goddesses who later scorned sent the Bull of Heaven to kill him, or Zeus seducing lowly Greek maidens to satisfy his libido, or Aphrodite, she the worst, her apple of discord launching those thousand ships more than pathetic Helen and Paris, all this came later on in our "evolution," clearly a "devolution" away from logical Logos unto and into chaos for as the further we progressed from our first parents stumble the more we stumbled into the darkness of our enslaving passions, notwithstanding heroic Hector meeting his fate outside the walls at Troy or those stars and stripes egalitarian Americans in the North African desert, the ancient Egyptians, whose logos variant "ma'at" dared claim that any man or woman, from Pharaoh to peon, could, by the merit of choosing good not evil, inherit the happiness of heaven.

And then the first true high point for man, and our history of Logos, the premier reconciliation, the Old Covenant between God and man, the moment when that Logos that is fundamentally Love decided enough was enough, and although our forbidden fruit eating first parents—and here's anti-Logos lies for you, *you will be like gods,* the enemy hissed, *knowing good and evil*—had merited not just expulsion but utter extermination, God himself reached out, speaking to Moses through the burning bush, beckoning him to remove dusty sandals from the sacred ground he was standing upon, declaring once and for all His essential nature—I AM[1]—for indeed He alone is He who IS and must be whereas all else can but need not be and if becomes then comes to be solely by His sovereign will. Finally came the Logos guidebook, the eminently logical instructions that, don't you know, can still be lived out today, the potentiality of a peace unsurpassed should we choose, in conformity of our own will to His, to put God first and above all, keeping holy His name and His day, honoring our parents while refusing to kill, commit adultery, steal, lie, covet.[2]

"The Greek Miracle," Dawson said.[3]

Miracle ×2, I say,

---

1   Exodus 3:14.
2   Exodus 20:1-19.
3   British historian, Christopher Dawson.

for the speech of the cavemen concerning what fillings of the fortnight's hunt paired best with available flora and fauna become the philosophical speculations of Socrates and his pupil, Plato; Plato's pupil, Aristotle, sent his pupil, Alexander the Great, and by extension all that froth-creamy rich proto-Christian Greek logistical syntax (*arete, ergon, telos*, the hoped avoidance of *aporia* with equal aspirations to, dare we dream, *eudaimonia*) all across the soon to be Hellenized world, tentacle stretching from Egypt in the south—Cleopatra was a Greek-Egyptian, after all, terminal stop on the Ptolemaic line—to Persia in the East (and look what the Jewish people had to say [rather what they explain *God has to say*] about Cyrus the Great[4]), to what would become Byzantium in the center, the middle, the rest, the whole, that grand city called Istanbul today formerly bearing the name of the great Roman Emperor who, in the year AD 312 at Milvian bridge followed the prompting to in that sign, that sign then *this* sign, conquer, and so he did, ending the night is darkest before the dawn most viciously anti-Logos Diocletian persecutions in one fell swoop re-orienting Rome into the bosom of Logos, the agent of Logos in the world (for the New Rome would now be carrying out the work long ago begun by Saul made Paul, Peter the Rock, and all those holy saints and martyrs of the first centuries AD whose perseverance unto death won for them a crown of imperishable glory and for us an example to aspire to) and even when Rome fell in the West in 476 to the rescue soon came Benedict and his men, *ora et labora*, the recipe for Logos in action, praying and working a new Rome into being until, three centuries and what must have seemed like three thousand barbarian assaults later, a new Roman emperor would take his crown, but this time, on Christmas Day AD 800, receiving it from the Pope, Bishop of Rome, whose Petrine authority could confer upon the head of a fallen man the title *Holy* Roman Emperor.

Augustine was right.

But two options present themselves to us here:

the City of God or
the City of Man.

---

4   Isaiah 45:1-6.

Right and just *Amor Dei usque ad contemptum sui* or the sinful *amor sui usque ad contemptum Dei.*

Yes, Medieval Europe had its glories, Christendom in full flower, God honored beyond the private sphere publicly, universities, cradles of all the science and speculative philosophies and historical analytics and the mechanical machinations to come, popping up at Bologna, Krakow, Oxford, Prague and Paris. And no one, I mean hardly a Harry or a Harriet near or far, knew how to get poly-mathematical ear-syrup poppin like ya girl Hildegard of Bingen (1098–1179). That she did not invent DJ'ing while beatboxing and bartending should not produce an imaginative failure concerning some composition of her's double speed playedback over a strobe-lit dance hall where she, simultaneously, could have treated dancing patrons to the latest home-brewed tripel with the option to read excerpts from her *Physica.*

Logos filled glories, aplenty, no question, but the Middle Ages also featured papal court scheming that would make even David J. Fillintheblank blush. At the so-called "Cadaver synod" of the late 9th century one pope pulled another pope's dead body from the ground only to desecrate it by a mock trial before throwing the corpse into the Tiber river. We talk about papal intrigue today, about the open antagonisms between Pope Francis and Archbishop Vigano, but, hey, at least things aren't this bad today, right?

Logos reached new, sky-scarping heights in the 13th century when the Angelic Doctor arrived on the scene; Gym, Tan, Laundry Tommy Fuhgeddaboudit, DJ Dumb Ox featuring No clothes Francis the Forrest Runner, aka MC Wolf Whisperer, for yes, amen in the latter, the seemingly *illogical* external appearance of stripping naked in the town square to renounce all earthly goods and follow the beckoning voice to "rebuild my church" was not just wholly logical but nerve center logic itself, Logos 101, the very Imitation of Christ. If Saint Thomas Aquinas is the greatest philosopher and theologian in human history it's because he's the most rational, most logical, most Logos, one. Christ Himself reportedly told him, sometime around the time when Thomas classified his life's work as "straw" relative to the beatific vision of Heaven, that "you have written well of me." That is enough of an endorsement, period. But further elaboration demonstrates two contributions that stand out in Aquinas' work (and I'm not even mentioning his reconciliation of Aristotle, of all pagan wisdom, to Christ, that in itself a monumental achievement), two contributions that form one organic whole.

How appropriate, for Our Blessed Lord himself is two, True God and True Man, in one seamless hypostatic union.

Aquinas's two—the five proofs for God's existence, and the definitive confirmation of God's essentialism, that He is the only non-Contingent Being, that "in God it is impossible that existence be distinct from essence"—are really one: one grand and eternal confirmation that, as God himself said to Moses "I AM," He is the only who Who IS and knowing this we can proudly declare "I am, therefore I think." This reversal, in four centuries anticipation, of Descartes *cogito* is the formula by which I will take you in skim-journey over the remaining eight hundred years of Logos v. anti-Logos history from Aquinas' time up to ours; up to right now, today, December 2020. For those eight hundred years, and indeed today, the choice between reason and irrationality, between order and chaos, depends on what side of this formula you fall on.

So, I ask you: Are you with Aquinas? Do you believe "I am, therefore, I think," (?) because, first and foremost in the only ontological inquiry that matters, God *is*. I am, therefore I think, therefore I love, I fight, I write . . . all that I do, all that I put my free will into action to activate, begins with the reality that I was created by God, God, the creator of everything, right back to the first moment of everything when there was nothing, absolute nothingness and God, the non-contingent Being, "I AM."

Or, are you with Descartes whose "I think, therefore I am" maxim (?), which birthed continental philosophy and its own children to come, posits man, not God, as the ontological point of departure. Here, one cannot be sure of anything outside of the *res cogitens,* one's own mind, out there in the catch-all everything else *res cogitens,* everything including God. (And here, in AD 1639, we haven't even arrived at the Newtonian pagan replay of all = love v. strife meaning all is inertia and gravity which then becomes, in money matters, the Adam Smith Scottish Enlightenment self-interest v.

competition binary which later on yet still is added itself to an admixture of Marx's the history of class warfare is the history of everything and Darwin's survival of the fittest. All this = forget the Logos of the societal and/or "common good" hope of a piece of the pie for everyone, the pie warm and homemade made with love because we're trying to be about that, love, of God and neighbor, and instead dive feet or head first into the chaos of "scientific reality" where individualism is the only rule and the most ruthless reaps the richest harvest; and if you're driving away from the village you just looted with a truck full of loot that you sit upon raising two middle fingers rigid back at those poor people you ripped off and made significantly poorer still, so what? Guess "natural selection" had selected them to be your doormat, them the weak evidently not yet "evolved" enough). But since I can only be sure of the I that is me, and cannot be sure of God or God's laws or anyone else's anything, does it not follow that truth is only what I perceive it to be, not absolute, and that morality is relative, as unique as a fingerprint and as prolific, and so all that's left to do is for each to do as each sees fit and let the strongest, the cleverest, the most convincing, the most wealthy—but not the most good or most holy, for such things hang on the absolute systems we have done away with—win?

Aquinas or Descartes,

a simplification, sure, but consider the following brief reflections on the rationality and goodness of the former rooted in the Eternal Logos versus the subjectivism, relativism, and ultimately illogical rooting of reality in the fallen, limited, and unstable mind of man. And I'm not even going to comment on the so-called "Protestant Reformation," nor frame it via the definition of heresy as choosing a part over the whole, for that's exactly what it is, Protestantism, picking out pieces from the complete Catholic pie and elevating them to prime importance while discarding the rest. For these choices are made by fallen people following fallible people who had themselves chosen their own truth, their own interpretation, over the assurances of Christ's Bride's protection against the Gates of Hell.

Aquinas or Descartes,

Logos or anti-Logos.

There are plenty of examples of Logos over the past millennium; the miraculous conversion of Mexico from bloody human sacrifices, mangled bodies flung down temple steps to the Hummingbird Wizard in favor of consuming the Body, Blood, Soul and Divinity of the One Eternal Saving Sacrifice made by God Himself, this transformation begun with *Nuestra Senora* and Juan Diego at Tepeyac Hill; the Catholic Counter-Reformation and the Baroque art and music that grew out of it; America, for all its many flaws, a nation born aspiring to high ideals, to happiness and fairness and the light of liberty guaranteed by a Creator who has made all men equal; the ending of slavery in that same nation, even if it took, sadly, a bloody civil war to achieve it; the telegraph, the train, penicillin and airplanes, proving that secondary causality—God himself really giving us talents to fulfill, and the means, the will, to do it—means we can produce works of art, that we can be artists and inventors and innovators; the concerted, free worldwide effort to defeat Nazism followed by, not so many years later, the crushing of the communist leviathan USSR, with St. John Paul II at the forefront of the struggle.

Nonetheless, a long list of the above good things made short by necessity can be matched, sadly, maybe even exceeded, by so many examples of anti-Logos, of hate, evil, sin, in short, in the world before and with us still now. "Paris is well worth a Mass," the Protestant king Henry IV said at the close of the 16th century French wars of religion, setting aside his religious convictions in an insincere conversion to Catholicism so as to become King of France. But, who cares, right? Religion isn't important, a private matter if anything at all. So the blasphemous French revolutionaries almost two hundred years later, when taking a break from guillotining their opponents and themselves, profaned Notre Dame Cathedral with the so-called "goddess of reason," which must have been a joke for their philosophy contained nothing rational at its core, declarations of "rights of man and citizen" a poor cover for will to power hatred of God and man. But, fret not, Darwin showed us we're not made in the Image and likeness of God, rather evolved sludge probably of lesser dignity and value than apes. Then Feuerbach explained that it was man who invented God, for a childlike "security complex" as Freud argued, it pathetically necessary to keep up the religious scam "opiate of the people" which kept the masses under control, as Marx explained.

So, armed with all this anti-Logos "knowledge" that began with Descartes opening the starting gate with it is not God first, but me, my mind first, through the above 19th century philosophers who assured us God does not exist, religion is nothing more than a coping mechanism, and that people are not a little below the angels but a few inches above the mud, it was not surprising when the prophet of anti-Logos Friedrich Nietzsche proclaimed—like Luther had before him—that all that mattered in life was will; not God's truth, not God's rational law and order, not God's immutable structure of love and goodness open to all by the salvific work of his Logos, His divine Son, Our Lord Jesus Christ, Incarnate and dwelling among us.

No to reason.

No to logic.

No to Logos.

All you have is you and the relative reality in your mind. Laws? Restraints? Rules? These are nothing more than social constructions designed by bad and mean and intolerant church men meant to restrict your happiness. Whatever you want, you can have it, so long as you take it by will, by force, so long as you, the uberman, are willing to reject the fiction of a singular reality and enforce your personal perspective on others. And so Stalin knew one had to break a few eggs to make an omelet, and Mao could justify killing tens of millions for his "Great Leap Forward," and Hitler gave us the Second World War and the Holocaust, and today, right now, today, we creak under the weight of the ever-growing numbers of the ongoing abortion holocaust, dedicated to an anti-Logos Moloch-type idol of I'll decide if that child is a person or a clump or cells, then I'll decide this and that, I, me, I will always decide what is right and wrong, what is good and evil, just like that snake in the Garden told my first parents so many years ago.

But so what can we do today, Advent, 2020? I'll challenge you with three items in closing. First, and for this Advent here and now, read St. John's Gospel cover to cover, it's all there, all that

Logos concerning Baptism, the Holy Eucharist, Our Lady's Christocentricism, and that Second Genesis poetic opening I opened this essay with declaring that God is, that before Abraham was he was, always, I AM, and, as we all know, that He is love, so loving the world in fact that He sent us His only begotten Son so that whoever believes in Him may not perish but have eternal life.

Read John's Gospel to get you in the right pro-Logos mindset, then do two and three, two things which are one for linked in a classic catchphrase of Benedictine spirituality referenced before they still today serve as a great blueprint for Christian action: ora et labora, prayer and work. If you want to serve the Logos and His Church, you must pray and work. Attend Mass and keep the commandments, love God and neighbor, pray the Rosary, the Divine Mercy Chaplet, the Liturgy of the Hours, everything. Pray without ceasing, let's truly try it.

Then get to work on becoming that which the Logos v. anti-Logos battle needs most: true artists, real artists in keeping with this essay's undercurrent of the coming Christmas season, of Our Lord's artistic masterpiece, the Incarnation, which is the perfect and seamless reconciliation of essence and existence. Essence and existence existing simultaneously and without conflict, that is what we're after. Real art is the manifestation of essence and existence successfully combined. Essence, baseline being, Form foundational reality, the "higher" things, transcendence; existence, baseline daily reality, foundational everyday existence, functions not Forms, the "lower" here and now stuff, immanence. You get one of these categories all the time and every day, the other one less frequently, but the two together harmoniously in tandem? That's art.

Sculpture is art because it does this. Sculpture begins with the everyday, the hard, the pressure-formed "real," some marble, let's say, and then brings something brand new into existence by impressing the essential idea—a/the Form of female beauty, for example—onto the existential stone. So when you have the final product, a statue of Maude Adams[5], you have art for the final

---

5 Turn of the century actress often found on lists of the most beautiful women of all time, in history, in American history, at least. While her religious affiliations are murky—her mother was Mormon and she was born

product is both existential and essential at the same time and seamlessly. The Maude Adams statue remains rock solid marble, as real as it was at the beginning, but it now declares the hard to pin down, amorphous ideal of feminine beauty in clear terms. Two disparate parts have together helped one another become more real.

But better still and best of all is the Christian doctrine of the Incarnation. God is an artist. God Himself, His consubstantial only begotten Son, is the ultimate expression of essence-existence art. God—ultimate essence, Being as in the non-contingent Being, the unique beingness Being—who bridged the gap between Himself and His creation via the Incarnation. Jesus Christ, "like us in all ways but sin," therefore like us in all ways pertaining to everyday existence, to eating ice cream and building block houses as much as playing with building blocks when younger, remains always the transcendent Logos who made the sky, the seas, the stars.

Get this about the coming Christmas season, about the Divine Child, about why Christianity is unique and incomparable to all other religions and philosophies: Jesus Christ is not simply a holy sage or wise teacher, not a specially designated prophet of God, all these types, even and especially the best of these types, all these are not art because they are not the two in one but only the one alone and disconnected like all of us humans are, of the existence, nothing more, the grocery store receipt and bucket of nails and paint and hard wood knock on that wood to hear it hollow out reality types. Only the Incarnation proposes the ultimate expression of real art, of the two in one harmoniously unified, the hypostatic union of the ultimate Essence tethered to existence in He Himself, the one True God, True Man. If we, poor sinners though we are, can imitate Our most artistic Master in the humble work of our own hands, it too aiming to reconcile essence and existence so as to help our more impoverished brothers and sisters sick with atheism, indifference, agnosticism, hopelessness and fear see the Truth about God and therefore themselves, what better Christmas present could we give this joyous, holiday season?

---

in Salt Lake City and lived in Utah for some time—she reportedly began taking long retreats at Catholic convents later in her life, donated personal estates to the Sisters of the Cenacle and there, at the Sisters' Cemetery, is her final resting place.

Jesus Christ alone is the bridge, he alone can bridge the gap, the gap between God and us, we, mired in daily everydayness, feeling alone and sometimes despairing, should approach the Christmas feast hoping to despair no more, for, behold, it is true, listen, and, especially, do not be afraid, now we find good news of great joy that will be for all the people. For today in the city of David a savior has been born for you who is Messiah and Lord. And this will be a sign for you: you will find an infant wrapped in swaddling clothes lying in a manger...Glory to God in the highest and on earth peace to those on whom his favor rests.[6]

---

6   Luke 2:10–14.

Catholicism
and Film

WHY MORMON-MADE
NAPOLEON DYNAMITE IS
A VERY CATHOLIC MOVIE

APOLEON DYNAMITE.[1] WHAT FIRST comes to mind? The dance? The "Vote for Pedro" T-shirt? Jealously stemming from your brother spending all day online, chatting with babes while you have to invent a girlfriend from Oklahoma, the one and same you took for glamour shots on her birthday, to keep up appearances? Maybe it's a mathematical postulation embedded in a physics calculation for the ages, namely, is it possible for a person to throw a football over distant mountains when adjusting for arm strength, wind speed, and the feasibility of time travel vis-à-vis destination 1982? Maybe it's more like one great mélange, a butter-crushed and whipped together now caramelized apple pie bottom crust, honey crumble like honeybee Deseret center leading to that southeast Idaho surface, yeah that barren high desert, yeah you see, it itself set against faraway mountains, plus a big orange van like orange creamsicle melt-marmalade spread-sprinkled on top plus UFO abduction insurance plus Lyle, Lyle the Lunatic he was not called but could have been, plus the Loch Ness Monster, Nessie—who, as far as lake monster women go, is apparently pretty good-looking—she plus dynamite making appellations spin cycle full circle, the appellations, the calls, like faraway cries, muffled, begging for her to be blown sky-high out of the water, because, yeah, that's how poorly the first date went for bad monster boyfriend prime example number one:

---

1   All quotations and citations, here and henceforth throughout this essay come from one source, the movie itself. *Napoleon Dynamite* (2004), Fox Searchlight Pictures, directed by Jared Hess, 95 mm.

144

the Abominable Snowman of Pasadena[2]; he and Nessie we tried to make it work. But also the internet is forever and if you saw some of the Snowman's archived tweets you'd be happy this dream couple didn't make it, because had they made it, maybe none of us could henceforth harbor hopes of love and happiness.

Speaking of sky-high eruptions, Old Faithful in Yellowstone National Park is only a hundred some miles away from Victor, Idaho, Victor, Idaho being in all the limelight of this talk southeast Idaho with Victor, Idaho also the home of the Grand Teton Brewing Company where one time not "once upon a time" because as if anything of real import, of note, ever happens in Victor, Idaho, c'mon, just a plain old Victor, Idaho type day in Victor, Idaho a Loch Ness Monster "historian" came to Victor, Idaho and proceeded to get prodigiously three sheets to the wind wet on beer then proceeded to go on and on to his formerly gracious hosts getting more agitated by the minute that did they know about the Teton Range and the French language etymology *les trois tetons,* "the three nipples," and he just kept laughing and even laughing IPA discharge out his nose and then he, because he just wouldn't stop, then he told everyone in the brewery he was going back to his university and changing his focus to the American Civil War just so he could quote "write a lot about Lincoln . . . Abra-hammered Lincoln, ha ha, get it?"

So, there you go, maybe *Napoleon Dynamite* means all or any one of those above listed connotations, the plus and plus and plus this and that of the whole matter yet, we can say with certainty, that this movie has a *minus* factor too, minus in associated recollections and calling card coffee punch card maybe koala-like kangaroo kickpunch me myself in my very own coffee pouch—the stomach—factor; minus Boise, minus potatoes. We, many of us here, may love Boise, even be from there, but can rejoice still, with those who hate Boise and their football team all the more, that *Napoleon Dynamite,* Idaho in cinematographic flesh, has nothing to do with Boise; nothing, also, to do with that staple crop ignorant Americans from other parts of the country think *singularly* symbolizes daily life in Idaho, the mornings and the nights too, but,

---

2   R. L. Stine, *The Abominable Snowman of Pasadena* (Scholastics Paperbacks; Reissue, Media Tie In ed. 2015).

ah-ha … wait, well, there is a lot, I mean a flippin' boatload of too much conversation dedicated to tater tots, especially in the middle of class Napoleon give me some of your tots no get your own tots in pants pocket crushed by kick to leg freaking idiot fashion.

What I bet didn't come to mind was "Mormon." Napoleon Dynamite is, for all intents and purposes, a "Mormon movie." It is set in Preston, Idaho—named after William B. Preston, a high ranking official in the LDS church at the turn of the century—a city of approximately five-thousand people where almost 90% belong to the LDS church (the second highest group? 4.8% Catholics! All the more impressive compared to the actually listed as 0.0% Baptists, Lutherans, Methodists and Episcopalians; even catch all "another Christian faith" members register but a paltry 1.2%)[3] Husband and wife dreamteam creators of this masterpiece, Jared and Jerusha Hess are Mormons (and Preston High graduates to boot). The film's leading man, Jon Heder, is Mormon. The film developed out of an embryonic short concocted by college film majors at America's premier Baptist University, Baylor—… just kidding, lol unto lmao, at BYU, at Brigham Young University, duh.

Napoleon Dynamite is LDS down to its core, then to the floor, then beneath the soil and through the roots unto magma; it's as Mormon a production as Mormon productions get, maybe even more so than BYU football and the Cougarettes dance team, and now that's saying something. I'm here to explain to tell you it's a very Catholic movie as well, perhaps unintentionally and surprisingly so, but so nonetheless. There are a few "Catholic themes" that run throughout the movie, some of them personified in the film's characters.

They are, in the order I will treat them:

1. rootedness or sense of place.
2. tranquil humility the helpmate of reason as a path to heroism (personified by Pedro).
3. blind hubris in the daily refusal to deal with the real, evidence of the fall (Uncle Rico).
4. Love covers a multitude of sins (Kip).

---

3   "Religion in Preston, Idaho," https://www.bestplaces.net/religion/city/idaho/preston

And, fifth and finally,

5. Heroism in the style of Saint Francis: rash vows realized (Napoleon).

Our first theme is *rootedness or sense of place*. Few things are more Catholic, and more particularly Benedictine in spirituality, than the concept of "rootedness." You've heard me speak about this multiple times in past lectures; on an approach to the environment, that we must be rooted in our common home in order to appreciate it and care for it properly; on beer, that loving the land we draw that golden drink from will make it go down all the more golden; on social justice in general, be it economic or political, that loving real places, real communities, will mean loving the real people who inhabit them, each of them, everyone, all, our neighbor, and in whom loving we fulfill the second half of the "law and prophets" greatest commandment reflected back onto point number one: to love God with all our heart, all our soul, all our mind.

It's Benedictine, rootedness, because it was the put down roots holy monks of the 5th century AD who stood firm like anchors and saved Western Civilization while simultaneously creating the Christendom to come while, also, perfecting myriad arts of the agricultural and artistic variety while also, here's the punch line, simply *being* as in not ceasing *to be* rooted while everyone else around them was decidedly *not* rooted, busy burning or being burned by the post 476 chaos of the Empire's fall. Rootedness, a Catholic value; non-rootedness, often not Catholic. Look at the world today, although 2021 still very much "2020" in ways I do not have to elaborate upon. Tell me who better embodies the Catholic values of religious adherence, the family, traditional morality, authentic community and, dare I say, simple human decency based in common sense and basic respect. Is it people who go about their daily work loving the land beneath their feet, the land that's part of the real place they love filled with real people, or is it the postmodern technocratic class for whom each place is this place and that place and ultimately no place at all so long as we can sell, sell, sell, buy then sell, short sell, so as to grow fat and rich our feet never touching the ground, that dirty, filthy ground truly *beneath us* in more ways than one?

Napoleon Dynamite is a movie with a strong sense of place, it is rooted. And those roots just happen to be put down on arguably the most beautiful place East of Eden: Idaho. To get paid in pennies—"that's a dollar an hour!"—working a day away trying to avoid the sharp talons of a chicken for the reward of your boss exclaiming mid-bite that over there, yonder, that field, he had recently found some Shoshone arrowheads, is Idaho. Napoleon's seemingly innocuous early movie trip to the guidance counselor's office asking for some lip balm is rooted Idaho, for a nearby poster below advertises an upcoming basketball game versus Bear Lake, the "only here, this place" Bear Lake! Bear Lake: turquoise watered Caribbean inlet in the Rockies. And lest you forget, the receptionist wears an "I love PHS" pin. We all love Idaho, this part of Idaho, here, in this movie, and from the houses in Preston, the school, the shots of the farm fields and the abandoned train tracks too, one quickly slips into the *feel* of this place and cannot be convinced it is anywhere else but where it purports to be. Idaho.

And that's cool, for there are a billion films that take place in the air above some megacity skyline that can be LA or Shanghai or New York or none of them or all of them together because who cares (?); superhero films exacerbate this problem, for their foundational unrealistic setting—film theory geeks know formalism when they see it; down with the tripartite categories anyways, that so long passe realism, classicism, and formalism, here's your automatic system update proclaiming "we know hyper-formalism when we see it, the less believable the better!"—sometimes literally on made up planets that are like one-third *Star Wars*, one third *Star Trek*, thirty four percent stupid,

> these you see,
> you lately feeling so free
> frolicking about with the birds and
> the bees in suntouched paths under green
> trees, the trails like the tails of
> snails dipped in Silvadene crème.
> Paths lacking we's, me's, even
> he's and she's, but if free you felt, it wasn't for lack of
> a belt, restrained you were

not, never, for the tighter you pulled it
taut you were taught
lessons too, that no place is no place to be
no matter how free one might

be, ah yes, we do now see that these films, they do not simply *lack* place, they do not just have *insufficient* place, they have none, and none is not fun, hun (not "hon" because Atilla, I mean, imagine a biopic about, starring Mr. Bean), no, they have none, no place, for they have obliterated it.

Rom-coms are the same thing: set in everyplace that is no place. Plentiful concrete and skyscrapers galore, what a bore, what sights to abhor, yet drunk on dreams you clamor for more, more, more coffeeshops on each corner, scenes of people running in central city parks next to people walking dogs walking past old men playing chess on weather-worn park benches like you wish it was a match-up featuring Magnus Carlsen v. Anna Muzychuk but yeah, right, as if, and cloudy weather with intermittent rain ready for that closing scene where the guy and the girl make-up with a long kiss under steady drizzle he holding his copy of the *New York Times* or *Los Angeles Times* or *Washington Post* or *Chicago Tribune* over her head so she, or at least the Starbucks Styrofoam cup she's holding, doesn't get wet.

Napoleon Dynamite does not suffer from the above stock photo, cookie cutter problems. And before you protest that lots of films have scenes of high schools in small towns located in U. S. states the high schools themselves with pin affixed guidance counselors and so what, let me tell you what, even what's what, okay? *Napoleon Dynamite* cements rooted sense of place with verifiable bombardment of the senses concerning the southern Idaho landscape, viewscape, the "surrounding scenery," the, well, "place." Go back through the film mentally and notice how many times southern Idaho—the flat Big Sky-open farmlands next to the unkempt dirt roads and boxy ranch style homes cloned one after the other all this set against jagged mountains in the backdrop the sky always a pristine and near cloudless blue—is omnipresent; from the first scene of the film when Napoleon drops the army guy out the back of the school bus window to have him bounce and pop-drag along behind, through Uncle Rico showing his first football film ("this is probably the worst film ever made"; "like anyone could ever know that, Napoleon"), through declaring he could throw a football over those mountains then hitting his nephew in the cheek with a beef steak, through taking his orange van out for a sales trip to nearby Bonida, through Napoleon feeding Tina, unto Deb and Napoleon playing tetherball under the building music of closing credits and that feel when "I caught you a delicious bass." Idaho, this part of Idaho, this rooted place and no other place that could not ever be mistaken for Boise or for Twin Falls—forget north of Riggins and White Bird—does not relent and so gives us the very canvas of a masterpiece that does not forget where it came from and proudly declares, yes, you can go home again.

Our second theme is *tranquil humility the helpmate of reason as a path to heroism, personified by Pedro.* The character Pedro Sanchez, and his role within the movie, seems predictable enough. Mexican kid alternately welcomed and not welcomed by the local community, which happens to be his own, too, but perhaps here is the classic middle ground story often felt by immigrants and children of immigrants and those to whom *where are you from?* manifests as a common question, a sentiment, this middle ground, well per-sonified by the former NFL quarterback J. P. Losman, he too of Mexican-American heritage, who said that growing up he felt "too Mexican for the white kids and too white for the Mexican kids."[4]

And that's what it seems like at first blush, that the Pedro character is going to be the vehicle for exploring the tensions of dual cultural identity in modern America, et cetera, et cetera, except, no, for just like in its rootedness *Napoleon Dynamite* is apart from the norm so too does it here progress past cheap cliches and stereotypes. Yes, the culture clash schtick is present in the movie, I'm not arguing for its total absence, but it's mostly there for absurd comic relief rather than pedantic virtue signaling about "tolerance" and "diversity." The best example being when Pedro, already then on the school presidential campaign, gets

---

4 Bruce Feldman, "Second Wind: J. P. Losman fought just to keep Tulane Football Alive. Now he's out to win it some Respect," *ESPN: The Magazine,* July 10, 2012.

scolded in the principal's office for making a pinata out of his opponent, "like they do in Mexico," school starlet and leader of the cliques, Summer Wheatley. The whole scene is a self-troll on schoolmarmishness, the principal explaining that the affair is an offense not just to himself and Pedro, teenage politics and Preston, but "to the entire Gem state."

Beyond this you'll find Pedro as an exemplar of the second theme, of a Catholic—one proud of his faith, too, statues of the Sacred Heart of Jesus and the Immaculate Heart of Mary displayed outside of his house along with countless images within of *Nuestra Senora y su hijo, Nuestro Senor y Salvador, Jesucristo*—who is humble, tranquil, rational and has both feet planted on the firm ground of reality, this ultimately leading to authentic heroism for to be heroic is to respond to that universal call to holiness to become a saint, each and every one of us, and this is possible, for each and every one of us, if we trust in God, rely on His grace, and be, like Pedro, humble, tranquil, and rational. Pedro is a great combination of Aquinas's embracement of the real and Augustine's focus on that which is above, his, Pedro's, citizenship in the city of God manifesting benefits for him in the city of Man.

What benefits? What can we learn from Pedro's Catholic behavior? Pedro sees through the vanities of life, the vanities of high school, and so is truly free, free to act. He asks out Summer Wheatly to the dance, and in unique fashion by baking her a cake, because he doesn't care that she's the supposed Queen of Preston High and he and Napoleon are peons on the peripheries of power. She says no. So what? He's not devastated, not even depressed. He asks another girl, Deb, to the dance. She says yes. Cool, so what, tranquil, tranquil, tranquil, he doesn't get too low or too high by rejection or requited feelings, respectively, for all here is vanity, vanity, vanity of already passing us by vanities, and he knows that, and what a lesson that would be for the Twitter and Instagram youth of today to learn.

While at the dance, Napoleon is stiffed by his date, one of Summer's friends. Pedro proceeds to fix the problem by setting up Napoleon with Deb, he the active ingredient of a budding romance soon to flower. Pedro runs for president because, why not? The principal makes him take down his flyers post Pinatagate. So what? Does he cry in a corner feeling sorry for himself before quitting and whining about how unfair everything is? No, you already know, no, he stays in the race, promises the student body that their "wildest dreams will come true if they vote for him," like every Catholic politician should do because are you or are you not a person of faith(?), and then sits back and allows Napoleon to repay him the favor of setting him up with Deb by absolutely crushing, I'm talking pop lock and moonwalk pwn'ing, a dance skit that secures him the presidency. Pedro never takes his feet of the rooted ground below him, he as rooted as the movie itself, and so he wins, and so too will we win if we take a cue or two from this modern silverscreen saint in the making.

Alas, if we can learn from Pedro in a positive sense—see and do, imitate—we can learn from our third theme guy, Uncle Rico, in the negative, see and do the opposite. Uncle Rico embodies theme number three, *blind hubris in the daily refusal to deal with the real, evidence of the fall.* Uncle Rico is the 180 degree opposite of Pedro. Pedro is rooted in reality and so reaps fruits real and lasting. Rico is completely detached from reality, head in the clouds and stuck back in time, and so reaps a continual procession of spoiled fruits mushy and already rotten.

But, here's the Catholic catch, the wow, this movie is so, so incredibly Catholic. In the vein of John 3:16 "God so loved the world...," under the umbrella of God is love, God IS love, even despite his own best efforts to ruin everything, beginning with himself, Rico finds happiness, and love, in the end. He finally finds the "soulmate soaking it up together in a hot tub" he's been craving all his life, his character arc a reminder that even if we try to engineer our own self-destruction God will not allow us to do so and should we be so eternally stubborn as to choose our own damnation, God forbid, it really will be our own choice for God wants all of us with Him, happy beyond measure for all eternity.

Okay, so two things first:

a. who is Uncle Rico? and

b. how does he embody "evidence of the fall"; (?), then to the examples.

Uncle Rico is Napoleon and Kip's (Napoleon's older brother, more on him soon) uncle, fifty-something years old, single, owner of a large orange van, lover of beef steaks, and infatuated with football, quarterbacking in particular. The second question's answer: because he's literally stuck in the year 1982 and in vast overestimation of his own abilities believing that if he could but return to that year and should coach put him in during the state championship fourth quarter, his team would win, he'd win a college scholarship allowing him to quit Preston, presumably star in college and then go onto a long and decorated NFL career. (Please note: former WSU Cougs star QB turned NFL legend Gardner Minshew [a Southerner too] has embraced comparisons to Uncle Rico, he being what Rico would have been had he made it, as Minshew did).

Unlike Pedro who's focused on the here and now, and so makes progress here and now, Rico's *literal* time travel obsession renders him incapable of productivity and being present outside of a voracious appetite for get rich quick schemes like selling various quantities of Tupperware kitchen sets, the 24-piece variety coming with a miniature sailboat included *gratis,* and *Bust Must Plus!* a natural herb-based system for increasing a woman's, uhm, top half, which because Rico is so disconnected from reality he of course passes out to a plethora of high school girls, a verifiable gaggle of gals, in the creepiest way possible. "You know, my friends, they call me *Uncle* Rico," he says while unbuttoning his shirt to hand a flyer to Deb who had mistakenly addressed him as "Mr." Rico, which leads to *Bust Must Plus!* flyers being taped, a cornucopia of them, all over Napoleon's school locker.

We are introduced to Rico via his homemade football tapes, the aforementioned "worst movie ever made" according to Napoleon. It's simple enough: a camera on a stand in front of which Rico throws footballs, over and past the camera, in the worst possible form imaginable. No worries, all he sees is athletic greatness, and when he claims that back in '82 he could throw a football over the mountains on the horizon we understand he is being literal, that he does in fact think he possesses the requisite arm strength to throw a football 40,000 feet, which, just for the *this is stupid enough so why not and you know what it'll be a fun image*, what this would look like in real life would be a person throwing a football from the goal line of one football field and it traveling through the air, like a plane, over one-hundred and eleven consecutive football fields until landing somewhere on the one-hundred twelfth. To get even stupider, hence more fun, one can imagine the muzzle velocity of this throw, the reading when leaving his hand, would have to be somewhere over three-thousand, four hundred miles per hour, more than sufficient to put a hole through one of his receivers. But, yeah, that's Uncle Rico for you.

"You ever look into time travel?" Rico asks Kip, the family's resident tech savant. Yes, Kip tells Rico, he has already looked into it for himself, but to no avail. Such polite dissuasion does nothing to stop Rico from purchasing a time travel kit from a guy in Florida that has users place crystals in the top of the machine, set the dial to the desired year, and then place a headset one one's head, obviously, but that's about the only sensible thing here, and a mini-pogo looking stick between one's legs before flipping on the electricity. Napoleon tries it out of curiosity and gets hurt and declares the time machine a rip-off. "I coulda told you that," Rico says, exiting the bathroom wincing in pain.

Rico is evidence of the fall because he well embodies all of our often obstinate refusal to get up and out of bed and on with our day, like Pedro. So many of us waste ample parts of our day, wishing we could go back, assured if just this or just that, everything would be different. In doing so we remain mired in a prison of our own making, as totally enslaved as Pedro is totally free, and so daily waste our time and talents and for what? "She said I was living too much in '82," Rico says in a moment of self-awareness to Kip over burgers and fries at some greasy spoon, referring to why his latest girlfriend had dumped him before assuring Kip that he would "contact the authorities" if he did not soon receive a full refund for the time machine purchase.

Don't be like Rico, be like Pedro.

But if you are or become like Rico know that God still loves you, God loves you so much and wants your happiness, your perfect joy, more even than you want to return to 1982. And so Rico, despite himself to the max, and after his latest flop—having his right arm broken by an angered husband not liking *Bust Must Plus!!* being shilled to his wife, this development forcing Rico to start making football videos of himself throwing left-handed, this in itself gloriously Catholic, truly Rico's most redeemable feature, his perseverance (the grace of perseverance precise fruit of the fifth Glorious Mystery), misguided though it may be—a woman emerges on a bike while he is filming his latest training session. She dismounts and parks the bike next to his orange van. He stops throwing, puts the football down, forever perhaps, and walks towards her smiling. 1982 is finally in the past and Rico is about to find the happiness he's long been after.

Our fourth theme is *Love covers a multitude of sins,* personified by Napoleon's older brother, Kip. Kip is, depending on your favorite insult, a tool, a nerd, a loser, or a geek; you got something else, go for it. He's thirty-two years old, so fourteen years older than his younger brother Napoleon, still in high school, and lives at home with Napoleon in their grandmother's house. Nothing is explained regarding the absence of a grandfather and, more curious still, their parents.

Kip is frail to the point of should be wind advisory worried, and wears glasses and button shirts fastened to the top bottom tucked into his khaki pants. He sports a mustache. He is unemployed, not in school, trade or graduate, and spends practically every waking moment in chat rooms online. That *Napoleon Dynamite* was made in 2004 is a delicious fact vis-à-vis online living, for 2004, if you remember, was the year Facebook was launched but MySpace and AOL chat were still "it"; Instagram, Twitter, TikTok and every single everything else to the billionth factor were not a twinkle in anyone's eye. "Yes, I love technology, but not as much as you, you see … but I still love technology … always and forever … always and forever," Kip will sing in the movie's epilogue, he, as mentioned, spending hours in the chatrooms of the 1990s web functioning via a truly old school dial-up connection. One can only imagine the disaster he'd be today with such evolved social media options.

Kip logs on and stays on and sits and sits and keeps staying online. He tells Napoleon he's training to be "a cage fighter," then gets smacked across the face and told he has the worst reflexes ever. He will later on tap out during an impromptu spar with his younger brother because his "neck meat" got bruised. Instead of rightfully criticizing Rico's training clip as "the worst movie ever," Napoleon was spot on there, blue-light zonked Kip squeaks, "that's pretty cool, I guess." Instead of properly demonstrating the resiliency of a Tupperware container—because, of course, he ends up working for Rico at one point in the story—by tugging on it, he places it beneath the back tire of Rico's orange van and backs up under the watchful eyes of a potential customer. It explodes, sale lost, nothing left to do but yell "dang it!" and drive away.

But love covers a multitude of sins, so said St. Paul, and so to us shows Kip. Kip really has been chatting with babes online; he has not been aimlessly wasting his life away as it has appeared to us, the viewers. And this woman, Lafawnduh, she comes to Idaho from Detroit, by bus, to prove her love to Kip. And it is a love story realized, for immediately they hit it off in person and although Kip loses nothing of his nerddom in full simpdom transformation from computer nerd to discount Eminem, they really have hit it off and for good.

It is to Lafawnduh that Kip sings "yes, I love technology, but not as much as you, you see" post-vows at their post-movie wedding. Because, the film shows us, we really should not judge. And behold the geekiest geek of them all, happiest in love at the end. Thanks to, not in spite of, his geekiness. And, and, and as we move to number five, our fifth and final theme, *heroism in the style of Saint Francis: rash vows realized,* where we at long last arrive at Napoleon Dynamite himself, we will one more time revisit Kip and his "love covers a multitude of sins" unseeming, below the radar, yet monumental contribution to the ultimate victory fit here between ninety-five minutes of tape from action to cut, from start to finish from, ah, okay, yeah, you get it. More on that soon.

Saint Francis of Assisi had crazy energy, was in motion, perpetually, and always gaining towards, if stumbling and falling forward, to some goal. Maybe his methods were crazy, but it was a crazy holiness and it got the job done. Napoleon, the man himself, protagonist of *Napoleon Dynamite,* is a lot like that, a lot like Saint

Francis. Like Kip, he's geeky and nerdy and awkward. Taller than his older brother by a foot, he has steel wool red hair and wears glasses and is a member of the "Happy Hands club" at Preston High and presents on the Loch Ness Monster for his current event and gets thrown and pushed and shoved into lockers with terrifying frequency. He invents a girlfriend, tells another girl, Deb, she could be drinking whole milk not one percent and asks if she's drinking one percent because she thinks she's fat, then draws the unintentionally creepiest pencil sketch of a classmate (not Deb) with an attached note asking her to the dance—the one and same dance Pedro will arrange for Napoleon to dance with Deb, igniting that classic romance—which he receives a "yes" response to only because the mother of the girl feels sorry for Napoleon and forces her daughter to accept. Rico, on a business trip to this house, had described his nephew as a "tender little guy who still wets the bed and whatnot." As mentioned, the girl, Trisha, dumps Napoleon the minute they arrive at the dance.

Napoleon seems to be a total joke—he keeps num-chuks in his locker and spends his free time drawing mythical creatures, the crossbred "liger" his masterpiece—and yet, Catholic lesson take note, he keeps on going, keeps on with that crazy insanity rooted in love. Napoleon, hard though it may be to see at times, and kudos to the film's creators for subtlety, loves. Napoleon loves his family, he loves his friends.

And so coming to the most critical part of the movie, often missed even by aficionados, LaFawnduh is sitting at the dining room table and Napoleon emerges from his room bathed in sweat following rigorous dancing. Intrigued, LaFawnduh tosses him a mixtape her cousin made. Napoleon masters a dance to this mixtape. This is the dance he performs as part of Pedro's obligatory "skit" and this is the same dance that secures his friend the presidency, his very best friend whom he loves very much, loves enough to dance solo on a stage in front of the whole school, which as far as the courage meter goes for high school kids registers right at the very top. And what a nice final twist, outsider and longshot Pedro, a bona fide Catholic hero, defeating establishment queen Summer Wheatley, predictive programming for the then twelve years in the future equally unexpected triumph of Donald Trump over Hilary Clinton.

Napoleon Dynamite is a Mormon made movie that, were it a pastry, would have an LDS crust but a Catholic filling. As firmly rooted in the fertile Idaho soil as a russet, it clearly lays out the benefits and pitfalls of a life based in reality versus the denial thereof and yet, final penitence be granted us all, Lord, it shows that even for those like Rico redemption is at hand, maybe just right around the corner. Finally, lest you be judged, do not judge. Last man you'd assume to have skills with the femalefolk lands his dreamgirl. Last man you'd assume to be a good dancer proves he can get any club poppin beyond belief. And last man you'd pick to head the ticket to take down the Summer Wheatley political machine proves to be the type of politician Idahoans have always wanted, the one who can finally make good on the promise to make their wildest dreams come true.

In Search of
a Catholic
Economic System

BEFORE I TELL YOU WHAT IS RIGHT, rather what might be right, might maybe be more right as in correct than the political and economic right and left binary choices both full steam to the extremes backs to the wall with wiggle room seen as weakness, I would like to begin with commenting on what is wrong. For us, sadly, what's good for the political goose is good for the economic gander. Capitalism or communism; often, capitalism "good" if not "great" while communism "bad" if not "evil." Fair enough in the latter, I certainly have little if anything good to say about communism, a totalitarian system in frontal assault against the Church, the family, fairness and freedoms of every stripe. But capitalism, a bit better sometimes barely, is often not significantly so. Capitalism: butter-greased slip and slide super-highway for oligarchic monopolies foregoing the concentration of wealth and power into a singular state source in favor of control by a few proprietors, a transnational one percent of the one percent elite who if they fall upon hard times fear not for there is always a government bailout to be found whistling Dixie around the corner. For you, common man, there is the "free market" actually free, free from safety nets and the security to speculate knowing the losses are covered. "Capitalism for the poor, socialism for the rich," indeed.

I'm here to tell you a different story. That there is a different way. I couldn't care less what you call the economic philosophy I'll sketch out for you tonight; distributism, localism, co-operative traditionalism. You can call it how much wood would a woodchuck chuck if a woodchuck could chuck woodism. But then a few woodchucks would undoubtedly form an invite only Marmot oligarchy beginning with banning lesser chucks from free discourse on forestfloor media platforms and ending with them seizing both the means of production and the fruits see: nuts and acorns flowing there-from for themselves. This would lead to a populist uprising resulting in much strife and sorrow culminating in one woodchuck trying in vain to proclaim himself king of the grand ground rodent family *Sciuridae,* claiming for himself direct descent from Punxsutawney Phil and the title *Emperor Marmota Monax* of all groundpigs, whistlepigs, thickwood badgers, and red monk land beavers.

Nobody wants to see these events transpire.

So, I propose to call this "system," better yet the "principles of a system," *The Palouse Co-Op Proposal.* It even has a neat as in clean and easy to remember acronym: PALCOP. Palouse because we live on the Palouse and so our ground level zero #A economic focus should be here, at home, in our own community, for this great Catholic principle of *subsidiarity,* that that which can be done on the local level should, partners with the second great principle of the Church's social doctrine, *solidarity,* we, all being God's children "all in this together," hence the Co-Op part with third and finally, "proposal," more disclaimer than titular guide.

I am not an economist. I will not be giving you mathematically interpolated and scientifically proven systems of economic praxis ready to be implemented with turn-key assurance. Rather, I hope this talk can serve as food for thought, lightbulbs flicked on, maybe for the first time, baseline questions and riddlecrack offerings, the proposal itself an invitation for any economists out there to go ahead and try, try putting these principles into a coherent system.

Six themes frame this talk. With these we can fight and flee from the oligarchy and centralized concentrated wealth and usury and debt and borrowing against our children's futures and monopolies and lack of purchasing power matching paucity of consumer choice that characterizes, albeit in different ways, both communism and capitalism. These six principles are, in the order I will discuss them:

1. That Economics is a distinctly *moral* science with moral questions at the very center quite unlike the "hard," "numbers only" sciences of physics or chemistry.

2. That Economic philosophy must place the person—never to be seen as simply a means of production or a tool for profit—at the center of its calculations and further still uphold the family, rather than the atomized individual, as the economy's most important entity.
3. That Labor is the Source of all real Value.
4. That private property is an inviolable right yet one that must work in tandem with the larger and general good of the community.

Points five and six bring us back to the beginning, back to the localism at the heart of this talk via the aforementioned

1. Subsidiarity. Subsidiarity in harmony with
2. Solidarity, the Common Good,

the dignity stemming from all of us being made in God's very image and likeness and so being commanded to love our neighbor as yourselves demanding likewise and furthermore that this love be expressed, as far as is possible for us flawed and fallen people, in economic systems fair, equitable, and just.

Point 1: *Economics is a distinctly moral science with moral questions at the very center quite unlike the "hard" "numbers only" sciences of physics or chemistry.* A flaw of both capitalists and communists is wanting to take man and morality out of their equations. For communists, people are but cogs in the machine, replaceable parts wholly material, with no supernatural components nor desires. Give them a few crumbs to eat, some levers to pull at work, and a place to rest their head at night, even if that roof above them is split and leaky, and they'll be happy.

For capitalists, people are but receptacles for credit cards, four in this wallet, two in the pocket, a new one just applied for. Happiness is consumption, an ever breathless bottomless pit of buying, buying, ad watching, buying, buying, need creating the non-needed need reproducing itself via asexual alchemy into four and five and six new needs not really needed expressed by swipe, swipe, click, swipe, swipe, swipe, card denied, wait this one, card denied, wait, this one, denied, maybe this one still in the envelope yes, accepted, my life is complete; at least for the next two hours.

Communists and capitalists agree that economics have nothing to do with morality. Whether their respective scientific methods aim at a state enriching planned economy where the enslaved populace's lowest common denominator needs must be met nothing more, often with the worst possible quality, or if they are aimed at a monopoly ridden and elite enriching economy where the enslaved population is encouraged to enslave itself to its basest passions and desire for instant gratification so that an ever growing pile of worthless products may continue to blight the earth, the means and ends are similar:

the economy is not about morality,

it is not about fanciful concepts like "justice" or "temperance" or "right and responsible use." It is about moving people like pawns, physically or by way of psychological warfare, so that a few select people can make tons of money before making tons and tons and tons of money before making the insatiably sought after *facil dinero* cashloot piles of dime-nickel Osaka Mint gallons of gold *suscio* bullion brick BonkBenjamins reduction, best poured directly over the head prior to showering, while showering, maybe afterwards too.

PALCOP, our system, proposes

a moral economic philosophy.

A moral economic philosophy is not utopian dream weaving. It is neither impractical nor impossible to define. I'll prove it to you right now; private property the example. Communists want property ownership reduced to one, the state. Capitalists want property ownership reduced to the few, look no further than justifications for pressuring allowances, some of them via eminent domain abuses, to bulldoze this or that neighborhood so that some Fortune 500 magnate can build his sixteenth hotel or 32nd apartment complex or 64th casino. Communists offend the right to private property by wanting ownership reduced to one. Capitalists lie about a "free market" justifying greed as good so an elite few can gobble up whatever they wish. But we, PALCOP, we believe private property should be as widely distributed as possible. Policies, laws, schools of thought, societal standards and etiquette, that classic "what we are all about," should encourage this type of thinking concerning property: the proper two in one dualistic balance that private property is both good and necessary but that one need not have too much of it, and never at the expense of one's brother. That is points five and six neatly themselves combined into an organic whole, "point 56" we can say, subsidiarity and solidarity bound by the glue of the "common good."

Private property distributed as widely as possible agrees with capitalism's supposed celebration of it. Private property is a noble right, one that should be enjoyed by all, one's home the very seat of liberty where you can do precisely as you please. If you doubt this, try walking into a restaurant in your underwear and asking to eat your meal on the floor. But you can dine like this in your own home, your own private space, the subsidiarity beacon of localism nothing more local than one's own little rooms and yard and nooks and crannies too. And yet, because private property distributed as widely as possible is an example of a moral economy, it declares that men and women should practice temperance and restraint and above all justice in their appetites out of love for their neighbor and the true common good, the solidarity driven common good that understands—because it is common sense—that a society is most healthy when many of its members are healthy and doing worthwhile work and receiving a just wage and contributing rather than being ripped off and maltreated day after day until revolution seems like a rational option. Or, maybe worse still, told not to work at all, but to take up residence in a dark basement and wait for the government to take care of everything while being encouraged to smoke X amount of Y until it's assumed Z, not A, commences the alphabet.

I'm not saying everyone has to be equal. That's communism. And communist equality is always the worst equality imaginable. It's looking at a room where 25 people sit, 6 of them with apples, and rejoicing that post redistribution of goods all 25 people have apples without reference to the fact that all 25 pieces are the size of one bite, and that one bite was the gross part of the previous whole, and, by the way, we dropped that one bite-size piece on a landfill before handing it to you.

Ensuring equality no matter what is not moral economy. People are born with different talents and different capabilities and will live different lives, materially as well. The problem is that those in the hyper-capitalist camp pervert this truth to claim there is nothing wrong with one man possessing billions of dollars while his employees can't pay their electricity bill, nothing wrong with him having seven homes and thirty-one cars while another employee lives in a studio apartment with nine family members, and we'll say that this man, well, he's just better at the free market free competition than we are ignoring the fact that there is nothing free about the tax exemptions, government bailouts, fixed and rigged prices, monopolization of the market and special loans and allowances et cetera *ad infintum* that have propelled this "self-made man" to such financial "success."

Rather than the amoral "just following the (economic) science" options of allowing the state or a select few to control everything, why not aim for an economy that—in true co-op fashion, in true homage to the American dream of no man a king, no man a pauper—is built upon a network, an archipelago better yet, of a vast number of private property owners for whom their own space is their one space and no one else's, and, yes, that space might be a farmstead in rural Idaho on 100 acres, why not, but where these one and same co-op Americans forsake the greed and avarice and rapacious gobbling up of more than their fair share so that others may too have a fair, a just, an authentically charitable as in *caritas*, piece of the pie.

Point 2: *That Economic philosophy must place the person—never to be seen as simply a means of production or a tool for profit—at the center of its calculations and further still uphold the family, rather than the atomized individual, as the economy's most important entity.* A flaw of both capitalists and communists is denigration of the human person and his natural habitat, the family. For communists, those intrepid usurpers who sent high school kids in the USSR on weekend field trips hoping the close quarters and raging hormones would soon bear promiscuous fruit, all the better to quash early in life any idea of traditional family roles especially the authority of the mother or father, a role which the State, in its all-encompassing benevolence, could so much better fill. Everyone agrees right? Less of our family and friends telling us what to do, more and more faceless government bureaucrats with bullhorns. For capitalists, the family is a shackle on the natural drive of the "individual" to fulfill his every consumerist need. Note, "individual," not person, for a person has rights, feelings, thoughts, some of them sometimes profound, faith, fears, faults and the ever-present hope for redemption. "Individuals" are as singular in their drives as the definition capitalists provide for them. People are complex, individuals are simple, individually focused on highly personalized and necessarily repetitious individualistic individualism best translated into the universal language of buy, buy, buy, spend, go into debt, so what, buy, buy, buy. Communists and capitalists love non-persons like comrades and consumers, they are simple minded and easy to control. Both hate people, who are often complex and capable of exercising freedom.

We want people to be part of our system. We want to place people and that most holy collective, the family, at the center of all our proposals. It is the family, not the individual, that is the "basic economic unit as well as the basic social unit," says John C. Medaille, author of the book *Toward a Truly Free Market*. Furthermore, the individual left all by himself, as many modern economists desire, is a "sterile and not a self-sustaining entity. Neoclassical economics thus has no way to explain how new workers come into the economy, and hence it has no way to explain growth." The family is a "true society," Pope Leo XIII wrote in his 1891 encyclical *Rerum Novarum*. Being a true society, and predating the State, the family "consequently... has rights and duties peculiar to itself which are quite independent of the State." Families produce independent men and women, people, whereas state control of the economy, John Paul II notes in his 1991 one-hundred year anniversary homage to *Rerum Novarum*, *Centesimus Annus*, inevitably reaches back into the family and against the person, rendering all "cogs" in a leviathan-like machine.[1]

---

1   John C. Medaille, *Towards a Truly Free Market: A Distributist Perspective on the Role of Government, Taxes, Health Care, Deficits, and More* (Culture of Enterprise, Wilmington Delaware: Intercollegiate Studies Institute, 2011), 39; Pope Leo XIII, *Rerum Novarum*, 7.; Pope John Paul II, *Centesimus Annus*, 15.

But while state ownership of the means of production is often a communist reality, listen to what John Paul cautions against as well. "Another kind of response, practical in nature, is represented by the affluent society or the consumer society. It seeks to defeat Marxism on the level of pure materialism by showing how a free-market society can achieve a greater satisfaction of material human needs than Communism, while equally excluding spiritual values." But "insofar as it denies an autonomous existence and value to morality, law, culture and religion, it agrees with Marxism, in the sense that it totally reduces man to the sphere of economics and the satisfaction of material needs." *Reduces man to the satisfaction of material needs.* Capitalism often strikes at the family and personhood by turning what should be a tight-knit miniature community of love into turned inward, selfish, consumerist robots. It is the family that is the foundation of both the social and economic superstructure, the "reason," as Medaille puts it, "for having an economy and the indispensable condition of the economy...a society that degrades the family degrades its own future."[2]

Point 3: *Labor is the source of all real value.* All that exists, economically speaking, is labor and nature. Modern economics, stuck in our point one problem of reducing the economy to mathematical algorithms and balance sheet statistics, focuses simply on the economy in motion, on exchanges, without ever speaking of the most important facet: the engine of the system, or the production process. This is same ontological problem the atheists face: how did we move from something to nothing? It cannot be turtles all the way down, it cannot be a perpetual moving line of box cars stretching back into infinity, an infinite regress, for something has to be moving the line, pushing it forward from a first-spark cause of motion.[3]

That moving agent is labor and nature. Imagine a thicket of strawberries and cows on a pasture and rows of sugarcane; nature. Imagine the workers, labor, that pick those strawberries and shuck that cane and the farmers who milk the cows unto another set of culinary workers who combine all these things, plus some more, into the final product: strawberry ice cream. Like the atheists who

---

2   *Centesimus Annus,*19; Medaille, 43, 100.
3   Medaille, 65–66.

claim that the universe brought itself into existence even though that would mean that the universe existed before it existed and that is impossible, modern economists, both on the left and right, pretend as if strawberry ice cream can exist as if having fallen from the sky finished, without nature and labor. For communists and capitalists alike, nature and labor are little more than taken for granted commodities to be exploited. Little wonder there is so much degradation of the environment, for how can one care about the land if fully disconnected from it? Little wonder so many rich people make their living off of usurious interest, literally profiting off of *zero labor,* by them, for *to them* labor is not honest but uncouth, judgment upon the losers of life and so better live up in some skyscraper collecting benefits which one does not deserve than to sully oneself with the peons working on the land, out there, somewhere far away.

But labor and nature *are the economy.* Only people—people, remember, from families, not consumerist or comrade robot wage serfs; people—willing to put their labor to the task of taking things found in nature and transforming them by ingenuity and hard work into products for the market make any of this possible. Without families that produce people that produce products there would be nothing. And the best thing about labor being the source of all value is that labor happens to be fun; really. It's better this way, more rewarding, very much like, *how nice it would be if we didn't have to eat but could take pills to fulfill all our nutritional requirements?* That would not be nice. That would be awful. Eating can be fun. Fasting can be rewarding. But taking pills in place of food, a plate of pills next to millimeter measured out beakers of vitamin water instead of real food beside your favorite drink, is never fun, not good.

So too making a profit without having put in the work, the labor, and yet how many capitalists make speculative fortunes in shady, short sold trade deals, perhaps the most disconnected from labor and nature "work" we can imagine, living high on the hog after having steamrolled a slew of mom and pop shops for no reasons outside of why not, I want to, that's life, and I can; and how many communist apparatchiks live pompous lives in paid for homes with paid for perks and pleasures, all of them paid for, in full, by someone other than them, probably you.

Labor is the source of all value.

Labor is rewarding and fun. "As regards bodily labor, even had man never fallen from the state of innocence, he would not have remained wholly idle," Pope Leo XII notes, "but that which would then have been his free choice and his delight became afterwards compulsory, and the painful expiation for his disobedience." *That which would then have been his delight.* Work was designed by God to be fulfilling, to make people feel good, like they matter, like they can and do contribute. One of the hidden secrets to life is that people love to work. Why have we heard otherwise so often? Thank you, communism and capitalism. If you spend your whole life in some factory making useless products for an unjust wage and both your co-workers and your supervisor look like the walking dead, staggering about, maybe even pretending to work, counting the ticking seconds until they can leave, leave to go anywhere but there, yeah, you too would come to the conclusion that work sucks. Notice I did not specify the above as belonging to the capitalist or communist sphere. It belongs to both.[4]

Be we, PALCOP, believers in a family oriented moral economy that honors people's work and the land they live and labor upon, we know work is meant to be meaningful, purposeful, useful and desirable. One, certainly not all, but one of the reasons to jump out of bed and take on the day, is being able mimic our Creator's ultimate creative power in the small creations springing forth from our unworthy hands. Work is good, people like to work. Listen to what Medaille says on the topic. "The truth is that people love to work. A man will come home from a hard day's labor and immediately go out to his workshop or into his garden . . . people love to accomplish things; they love to contribute; they love to demonstrate their skills and their mastery over some productive technique . . . it is only since the invention of television that people could be diverted long enough from the boredom of idleness to engage in it for very long."[5]

---

4   *Rerum Novarum,* 17.
5   Medaille, 97.

I will discuss **Point 4**: *Private property is an inviolable right yet one that must work in tandem with the larger and general good of the community in conjunction* with **points 5**, *subsidiarity* and **point 6**, *solidarity*. Private property is a non-revokable right in a fair and just economy and society. Furthermore, a person has a natural right to what he produces. If you have made the strawberry ice cream by your work and ingenuity, it is yours, it belongs to you, and you may consume it or sell it for profit as you see fit. Just as people have a right to living spaces that are theirs, the necessary privacy prerequisite to freedom, they have a right to the products they produce. This is right and just, this is subsidiarity, here an intellectual localism that that which springs from these hands not those belongs to these and not those.[6]

But yet solidarity soon enters into this two-sided, authentically whole, equation. No matter how singular your effort was in making, perhaps "designing" and "creating," the strawberry ice cream, it's doubtful, if not impossible, that you did it fully alone. It was probably others who gathered the ingredients, made the machines with which you made the ice cream, packaged the product, so on and so forth. And everyone getting his *just* due here fulfills the full intent of this essay, fulfills the moral economy based on real people not caricatures supported by fair wages and fair shares properly acknowledging what is mine, private property, and what has come from and must be distributed back to the community for the common good.

If this sounds simple enough, why do so many employers pay their employees such horrible wages? Why is there so much greed? Why so many laws and loopholes seemingly designed to funnel as much money, much of it usurious non-labored for unearned money, into the coffers of the few at the expense of the many? Why, unlike our strawberry ice cream which is made from the best ingredients and to the highest rung of quality—because our moral economy knows real people and their families will be eating this treat—are there so many garbage products, food and otherwise, on the market?

---

6   Medaille, 117.

The balance between private property and subsidiary driven localism with the communal good is as true for products as it is for living spaces and land ownership. "Every man has by nature the right to possess property as his own," Pope Leo XIII says. "This is one of the chief points of distinction between man and the animal creation . . . not just self-preservation and propagation of species but more, but to have and to hold them in stable and permanent possession; he must have not only things that perish in the use, but those also which, though they have been reduced into use, continue for further use in after time." Furthermore, the pope says, stating the issue plainly: "The first and most fundamental principle, therefore, if one would undertake to alleviate the condition of the masses, must be the inviolability of private property."[7]

There are, however, limits to this right. Leo XIII points out that St. Thomas Aquinas said it is both "lawful" for man to hold private property and "necessary for the carrying on of human existence." But when the question turned to how one's private goods and wealth should be used, Leo, building on Aquinas, wrote, "the Church replies without hesitation in the words of the same holy Doctor: 'Man should not consider his material possessions as his own, but as common to all, so as to share them without hesitation when others are in need.' "[8] John Paul II builds on this insight in *Centesimus Annus*, stating,

> The original source of all that is good is the very act of God, who created both the earth and man, and who gave the earth to man so that he might have dominion over it by his work and enjoy its fruits (Gen 1:28). God gave the earth to the whole human race for the sustenance of all its members, without excluding or favoring anyone. This is *the foundation of the universal destination of the earth's goods.* The earth, by reason of its fruitfulness and its capacity to satisfy human needs, is God's first gift for the sustenance of human life. But the earth does not yield its fruits without a particular human response to God's

---

7   *Rerum Novarum*, 6, 15.
8   *Rerum Novarum*, 22.

gift, that is to say, without work. It is through work that man, using his intelligence and exercising his freedom, succeeds in dominating the earth and making it a fitting home. In this way, he makes part of the earth his own, precisely the part which he has acquired through work; this is *the origin of individual property.* Obviously, he also has the responsibility not to hinder others from having their own part of God's gift; indeed, he must cooperate with others so that together all can dominate the earth.[9]

Both communists and capitalists fall sort of this tripartite ideal regarding subsidiarity, solidarity, and private property vis a vis the common good. Communists reject subsidiarity in favor of a centralized, bloated bureaucracy that in enriching a select few works against solidarity, swallowing up private property and crushing into dust any conception of the "good," forget common. And yet capitalists, sure, I've already said they are the lesser of two evils, okay, but still, capitalists reject subsidiarity by never finding a local business or shop they won't willingly sacrifice to the big business box store thereby crushing the local community solidarity necessary for healthy, thriving towns and townships, they too, the capitalists, less concerned for the common good than the bottom line, they too about that small special group of the benefitting built on the backbreaking labor of the thought benighted masses. And, lest you think, well, at least capitalists respect private property, I ask you, do they? "I am well aware that the word 'property' has been deified in our time by the corruption of the great capitalists," G. K. Chesterton said, many years ago. "One would think, to hear people talk, that the Rothschilds and Rockefellers were on the side of property. But obviously they are the enemies of property; because they are enemies of their own limitations ... it is the negation of property that the Duke of Sutherland should have all the farms in one estate; just as it would be the negation of marriage if he had all our wives in one harem." Or, like John Calvin is reported to have once said, and, take note, the following might be the first and last time I favorably quote a Protestant:

---

9   *Centesimus Annus,* 31.

"Wealth is like manure; it works best when it is spread, but stinks when it is in one big pile."[10]

Ok, so what?

A recap-plus, the plus being that which is in addition to our six themes, with a final call for those who might know this moral science, economics, so much better than I do, than I could ever hope, to attempt to put the pieces of the puzzle together, for the betterment of their own, local communities and maybe then for the betterment of us all.

First, to recap on our Palouse Co-Op Proposal six theme approach, a healthy, and truly third way economic paradigm shift away from the communist and capitalist poles requires a distinctively moral approach to economics with the person and family at the center respecting labor and the land, those two together the *sina que non* of authentic social and financial progress, a system respecting private property and privacy/individual freedom to the maximum without compromising the ever necessary submission to the common good willed by God, this delicate balance fulfilling the subsidiarity and solidarity pillars of Catholic social teaching.

Furthermore—plus one—in response to some of the problems mentioned above, we should, as Medaille argues, do the exact opposite of that which is in practice now and afflicts us: "so then," Medaille writes, "in place of a claim of a physical science, we should *re-moralize* the markets. In place of globalist claims we should *re-localize* the economy. In place of capitalist claims, we should re-capitalize the poor...the small farm, and the small businessman."[11] Furthermore—plus two—we should teach these principles to our ourselves and our children, until they become as second nature and reflexively natural as "America" and "capitalism" are now linked, and elect officials who think locally and will act locally, act in the best interests of their local communities, the actual people they represent instead of the faraway special interests whose bidding they jump to do. Furthermore—plus three, the final plus—behold the genius of the co-op model in its ultimate essence, the only co-operative

10   Medaille,124.
11   Medaille, 238-239.

philosophy worth speaking of, a true co-operation between the workers and the bosses. Capitalism and communism are each based on class warfare and hatred, on enmity between laborers and management. It need not be this way.

As Medaille writes, "The simplest way to overcome the opposition between capital and labor is simply to dissolve the difference between the two, to make the workers the owners of the capital they create." John Paul II goes further and claims that an economic systems moral legitimacy and intrinsic authenticity depends upon "if in its very basis it overcomes the opposition between labor and capital." Labor and capital united; all of us in it together; solidarity; the common good; the family; a just and real wage for a real person always in need of justice. Leo XII notes laconically, "the law, therefore, should favor ownership, and its policy should be to induce as many as possible of the people to become owners."[12]

That's it, and that's all. Those six principles plus direct *mirror* action, doing the right thing by doing the precise opposite of the wrong things we've been suffering to date, plus good teaching and good laws, i.e. good elected officials who actually do the people's will, *their* local community people's will, plus the elimination of imaginary strife between labor and capital, between workers and employers, for when all share risk and the hope of reward, when all know they will sink or swim together, and that bad decisions will hurt real people in the real places the leaders themselves live and love, then we can hope to make some progress in this ever confusing, confounding, and always puzzling facet of society and life.

First, and most importantly, we must be convinced that something more than communism and capitalism is possible. That what can be worthy to be called a "Catholic Economic System" is possible.

Then, we try.

---

12 Medaille 135, 134; *Rerum Novarum*, 46.

On What a Catholic College Should Be

OR, CPPCL-M[1]

WHEN I WRITE I OFTEN CREATE A "messsheet," a sidebar post-it notes file emphasizing structure. For example, "Title: Magnificent Marsupials; those to eat, those who might eat you, those you'd wish you could sit down to a meal with." Below that, picture section headings labeled

A. Wombat Wonder Stew

B. Getting Kicked by a Kangaroo will equal pain that is True, I'd avoid it all costs

C. Bubbly Night #6, David J. Koala Beergoggles Right Honorable Red-Necked Wallaby IX

Often, I leave the messheet on the side and discard it into the trash bin once the refined and more focused material has taken shape, the shape of things, things formerly thought now spoken now known. But tonight, I'd like to share with you a small section of this essay's messsheet because if Hemingway's maxim is correct—write the truest sentence you know—then ... but, wait, you know what? On second, thought, no, I'm not going to read you my messheet, and never mind, forget all that, but you should mind, that one and same way Ms. Mind your Manners reminds you to be minding those Ps and Qs, mind keeping your mind and mine on the following, this goldmine method of before getting into the crux of the original argument citing from reputable sources so as to provide a solid intellectual foundation from which we can take off together into the deep.

And that water better be deep and blue and cold, that's the most important thing, cold, because in aquatics cold *is* gold, for

---

1 Chernobyl on the Palouse Polymathematical Catholic Laboratory—Москва (ID)

who wants a tepid pool for dipping in your overheated self and your own pools of sweat on sweltering summer afternoons? Cold truly cold also because the previously thought goldmine method has proved to be pyrite, cheap tricks of the second-rate salesman, "citing from reputable sources," basic even threatening to bore, and yet, go head, and please, read John Henry Newman's *The Idea of a University* and John Paul II's *Ex Corde Ecclesiae*. These both, the two of them, are neither boring nor basic but basically, as in just, see: simply, good sources; so read them. Or, maybe you prefer what John Paul II said on June 1, 1980 in a talk to students of the Catholic University of Paris, that being a Catholic intellectual means searching for the truth while at the same time assured, by faith, that we possess as in have already been given the foundation, the seed of truth. Or, perhaps you prefer another scholar he too Catholic and associated with Paris all the same who opined that *"ultimus finis totius Universi est Veritas."* Aquinas himself would agree that the whole universe cannot be reduced to a word of the same root, namely (the) university, but that truth, *the truth*, the sole true end of learning and of life remains as such, in and out of the classroom, is of course indisputable and more humbly still, it follows, it works, yes, this is it. So now, begin. But leaving that to you and your own time management, I want to come back to here and tonight, just us, just about us, in Moscow.[2]

Concerning what I'm about to describe to you, please first consider an imagined "ideal professor" for us, a Platonic Form or the formless definition of platonic science-nerd affections, behold the late Nobel Prize winning chemist Kary Mullis. If Kary Mullis was alive today, he'd be the first call I'd make when assembling faculty and staff.

Why?

Because he combined something lacking yet sorely needed in today's academic world. He had genius and scholarly seriousness and purpose and a readiness to make contributions so as to make

---

2   John Henry Newman, *The Idea of a University* (introduction and notes by Martin J. Svaglic) (Notre Dame: University of Notre Dame University Press, 1982); Pope John Paul II, *On Catholic Universities: Ex Corde Ecclesiae* (United States Catholic Conference, 3rd. ed, 1996); Jan Pawel II, *Kultura i Wiara*, 288, 213.

improvements so as to help us, help the world, etc., etc., in short, the stuff that makes outstanding scientists and academics. Fine. But, more importantly, Mullis had true sense of humor, authentic weirdness, frivolous joy, and the refusal to take himself too seriously, the last thing most damaging of all (lacking it) for any would be thinkers and problem solvers on the make. Our place here will need people like Mullis in this precise way: brilliant but bubbling with joy, goofy joy, a mirth in addition to, meaning in support of, never in subtraction from, a mind at work minding the business of one's own particular business the business of pursuing excellence in all its forms.

Mullis' autobiography, *Dancing Naked in the Mind Field*, features the following description on the front cover: "a chatty, rambling, funny, iconoclastic tour through the wonderland that is his mind ... perhaps the weirdest human to ever win the Nobel Prize in Chemistry." Following his death in August 2019, *California Magazine* called him "Berkeley's most controversial Nobel Laureate," subheading his *in memorium* piece with "Kary Mullis revolutionized biology and pissed everyone off. Now that he's dead, how should we remember him?" His "revolution," and reason for the Nobel, for your information, was inventing the DNA replicating polymerase chain reaction, the PCR test, in the spotlight recently for its use in COVID testing.[3]

Mullis was drunk the morning he learned he had won the prize; drunk, not hung over, the rarely seen morning inebriation leading to a once in a blue moon hung-under evening, best spent in warm natural spring water—here the aquatic etiquette centers on cold is *not* gold—with a warm compress on the forehead and virgin mint julep in hand, the last accoutrement essential equipment for properly appreciating a violin solo of "My Old Kentucky Home"[4]

---

3   Kary Mullis, *Dancing Naked in the Mind Field* (New York: Vintage, reprint, 2000); Coby MacDonald, "Intolerable Genius: Berkeley's Most Controversial Nobel Laureate," *California Magazine*, Winter 2019. https:// alumni.berkeley.edu/california-magazine/winter-2019/intolerable-genius -berkeleys-most-controversial-nobel-laureate;

4   ... bye and bye hard times, will come a knockin' at my door, then my Old Kentucky Home, good night. Weep no more, my lady, weep no more today. We shall sing one song, for my Old Kentucky Home, for my Old Kentucky Home far away.

under a late summer setting sun. Not long after receiving the announcement of a lifetime, he went surfing. Mullis liked to surf. Mullis surfed a lot, like a lot, like so much. In high school, he designed a rocket powered by sugar and potassium that launched a strapped-on if not glued-to frog 7,000 feet into the air. Apparently, it returned to solid ground unhurt thanks to a farsighted parachute feature.

An avid LSD user while a graduate student at Berkeley—which considering drug use and the 1960s is without question the most boring, unoriginal facet of his biography—one hallucinogenic experience inspired an academic paper on time travel later published by the scientific journal *Nature*. After completing his PhD in 1973, Mullis put science on hiatus to write fiction and work as a baker. Other memorable moments include Mullis once describing an alien encounter; Mullis once recalling his dead grandfather paying him a visit in California and a nice catching-up talk over beers, he having to drink his grandfather's beer for him, for obvious reasons; Mullis once encountering what he termed a "luminous alien raccoon" in the forest. Mullis was renowned for, what many deemed to be, outlandish behavior, "public lovers spats" at the office one example, as so was described thusly by a fellow scientist: "He's the molecular biology equivalent of Donald Trump."[5]

Why, you may ask, am I holding up Mullis as an example when I could have picked anyone else throughout history? Why Kary Mullis? Not because of his supposed extraterrestrial experiences. I'll confess to remaining a skeptic in this area. Not because of his rampant drug use. I am opposed the use of illicit drugs and have myself never consumed anything stronger than the caffeine found in coffee and the alcohol in beer and wine. Not, also, because of his personal actions drawing comparisons to the 45th president of the United States; not for any of these reasons.

---

5   Dorany Pineda, "Kary Mullis, quirky Nobel Laureate whose DNA discovery changed the science world, dies." *Los Angeles Times*, Obituaries. August 13, 2019; No Author Listed. "Kary Mullis, the Genius of a Scientist, the Eccentricity of a Celebrity," December 27, 2019. https://www.bbvaopenmind.com/en/science/leading-figures/kary-mullis-the-genius-of-scientist-the-eccentricity-of-celebrity/

I have chosen Kary Mullis as an example simply because he is the most extreme, and the best, example of a true scholar maybe intellectual giant blessed with the jovial virtues of the unlettered peasant, as of the earth as medieval serfdom, laughing because something was funny, being petty because pettiness is more comely than pride, above all not being blinded as in tricked by his own talents into assuming delusional airs about his own superiority for he knew he was not superior, so why would he, would anyone, act that way?

Mullis was the King and the Court Jester, and while these qualities can be mistaken for a lack of professionalism or a lack of professorial dignity they are, in fact, symptoms and signposts of that rare and precious Catholic virtue of humility. I know nothing about Katy Mullis' personal views on religion. I don't care. And I'm certainly not pointing to him as a model of Catholic virtue or the "ideal Catholic scholar." What I'm saying is that this just mentioned combination is what all of us, from the faculty down to the students, should strive for daily here, here and now at St. Augustine's, and in the future at the place I will soon take you to. We should honor the intellectual talents God has given us so completely that we aim for, and expect, to produce significant breakthroughs in our respective fields and compete for the highest honors, all the while realizing that we are nothing, God is God while we are humble little specks, and so should any of us become true academic stars we will eschew the haughty and arrogant pretensions of the ivory tower in favor of Mullis' goofy and friendly comportment, minus the "outlandish" stuff, of course, that should go without saying. "I think really good science doesn't come from hard work," Mullis once said. "The striking advances come from people on the fringes, being playful."[6]

Okay, so, here it is: the vision, the rough-hewn sketch of a thing still the outlined shadow of a thing that might one day, God willing, materialize into something that's really something. Intellectual spadework break that ground, shovels turned to dirt perforation mode, prime those muscles, kids, and stack that foundation of, like

---

6   Pineda, "Kary Mullis, quirky Nobel Laureate...," *Los Angeles Times*, August 13, 2019.

towards, the establishment of our very own Catholic college here on the Palouse, right here in Moscow, Idaho. This forthcoming explanation will aim to explain what I believe a Catholic college should be. So listen up and allow me to get numerical on the step by steps explanations of this and that and all those things that should this come to fruition will be spoken of as *these* things in the now future but then present tense.

Number one: This place will never be called an "Institute." "Institute" is boring. "Institute" is so prolifically attached to Catholic think tanks and collectives alike all sense of uniqueness and place is lost. "The Catholic Institute of blah, blah, blah…" See, one cannot even make it past the word before zoning out, even being zonked out by, boredom. "The Catholic Institute…" where exactly, what exactly, how exactly, how as in how is this new institute any different from every other place in Yawnville City in the State of New Evangelization growing older by the day kitty-corner from the EveryspeakeratEveryCatholicConference Co. crumbling building camouflaged into irrelevance even in its deteriorated, dilapidated state? You tell me.

So, *number two*: Our place will be called a "Laboratory." Laboratory for multiple reasons. First is point

2A. Catholic thinkers such as ourselves should fight to reconcile the false dichotomy between the humanities and the hard sciences because contemporary life is rife with many false dichotomies, one example being the heretical separation of the body and the soul. Choose one they say, be so "spiritual" you see your true self as trapped within the prison of your flesh; or, deny all things to do with God and live as the mud-sloshing evolved ape-pig you are, give in to all your passions, all the time. Now, that's freedom, they say, forgetting, both sides, that man is the seamless combination of soul and body, both angel and ape-pig, and only by living both to the full can we be fully human. Our laboratory will be fully academic then, me, the historian and writer humanities specialist claiming the identifier usually reserved for hard scientists because here we will shy away not at all from all and any knowledge, our sights set firm on the *undivided* Truth Himself, He the sole standard of what constitutes learning in its integral, organic form.

Point 2B is an etymological one; laboratory, based on *labor,* labor the sole source of all value, labor, because we will pursue the truth with indefatigable *effort,* old school grandfather style up snowy hills walking forty miles to school both ways without a word or complaint hard work. At "Institutes," pretentious people sit around smoking pipes[7] pretending to be smart, assuring each other they are smart to assuage the doubts of not being so because, ah, gentlemen, once more we are idling the day away. At laboratories, people work. The unlisted and therefore clandestine point 2C is the most obvious of all. Kary Mullis spent his life working in laboratories, so, so will we.

Number three: The full title of our laboratory will be the Chernobyl on the Palouse Polymathematical Catholic Laboratory—Москва (ID); *CPPCL-M.* You may recall a fiction piece I presented here in January 2020 entitled *Chernobyl on the Palouse,* and if you do remember so many months ago—before Covid and with Kobe Bryant still alive, but a few days before he died, in fact, God rest his soul—I titled my piece that way to draw your attention to the similarity between the Idaho Vandals football stadium, the Kibbie Dome, and Nuclear Reactor No. 4 at Chernobyl. We, I argued, and still proudly declare, have our very own Chernobyl on the Palouse a stone's throw away from the Augustine Center. That, that's cool, full stop. Aesthetics matter. Myriad institutes work in cookie cutter box buildings trying to lure funding and faculty to the next front glass façade beneath a flat roof and flatter ambitions. Our lab will work in the shadow of the greatest nuclear disaster in world history, ambition on overdrive, the catch being we don't aim to meltdown.

"Catholic," of course, but for *number four* focus on polymathematical. A polymath is a Renaissance man, someone of diverse talents both wide-ranging and deep. We live in a specialized world beset with experts who can't see the forest for the trees. Although they know that small clump of trees before them better than anyone

---

7　Unless you are Dr. Alan Harrelson. Then—you being him—you can smoke as many pipes and for as long as you want. And if Grace Martin is on the piano, fine, okay, then, but only then, you can call your Institute an "Institute."

who has ever existed, they cannot fit their small piece into the larger puzzle. Even if they made an open field charge converging at a clump of trees for this very purpose: clarity, nation making or breaking clarity, they would surely and sadly fail. Polymaths, making them and being them, that's our goal, to know a lot about a lot, and knowing all of that well, a few things to a peerless expertise. It's about the lens. We have to possess the requisite skills to zoom out for the panorama and go microscopic; each when necessary. The Chernobyl on the Palouse Polymathematical Catholic Laboratory will therefore be polymathematically organized as such: me as director—really no different from my title now as Director of Intellectual Formation, for this laboratory will be the fruit and beating heart of our Intellectual program; *CPPCL-M* will equal Vandal Catholic Intellect—overseeing five departments: History, Literature, Evangelical Sciences, Social Sciences Whirlpool, and Free Ambition.

Concerning these four, I will elaborate in detail in the forthcoming section. But, before we arrive there, remember when I just said "Catholic, of course"? Indeed, but let's plant the first flag firmly declaring that before anything can be said about the four departments we must have orthodoxy, prayer, the faith in motion. *Ora et Labora*, yes. Just like the Benedictine monks and their monasteries I can't take my mind or my beer mug off of. For we will begin, end, and saturate our days with prayer, constant prayer, this alongside an uncompromising defense of orthodoxy. Unapologetic Catholicism must be the defining feature of our lab as it is the *sina que non* of any school, college, or university pretending to the title of "Catholic." That before publications and grants and newspaper clippings and football teams and endowments a Catholic college should be about people on their knees with moving beads in hand, preferably in adoration before God Himself, praying for themselves, the world, the suffering souls in purgatory. That fail all else, we do this, at a Catholic college.

Okay, so what about those detailed descriptions of the five departments? The History department will focus on "big history," wide-ranging, time and thematic sprawling studies of all things relative and riveting. We, all of us Americans, nay the world, do not need another study of grassroots political agency in this singular county of southeastern Nebraska in April, not March, not May, 1909. Professional historians are far too specialized today. Sure, specialization is good, and the expertise that's supposed to come from it is necessary. Ask anyone off the street if they'd prefer a specialized pilot flying their commercial aircraft or someone who "dabbles" in aviation on the side as a hobby. The problem is that specialization has become exclusion, soon metastasizing into hyper-specialization ending at absolute zero unintelligibility. When three specialists of the American Civil War find themselves silent at a conference table, each unable to understand the ins and outs, the jargon-laden terminology, of what the other two are studying, you have a problem. And we do have a problem. We'll aim to fix that at our lab, for a Catholic college should never, ever, sacrifice the larger picture to the tiny details. Be as good and as thorough a specialist as you want, that's great. But when you can't connect simple dots, forget the larger ones needed to tell any coherent story, you need to go back to the drawing board.

I, therefore, envision hiring a historian in the mold of Will Durant, Warren H. Carroll, Oswald Spangler or, dare we dream, Christopher Dawson. Here's an assignment for you: read Dawson's *Religion and the Rise of Western Culture* or *The Formation of Christendom*, and Carroll's books on Our Lady of Guadalupe and Isabel of Spain and the First World War and you'll see what I mean, what I want, what we need, here. Our students, too, they themselves, will have a deep and thorough understanding of history via a long-forgotten tool, timelines. Same critique I made above: super cool if you know the historiography, and all the recent scholarship trends on a topic, but a historian proves he or she is in fact a historian by being able to tell you what happened in 1648, 1865, 1919 and even 31 BC, and, no, no that didn't happen in 1490, rather it was 1517 and, by the way, here's a quick two-minute footnote on the important contextual information pertaining to the first half of the 16th century in that place we're talking about. The history department at our lab, as it should be at any Catholic college, will produce scholars who can always, in first order, tell you where the pieces fit together and how and why, no matter how focused and microscopic they prefer to get, and will house students who, downright shocking in our day and age, will not only appreciate and understand history but be able to place it and perceive it one event relative to another.

The literature department will be headed by a novelist, not by an "English educator" etc. No offense here, the point is that our lab will be all about the producing of original material, and prolifically so, I hope.

Orthodox faith,
Polymathematics,
Publications.

Remember those three and you'll know what we're all about. Novelists, writers and artists in short, can and will teach classes and instruct students no less than our history department But as I'll hope that our historian can produce articles and manuscripts on a steady flow so too will I be looking for a new short story every half year or so, a new collection of essays in between that anticipated first book, from our novelist. Publications because that's what faculty should fundamentally *be about* at a Catholic college vis-à-vis their labor, at any college, first rate scholarship, and, furthermore, these publications, flowing from the well of orthodoxy and from the breadth of polymathematical appreciation, serve the needed promotional aspect of all schools. We know we're good, we need the public to know it too, to be the sunlight that grows the seed we're watering daily. There is no better way to fulfill this ambition than to become quickly known for producing high quality history and fiction at the intersection of Catholic orthodoxy, polymathematics, and the timely, the timely as in just yesterday you didn't know this book or argument or article you needed even existed. Now you can't imagine how you ever made it so far without the insight gleaned therein.

So, history and literature, two separate departments headed by two individuals but with much synchronicity, offering students polymathemtaical courses in the respective disciplines in support of robust publication. The third department—and we're still on *number five* of the overall description, keep that in mind—will be called "Evangelical Sciences." We already do that so well here at

St. Augustine's, being blessed with such a talented pastor, staff, Focus missionaries and parish community in sum. The Evangelical Sciences department, perhaps headed by a professor who previously was a Focus missionary, will be in the business of something I call

identify,
improve,
interpolate;

three "I's," simple enough to start. First, identify what are the leading trends in evangelization, in the now getting long in the tooth "New Evangelization," by, surprise, surprise, the polymathematical method of broad-brush turning over every rock and stone, reading every book and watching every YouTube channel and listening to every podcast and on and on and like that and like this *ad infinitum*.

Identify what is good and what is bad, what works and what does not. Then, improve it.

You are faculty at The Chernobyl on the Palouse Polymathematical Catholic Laboratory because you're a genius, you have what it takes. So get to work. Improve what has already been identified as the best and then, the final "I," interpolate it, insert it into the curriculum you will teach your students and to the larger Catholic culture you'll reach with your essays and articles.

The two remaining departments are two plus one, the one being the final one but the one that just might prove to be the most fun and certainly will be the most full circle, it, like the foundational orthodox prayer life we'll all cultivate and share in, it too will be common to all, making the most common of us, via participation in it, common no more. This, in the shadows, perhaps "Catholic deep state" department number six—which, yeah, duh, we'll acronym as CDS-006—is "Yolk Center United," but more on that soon, in conclusion.

First, still, yes still, in this number five vein, departments number four and five: Social Sciences Whirlpool and Free Ambition. Social Sciences Whirlpool will be run by someone with an economics background with the focus being intense study and scholarship concerning the diverse amalgam of distributism, the papal encyclicals on economics, Heinrich Pesch's (SJ) work, and the general search for a third, most Catholic way between capitalism and communism vis-à-vis social studies on contemporary demographics, politics, and social activism in the U. S. Hence the catch-all "whirlpool" part, with once more the polymathematical reach our of lab on full display.

The Free Ambition department will be free, simple as that, as simple as it sounds. As free as American freedom. Like a Bald Eagle in full flight over the Grand Canyon on the Fourth of July where, down below, authentic hillbillies from northwest Arkansas shoot illegal fireworks from an illegally parked positioning of their Sprinter Van, everything on it illegal, see: expired, tags and licenses and emission tests too. Look, we've got a history department, a literature department, Evangelical sciences, and a tight focus on economics and their relation to social realities. That's pretty cool, pretty good for a Catholic college, pretty freaking great maybe. So, because Chernobyl-Moscow is going to be like Harvard and Oxford meet the University of Hawaii at Hilo on a Mardi Gras trip to Bourbon Street in New Orleans, *verso l'alto, non e vero? Mi scusi, pero, abbia la bonta, allora, ma, guardi:* if you're thinking about Blessed Pier Giorgio Frassati plus Kary Mullis when hearing that previous sentence, in the phrase and the phraseology pertaining to a few institutions here and there all across the map smash-jam spread like apricot jam across fine toasted bread, rest assured that you're thinking correctly.

The Free Ambition department will be headed and formed like formed into being out of love for the One who originally made it all out of nothing, something out of nothing, via His Word going out over the formless void illuminating the darkness covering the face of the deepis HIs by the man or woman who presents to me and to you, to us, the best and boldest and ultimately most necessary focus-topic the people, Catholic and otherwise, need at the moment, that moment being now. They, that professor to come, they will decide what Free Ambition will mean. Maybe that person will be recently released from an insane asylum. Maybe they won't speak a word of English, communicating via morse code tapped out in punches to the shoulder. Maybe it will be an alien from a faraway galaxy who is claiming to be Kary Mullis and while I won't believe that it will at least make me believe in aliens and then my respect for Kary Mullis, currently at like 11.2 on a 0–10 scale, will climb so high it'll threaten unregisterability. Maybe they'll be so normal they'll make boring look exciting. I don't know, but I'm eager to find out, aren't you?

Eager too, you and me, to finish number five by talking about six, CDS-006, Yolk Center United. I want you to imagine an island and on the island one large hill on the left and one large hill on the right, in between a bunch of miscellany, buildings and shacks and discarded surfboards washed up on shore next to chairs and parasols and on and on even empty drink containers the synthetic syrup still clinging to life on the sides of the plastic receptacle and the plastic straws long after the ice has turned to liquid and then evaporated altogether. The island is the Chernobyl on the Palouse Polymathematical Catholic Laboratory, the water around it the Catholic faith for the faith envelops and overwhelms and informs all we do. That in between the two hills, the shacks, the straws, the solidifying syrup, that is our own specialty, our own specificity. The two hills, however, are what tie us together, the first hill being the daily prayer life we'll cultivate together and already do here and now, at St. Augustine's. This second hill is Yolk Center United, the physical exercise component of Chernobyl on the Palouse where we bring the polymathematical vision of the whole person, the orthodox Aquinian body and soul amalgam, to fruition.

For a human being is most human when he or she exercises the full spectrum of their physical, spiritual, and intellectual capacities.

CDS-006 Yoke Center United will bring out our best physical selves; a daily half hour class of push-ups and ab work in the arboretum, no rest rather hill sprints in between sets? Full on max deadlifts, full throated encouragements threatening to sound decibel down walls? We'll see. The point is that at the Chernobyl on the Palouse lab we'll aim be jacked, ripped, absolutely *yoked* out of our full spectrum selves; in the soul first and above all, but in the mind and body too. And this is what a Catholic college should be: expert level focus with polymathematical breadth on everything it means to be human; for the love of man, yes, but for love of God above all. And while earnest and serious and committed to the perfection of all gifts from God for the glory of God and love of our neighbors, so gratuitously easy going and happy and joyfully laidback too. And you already know who I'm thinking about here. Go ahead, say his name, whisper it. Then consider this most outrageous and absolutely scandalous, impossible to believe he said it until it's confirmed he did, Mullis quote. But, I warn you, brace yourself, it's pretty shocking stuff. "My mother would give my brothers and me a pile of catalogues and let us pick what we wanted for Christmas."[8]

Okay, so I'll keep my *final two sections, six and seven,* brief then, because I assume you get it by now. You see the vision, you understand. Skipping to the very end, *number seven* concerning the practical how, I'll simply say, God's will be done. How would such an endeavor be funded? I don't know; from grants bequeathed by national foundations, or the support of Catholic oligarchs, the kind of people who post morning prayer eat caviar on yachts and take rich people vacations to some Siberian oblast where for a few million rubles you can watch Russians wrestle polar bears while you sip French champagne? I don't know. Rome wasn't built in a day, so should the Chernobyl on the Palouse lab take years even a decade plus more to be realized, so be it. God's will be done.

What I want to finish with is section *number six*: the recapitulation of all we discussed in imagining what this place would look like running at full, RBMK reactor steam. The whole lab gathers for morning Adoration of the Blessed Sacrament, morning prayer besides, and the Holy Rosary and Divine Mercy Chaplet included, reconvening on the spiritual node for Daily Mass when offered and the Noon Angelus to Our Blessed Mother as devoutly as if we were, are, would be, could still be but in a different way 14th century peasants hats off under the sweltering summer sun urged on by the bells in the distance. Everyone has arrived at morning prayer calm and calibrated, having just begun the day before the crack of dawn on Palouse hills outside the city limits attending Yoke Center United. Before the dew left the verdant dunes the

---

8   Google search for "Kary Mullis quotes."

collective legs were properly crushed from up and down, up and down, up and down again, but no one, not a solitary soul, complained when at conclusion Father Chase declared it was high time to find max points on the bench and squat. And so the intellectual work for the day began just like that, immediately after the body had been fully primed, and the soul fine-tuned to point proper, unto God, and so no one was surprised, nor should they be, if day after day following such a simple yet powerful formula led to some of the brightest minds the West has yet seen, that moment when our Professor of the Whirlpool department delivered the annual Jefferson lecture, that moment when our History department head penned the definitive biography of Lewis and Clark, that moment, that most proud moment, when Free Ambition was revealed to mean Ambition unchained, and the head of this department went on to become Governor of Idaho and then the President of the United States.

Is this too much? Stupid? No, it's The Chernobyl on the Palouse Polymathematical Catholic Laboratory. That'll be our official slogan by the way; "Is this too much? Stupid? No, it's The Chernobyl on the Palouse Polymathematical Catholic Laboratory."

Thank you.

A Conversation
Among Friends/
The Hope We Have
in Jesus Christ[1]

MY FAVORITE LDS HISTORICAL FIGURE is Increase Franklin.[2] A graduate of Utah State University, he created the aversion to power political theory "Pharyngeal Reflex Authoritarianism" and mastered French, Italian and German while studying in Europe before returning to his native Idaho to run, successfully, for the nondescript post mayor of Preston. In Preston, Franklin devised his plan of secession, the pacific removal of Idaho and Utah from the United States to form *The New Republic of Desert and Dixie.* Dixie an homage to the so-named southwestern Utah region around St. George.

Franklin failed.

The N. R. D. D. failed to take shape.

But what took flight was this man's legend. *The Salt Lake Tribune* wrote a glowing feature about Franklin asking, "What do Patrick Henry, the North Carolina NAACP and Spartacus have in common?" Despite holding no academic post previously, the University of Idaho appointed him a full professor in their Department of History. Dr. Franklin lived, and loved, and worked among us for many years, here, in Moscow, Idaho on the golden, gilded dirt and lentil-laden Palouse. Someone you know may have passed him out on the gravely properly gorgeous Old Moscow Highway, it connecting Moscow with Pullman from the Kibbie Dome to Kruegel Park by way of Stratton's Cutting Garden pick your own

---

1 Lecture presented at the Moscow LDS Institute, on the campus of the University of Idaho, April 16, 2021.

2 The protagonist of the novel, *Thermonuclear Mirth* (Arouca Press, *forthcoming*).

flowers post-coin clanking the deposit box nailed to a tree as if to intimidate the owls; or, waved hello to him at the farmer's market some Saturday morning in June; or, had the opportunity to see him *in actum professorius,* experiencing first-hand his seven language hyper-immersion polyglot lectures.

But the Palouse, poor Palouse, it could not keep him. Not when his nation needed him. Not when an unprecedented threat to American freedom in the form of technocratic oligarchy at the controls of a genocidal Artificial Intelligence army declared their intent to be utter elimination. Not when you, Dr. Franklin, are the secret heir to a Manhattan Project-like think tank that built not the atomic bombs but something far greater than the Tsar Bomba. Not when you are forced to decide whether to use this weapon or not against the A. I. army, and not when you choose to use it, and not when the same people who mocked your N. R. D. D. project beg you, in the outpouring of gratitude that followed, to assume the presidency of the United States.

You've probably surmised by now that Increase Franklin is not real, that he is a fictional character. You're right. I have begun tonight's talk with Increase Franklin's story, he being one of the prime characters of my novel *Thermonuclear Mirth,* as a sign of my bona fides, evidence that I, a Roman Catholic, have a genuine respect for the LDS community, for making a Mormon one of the heroes of a long and laborious novel is not without specific intention. And if I were to tell you how much I like the movie *Napoleon Dynamite,* as much an "Idaho" production as it is an "LDS" one, sprung from the seedbed of a BYU film class, or that I enjoyed watching Taysom Hill play quarterback in college in 2013 long before his current fame with the New Orleans Saints, or that I agree with historian John G. Turner's claim that Brigham Young does not get enough credit for his political acumen as he deserves, he the founder of the largely unknown original State of Deseret which between 1849 and 1851 made claims on one-sixth of the contiguous United States and is the inspiration for Increase Franklin's own "New Republic of Desert and Dixie," I'd be saying something, the same thing: respect, all the same. I do come here tonight in equal measures respect and excitement. It is good to be here. Thank you for the invitation.

Much separates Catholics and the LDS theologically speaking. This is not a secret, and to obscure our differences does a disservice to both sides. But much unites us as well. And I come here tonight in that latter vein, on the commonalities, the connective threads between our two communities. Four sections frame my essay. They will hopefully make clear the details of our shared hope in Jesus Christ, happy contemplative fodder, indeed, during this, the Easter season.

They are, in the order I will discuss them:

1. The corporal works of mercy, Matthew 25 as wellspring.
2. The principal of subsidiarity, or localism, as relates to community.
3. The ongoing fight in the so called "culture wars" for a healthy sexual ethic.
4. The Mission as evidence of a lived, living Faith.

Number one, *The corporal works of mercy, Matthew 25 as wellspring.* For those not familiar with these, there are seven: feed the hungry, give drink to the thirsty, clothe the naked, shelter travelers, visit the sick, visit the imprisoned, and bury the dead. Minus the last one, they are taken verbatim from the 25th chapter of St. Matthew's Gospel[3] and are held up by Jesus Christ Himself as the yardstick by which our eternal destiny will be decided. Having done them, we will have done them to Our Lord; having failed to do them, we will have failed Him. Both the saved and the damned plead ignorance to having done or having failed to do for the Lord. To which He replies that whatever we did to or for the poorest of the poor, the most neglected and forgotten of society, we did or did not do to Him, to God.

Catholics have and continue to do much in the way of the corporal works of mercy. In many countries, and here one must jog memories back a thousand years plus, the Catholic Church founded the first hospitals, charitable organizations, community center-like food and soup kitchens, and monasteries. Monasteries,

---

3   "I was hungry, and you gave me to eat; I was thirsty, and you gave me to drink. I was a stranger, and you took me in; naked, and you clothed me; sick, and you visited me; I was in prison and you came to me." Matthew 25:34–36.

omnipresent on the medieval European landscape, were renowned for their charity—charity as in the first of the Three Theological virtues, *caritas,* that agape capital L Love, of God and neighbor—sheltering and feeding and clothing world weary travelers, outcasts, anyone and without cost or attached string.

It was probably the Europe and Western Civilization creating Benedictine monks, spurred on by their *ora* et *labora* motto, that lived the corporal works of mercy to their maximum output value. The hospital built at Monte Cassino in 543 was the first of its kind and became the blueprint for similar "Monastic hospitals." The Catholic Church remains today the largest non-government provider of healthcare in the world with more than 23,000 hospitals and clinics. The Society of Saint Vincent de Paul, you may be familiar with their same named soup kitchens, serves more than 150 countries in the world. In the U. S. in 2015, SVP programs, which cover the full range of the corporal works of mercy plus some including helping people with utility payments, elderly care and natural disaster relief, listed nearly half a billion dollars in expenditures. And I'm sure, judging from what I know of the many Catholics in my own life, that of the 1.3 billion Catholics worldwide countless numbers of them do much in the way of serving the poor and needy. And if they really are true Catholics they follow the injunction of Our Lord to do it covertly, not letting one's left hand know what the right one is doing so that seeing in secret God Himself may arrange the repayment.

Catholics, God help us, try to live the corporal works of mercy. So too do the LDS. LDS Charities service more than 142 countries today boasting an impressive 11,000 specifically health service missionaries. These humanitarian efforts are geared towards all aspects of the above-mentioned corporal works of mercy and from this base extend out into the domains of both natural and man-man disasters. Furthermore, specialty service branches include, but are not limited to, food and clean water delivery, maternal and newborn care, and refugee assistance. All this to follow Our Lord's words to feed and quench the thirst of the needy, clothe them, visit them, help them heal. And that one hundred percent of the donations go to this humanitarian umbrella—not 99.2%, not 98.7%, 100% —perhaps says it all concerning the authentic love of neighbor to be found here.

Number two, *The principal of subsidiarity, or localism, as relates to community.* Subsidiarity means that what can be done on the local level should be. Before rushing off to involve faraway central authorities, start from the bottom up, begin in the local community. Subsidiarity works best in tandem with solidarity, the second principle plank of Catholic social teaching. Precisely because we are all equal in dignity equally made in the Image and Likeness of God Himself, we should not in knee-jerk fashion privilege the large over the small, the far away bureaucratic leviathan over the leaky-roofed, drafty windows, city hall around the corner. Never forget: Our Lord Jesus Christ, the Word Made Flesh, the Son of God, 2nd Person of the Holy Trinity, our common hope the only hope of all mankind, did not disdain the lowliness of the manger nor the humiliation of the Cross; and as he did if for our redemption, and as the ultimate act of love, perhaps he did it too so that we may learn humility ourselves.

Because if He who did not have to be humble choose humility we have no other choice. Be humble and do not despise the small, the meek, the local. Alas, sadly, we do do this. We all know the president's name, do you know the mayor's? We look to the Supreme Court to pass paradigm shifting laws, do we ever consider speaking up at a town hall meeting? We love to push buttons on technological devices so some oligarch-run big box store can send a drone to drop products at our doorstep. How many of us support our local baker?

Subsidiarity is based on the love of the real, for honoring the local means cherishing real people and real places; the aforementioned monasteries dedicated to the principle of rootedness, of remaining, anchors down, in a single place to love it into being; agriculturally, politically, socially, each and every of the ties that bind. Solidarity is based on advocating for decentralized models of governance and culture; local music, local customs, and local languages most of all, the last bit, language, your solidarity-subsidiarity amalgam most pronounced. For in all finding solidarity in Latin, one was free to cultivate and ultimately let run wild the languages of one's particular nation, in the realm of literature and art above all. See Dante's Italian language creating *Divine Comedy* to see what I mean. And lest I leave out economics, it was this pro-local, proto Co-Op philosophy of subsidiarity that one can trace as the seedbed of the distributist philosophy, arrayed against the avarice and tyranny of capitalism and communism alike, each enriching the men at the top at the expense of the neighbor next door.

The LDS know about the neighbor next door, about taking care of the brother down the street, and how this manifests in a real place, the real red dirt of the St. George environs or that impossibly aqua-blue turquoise water of the so-called "Caribbean of the Rockies," that petite shoreline on the southwest side of Bear Lake, somewhere out there on Bear Lake Boulevard itself, doing its best Lake Michigan Lakeshore Drive impression a few miles south of Garden City. Real places in the real state of Utah, a buzzing beehive bound geographically by lines on a map within which LDS members aplenty live this communitarian, local, subsidiary philosophy.

Is Utah a "Mormon state," one may rightfully ask? Yes, for all intents and purposes, yes, it is. Sixty percent of Utahans, three of every five people, are members of the LDS faith. If 60% of Mississippians were High Church Anglicans I'd conclude that Mississippi is an "Anglican state." LDS Utahns, stemming from their tight knit communitarian fabric, tithe 10% of their income and even more of their time. Unsurprisingly, Utah ranks number one in the nation in charitable contributions. Estimates put the yearly tally at approximately 5 billion dollars. Owing in some measure to the LDS prohibition on alcohol consumption, Utah is also number one in the lowest number of drunk driving fatalities. The state is also in the top 10 for workplace safety, emergency preparedness, and overall safety while tying with a few other states for another number one national ranking: low unemployment.

Labor is the source of all value.

A labor-based economy, one structured upon honest work and the common good, not exploitative greed and usury, makes for a healthy, thriving, local community. One does not have to look far to locate the catalyst in a state where more than half of the population identifies as "very religious." It is the lived practice of the LDS faith, these faith values in action.

Number three, *The ongoing fight in the so called "culture wars" for a healthy sexual ethic.* Catholics have long advocated for a proper sexual ethic—God's vision for sexuality and marriage one can say—and have been, and remain, at the beating heart of the pro-life movement today. This movement was, without exaggeration, a Catholic creation. Already in the late 1960s, a few years prior to Roe v. Wade, Catholic laymen, a smorgasbord of doctors, nurses, lawyers, and the assorted concerned, joined Catholic bishops in opposition to growing sentiment for legalized abortion. Catholic couple John and Barbra Wilkes are credited with authoring the founding document of the pro-life movement, *The Handbook on Abortion.* The National Right to Life Committee, the nation's oldest and largest pro-life organization, was founded by the National Conference of Catholic Bishops. Nellie Gray, who organized the very first March for Life in Washington D.C. was a convert to Catholicism; so too, converts to Catholicism, NARAL founder Bernard Nathanson and Planned Parenthood Clinic Director turned activist Abby Johnson. Nathanson explained his conversion succinctly, stating, "no religion matches the special role for forgiveness that is afforded by the Catholic Church."[4]

Returning to point one here, that Catholics have long fought for a proper sexual ethic, the just mentioned information on pro-life is but the latest manifestation of a connected thread stretching back centuries to Saint Augustine who in his magnum opus *City of God* claimed that God's city is populated by people who love God to the extinction of self, whereas those in the fallen City of Man reverse the equation loving themselves unto the contempt of God. To have contempt for God is to be governed by one's passions, "libido dominandi," and this inverted Platonic formulation of the passions ruling the will and the intellect often manifests most destructively in the arena of sexual sin; the story of King David, Uriah and Bathsheba quickly comes to mind. And so Catholics, for centuries, from Augustine through the papal encyclicals condemning contraception in the 20th century up to John Paul II's famous *Theology of the Body,* have insisted on a moral and theological values based sexual ethic.

---

4   Facebook, *Catholic Answers Page,* post dated February 21, 2014.

One can see the same values that animate Catholics in the pro-life movement shared by the LDS. Allow me to present to you two recent examples. Two themes:

1. the fight against pornography—pursuant to this, don't forget that sexual liberation is political control, those who push the subversion of sexual morality do so not to give men and women freedom but rather the opposite, to enslave them to their passions so they can be more easily manipulated and controlled—and
2. a "winning pro-life strategy."

"Utah Governor signs divisive measure to require porn filters," reads a recent headline from March 2021. Claiming the measure would send an "important message" supporters hailed legislation that would automatically block pornography on all cellphones and tablets sold in the state. The paper correctly squared the issue when writing, quote, "Combating porn is a perennial issue for Utah lawmakers, who are predominantly members of [the LDS Church]. Lawmakers have previously mandated warning labels on print and online pornography and declared porn a 'public health crisis.'" Imagine, following the logic of Kant's categorical imperative to act so that what we will should become a universal law, if more states took inspiration from Utah and worked to ban pornography. What would society look like if people spent hours on improving their communities, families and themselves rather than gratifying their basest passions, ones that slowly and steadily eat away at the soul? I hope Utah may be an example to us all.[5]

The second subpoint here has special resonance for us tonight. For it is within a Catholic periodical, *The National Catholic Register,* that one can find an LDS example of the next positive step in the pro-life fight. "Utah's New Law Could Be Part of a Winning Pro-Life Strategy," proclaims a headline paired with the subheading "new pro-life measure recognizes the father's responsibility for his unborn child, and financially empowers the mother." Wise words. For how many young women have turned to abortion because the

---

5   Sophia Eppolito, "Utah Governor signs divisive measure to require porn filters," *Associated Press,* March 23, 2021.

man they thought loved them abandoned them the day of the positive test? How many women who have had abortions would not have, had the other half of the equation done even the bare minimum regarding support? The hope we have in Jesus Christ centers upon providing hope for life in all its forms, for protecting the most vulnerable, none more so than our brothers and sisters in the womb. As one legislator said, "… there's an issue of responsibility that I felt like men weren't really stepping up to the plate on," he continued, "I'm a father of five and I can tell you that it wasn't the moment that my children were born that I felt responsible, it was the moment that I learned that my wife was pregnant and I don't think I'm unique in feeling that way."[6]

Number four, *The Mission as evidence of a lived, a living Faith.* The history of Catholic missionary activity—commenced from the last chapter of St. Matthew's Gospel straight from the lips of the Risen Christ, He to whom all power has been given in heaven and on earth, founding the Great Commission to "go and make disciples of all nations, baptizing them in the name of the Father, and the Son, and the Holy Spirit, teaching them to observe all things whatsoever I have commanded you: and behold I am with you all days, even unto the consummation of the world"[7]—is so wide and deep and universal it would be impossible to give even a basic primer.

Because where to begin? With Saint Paul? With Saint Francis Xavier, missionary to Japan, Borneo and the Maluku Islands? (Saint Maximilian Kolbe? Yes, of Auschwitz rightly earned eternal fame but, none the less, SMK of Japan, of Nagasaki, for his role in building the Immaculata Garden the location of which on the slopes of Mount Hikosan helped save that sacred place from destruction on August 9, 1945)[8]. With the Jesuit fathers and the Gaurani natives of Paraguay? With Augustine of Canterbury and the creation of Christian Britain or "Apostle to the Germans" Saint Boniface or arch enemy of snakes and superstition, green clad Saint Patrick

---

6 Lauretta Brown, "Utah's New Law Could Be Part of a Winning Pro-Life Strategy," *National Catholic Register,* April 9, 2021.

7 Matthew 28:18–20.

8 So, SMK of the Atomic Bomb? SMK of *God's Divine Mercy in the Midst of the Atomic Bomb*?

of Ireland? With the brothers Cyril and Methodius, apostles to the Slavs and inventors of the Cyrillic alphabet prominent vessel of the Russian language today?

Maybe with the Blessed Mother herself whose 1531 apparition on Tepeyac Hill shortly thereafter led to the conversion of 6 million Aztecs to the Christian faith and whose famous Image on that famous tilma is honored throughout Mexico and the world today; *Nuestra Senora de Guadalupe,* Patroness of the Americas. Maybe I should look locally, for that has been a theme of this talk, subsidiarity, and looking local I'll look to us here, on Increase Franklin's beloved Palouse and to the FOCUS missionaries who work at the Saint Augustine Center each one of whom I am privileged to call my colleagues and my friends.

The connective point of the above to that which follows forthwith is that as Catholics proclaim their faith with evangelical zeal so too do the LDS set out on mission, and prolifically so. To speak on the LDS mission is to speak on what is perhaps most familiar. I can recite for you some statistics and facts—that there are 10 missionary training centers, almost four hundred missions, and 67,000 missionaries, etc, etc—but I think for you this might be well trod ground.

So, instead, what I want to focus on is two things. First, my respect for the LDS community probably comes, first and foremost, above all, from the missionary commitment of the young men and women who make it. How many kids, teenagers, some of them but a few months past twenty, spend day after night after day partying, enrolled in college but majoring in drinking, promiscuous the way people used to shake hands pre-Covid, because for them sex is nothing more serious than a handshake. I don't have to continue down this road, we are all aware of the problems of contemporary society. What I want to call attention to is how different, and how much loftier, is the personal moral ethic aimed at by LDS missionaries. Kids themselves the same age who leave home and hearth for 18 months or two years and forsake so many of the pleasures and comforts of life to spend hour after day after week, months on end in full dedication to their faith. That deserves respect.

The second point I'll make is a personal story, but one which circles back to the first, an anecdote illuminating the aforementioned frame. I was visited at home in the fall of 2019 by two missionaries, two young women the two of them as kind and as nice and genuine as these terms get in real, lived experience. Our conversation did not proceed far, theologically speaking I mean, for in explaining that I was as devout in my Catholicism as they are in their Mormonism we had reached what can only be called an impasse, a roadblock of agree to disagree wrapped in mutual respect and friendship. And they were precisely that: respectful to the maximum, friendly without the fakeness that characterizes so much of our Facebook friend online-only fraudulent interpersonal relations today. Once they left (this after a pleasant fifteen minute conversation on who they were, where were they from, and how was their day going, by the way, how's their week been?) I was left with the confirmation of the original sentiment I just expressed. That these people are good people. And that we can never have enough good people. And that I, a Catholic, would have no qualms should more and more LDS people assume roles of import in our society and states throughout the Union, "Utahisizing," our collective American community with those glorious virtues of brotherly love, care for the poor and neglected, love of family and country and an ever-present eagerness to, simply put, make things better.

"The Hope We Have in Jesus Christ."

I hope, my personal hope you see, is that we, all of us here will realize that it is a hope rooted in doing what Jesus says to do. "If you love me, keep my commandments," He Himself instructed. And so when Catholics and LDS live the corporal works of mercy, and take care of our local communities not disdaining the small and simple but building it up and for the betterment of all, and when we fight for God's plan regarding sex in our own behaviors and on behalf of those without a voice to speak themselves combining this caritas into one, seamless intention to go out and proclaim these values to a society so often arrayed against them, against us, it is then that we begin walking the road towards that ultimate hope we have in Jesus Christ

2ND FICTION INTERMISSION
Margaux Himmel

OUT OF DYSTOPIA, HOPE.

X.[1]

Y.

So, here they are. She and him, the two of them, Margaux and Greg, in a room inside the *Two Mallards Motel* in what was once called Mississippi but is now New Bavaria, a place, the motel, you arrive at on gravel crunched country roads, way out in the country, and it has a neon sign, and complimentary breakfast, which includes a waffle making station and unlimited syrup and honey, and a woman who sits at the front desk watching old re-runs of the *Mary Tyler Moore Show* while she chain smokes cigarettes as if it's an assignment, as if her job is to smoke and Mary Tyler Moore is the addictive habit that helps her focus on the next drag, the next exhale, and it's so robotic, so robotic it's almost an artform the way she smokes and watches that TV and says something snarky to patrons who walk in or, when she's really deep in her métier, nothing at all. She just stares at the screen and shuts off the world and smokes and doesn't even make time to smile. "Well, it's you girl and you should know it, with each glance and every little movement you show it," the opening credit song sings.

---

1   The Russo-Chinese Confederation launched a nuclear strike—one bomb— intended for New Vienna but it missed, landing three hundred feet away from the front door of *Two Mallards Motel*. This took place in the middle of the night, the early morning hours of the following day, 2:26.23 a.m. local time, after Margaux left Greg and walked over to Saint Edith Stein's for a final visit. And her final visit there would be the final visit for anyone anywhere there for everything in that small town was destroyed. That's what a twenty plus mile radius of complete destruction will do. But by that time, when the bomb hit, Margaux had already, by the grace of God, put everything into place. The first words she heard post mortem were from the Master Himself, "Well done, my good and faithful servant . . ." For that's what a contrite heart, authentic repentance, and all the sacraments will do for a soul. No purgatory time. Straight to heaven. And here is where it all became interesting and hidden all...

Nothing, this elicits no emotion from the front desk woman. Not even when Mary throws her hat skyward into the frigid Minneapolis morning. The woman's placid stare is unbreakable, her commitment to staring while smoking, impregnable.

Greg is a seasoned journalist himself, an investigative reporter specializing in "religious and extremist cases" precisely like the Crawford story they, he and Margaux, have been sent to New Bavaria to cover. Greg, unlike the average mid-21st century American man, is rather musclebound, certainly in shape and perhaps even objectively handsome, but in an old school, toxic-masculinity way. It's not that he doesn't have the correct views. He lists "Environmentalism" as his religion of choice on official, government issued documents and won a national DeColonizing of the Masculine Idea Space essay contest in high school with "Men Really Suck: Whatever we did before, I'm sorry, and I beg your forgiveness for all my future faults," with one of the judges remarking that his piece was "especially noteworthy in its no holds barred hatred for all things masculine. Well done!" A few years ago he found artistic success when a collection of his poems was adapted for the stage. Entitled, "My bad, Baby Girl. Wait, I'm sorry for calling you baby and girl," it is the story of a man who makes mistake after mistake that progressively enrages his female partner. *The New York Times* summed up it as "a ninety minute play where, for ninety minutes, one woman yells at one man. Five stars; visionary; bold and brilliant."

A noticeable demerit in an otherwise stellar resume is his athletic background. Greg was a college football star, tackle football, at the University of Iowa, and so one can ever be too sure that someone who would do that might not be harboring a few dark secrets as well. Play tackle football and most likely you hate democracy, that kind of thing. In fact, all public school students are required to watch a PBS documentary upon entering high school entitled "Football: the Slippery Road to Fascism."

Speaking of sports, in contemporary America, 2064, two past times of yesteryears gone by have long been related to the dustbin of history. Baseball a long time ago, football, the kind Greg played in college, more recently. The current #1 national sports league is the NTFFL: National Touch and Flag Football League. The Windy

City Powder Puff Lion Cubs are last year's defending champions. Last season they finished one game ahead of the Orange Man Bad Browns to qualify for the playoffs. After defeating the Reproductive Rights Raiders in the first round they overcame a slow start to beat the Low Carbon Footprint Cardinals, after which, they defeated the Social Justice Steelers to win it all.

Once at a bar, after hours and off the record, Margaux asked a colleague who covers the sports beat about the old football vs. new football dichotomy. He explained to her that if a collegiate team from, as is Greg's alma mater, the Big Ten conference, where the old rules are observed were to play a team from the NTFFL in a game of touch and flag rules "it would be 50-0 after the first quarter in favor of the real football players…[he then laughed out loud] don't you dare mention that, that part to anyone!" What if the two teams played a game of contact, old football, Margaux asked him. "The touch guys would die. No, I'm not joking. They'd get killed, a bunch of them would actually get killed on the field."

Greg has just gotten back from America. He looks haggard, maybe more like half dead. He has tears in his eyes. Noticing, Margaux looks away, and returns her attention to the tea making.

Peach tea for him, peach tea for her.

Two cups, two chairs, the silence of the room, nothing but the usual nothing-buzz and hum of the night outside, outdoors. It's been about two weeks since they last saw each other.

"What happened next?" she asks. "You get this plane back to D. C. and what?"

"More of the same. You get a good look at everything out the window in these rides. Completely wrecked, ruined, everything from the border back to D. C. I see plenty of their flags, little of ours. Like Smith said, and he was right, the president is gone, the whole of the leadership is MIA, the country, I mean it's just completely burnt over, wrecked, bombed out, flattened, everywhere, all the way back and it's a slow flight in these things. Finally arrive, land, get out, and it's freaking," he starts shaking his head side to side, hands raised again, "like animal far-,lord of the flies, post-apocalypt-, it's just, it's crazy, ok? D. C. is *not* anymore, you get it? Do you understand? It's not that it doesn't exist or has fallen or something. It just *does not be* anymore. You've got RCC flags being thrown up, RCC soldiers marching around and trying to, I don't know what. Organize? Bring under control? Calculate? Compute? It's total chaos. I don't know what Smith was talking about in his report, about them being somewhere by Cincinnati or something. That he was wrong about, totally wrong. That's what I'm saying, like I look at the whole scene, and I don't know what has happened. The whole world's gone nuts, everything's destroyed, all communications, all sources of information, it's all destroyed, it's like caveman palooza out there, it's a complete and utter cluster, a—"

"So what did you do?"

"I did what everyone was doing, trying to do. I tried not to get killed. Tried to find food. Got a gun. Got another gun. Slept two nights in a broken stormwater pipe outside of the city sleeping on one gun the other in my hand, loaded. I was attacked by a pack of rats after midnight in the pipe one night. You know what a bunch of rats blown to pieces by machine gun fire looks like? It's not pretty. Tried to get food, like I said, because I had failed to before. Grocery stores, completely stripped bare. Every store, literally *every store*, windows smashed, jars and containers smashed, smashed glass everywhere. I finally made the rounds about the city and found the camp."

"The camp?"

"The prisoner of war camp. Got a good peek inside and, finally some order, some kind of calm, even if it's people lining up in long lines for food. But at what price! Those that haven't been killed have surrendered. It's over, do you get it? Here we are, and it's over. America never made it to 300 years. Here she lies, RIP, America. 1776–2064."

"It's over," he says, again. "It's over."

"How did you make it back?"

"I don't know. I left the city. I don't even know how I made it back here. It's over. It's over. I don't know. It's over."

She takes his hand in hers. They hug. Soon she is holding him, consoling him. She feels broken, he is. She holds him for a solid five minutes. His head in her lap he eventually lifts his head, his eyes now at the same plane as her stomach.

But when the Son of Man comes, will He find faith on earth?

Depends, it would seem. And maybe there are two kinds of people. There are those who believe and have repented of their sins and do continue to repent and trust in the Lord and will, by His grace, preserve to the end and be saved. Those kinds of people probably start praying at this moment, at moments like these, readying themselves. Other people, a second group of non-believers, these too sensing the end must be near, break down and give in, totally, to passion and their most base desires. Margaux and Greg are in this second group and Greg, at this moment now, the ongoing and developing situation, wants nothing more than to have sex with Margaux.

"Please," he says, looking directly into her eyes.

"I can't," she says, taking his face in her hands and kissing him on top of the head. She kisses him in the same spot again and then pushes him away, gently, before standing up.

"Please," he says again, this time in a lower voice, almost a whisper.

"No," she says, now holding the tea pot in her hand, caressing it. "You don't understand. *I* don't understand, okay? I've been with many guys. I assume you've been with a million women. You are, by far, the best looking man I have ever seen. By far. Sex has always been a handshake, an ice cream cone, take it or leave it, regret it the minute you eat it, just something *to do.* You're the first man I've ever actually wanted to—

"Yeah, okay, me too. I agree. What's stopping us?"

"I'm saying it's only a true sacrifice if you don't do something you actually want to do. If you don't want to do it in the first place, it means nothing. But if you do, and believe me I do, then it's actually worth giving up."

"What are you talking about?"

"I don't know. I just know I can't. I've, I can't."

'You've been spending time at the church. Right? That's what—

"What?"

"The church, this is what this is, right? Shit, you've—

"I'm not a believer," Margaux protests. "Is that what you're asking? I'm Pure Voidist, like you, like everyone."

"You've been at the church," Greg says, "nope, nope, nope, this is it, that. This is that. Nothing to do in town and here's this, what, this beautiful space and, what, you've gone there and now all these people have been filling your head with these stupid ideas—

"Don't talk to me like I'm a child. That's not it. Yes, I've gone there, I go there for cold air, for some reprieve from this death valley one horse town. Don't act like you know me or can get inside my head or something. I'm telling you, so listen. I want you. I'm trying to explain to you that you're the first person I have ever wanted in my entire life. But—

"You're literally killing me," he says, head in his hands.

"I'm saying, what if what the critics say, what if that's right—

Her speech breaks off abruptly. Greg just stares. He says nothing.

"What if our whole, our, our entire society is based around this type of sexual manipulation?," she says. "Like, they, by they I mean the 'leaders,' the people we are a part of, they try to get people to have as much random and meaningless sex with as many of these losers and tools as possible, all of them as depressed as they are, just so having given away this thing, this thing that's supposed to be something insanely precious, your sexuality, your like, *purity*, your 'innocence,' having given it away you'll give anything away to anyone and then you're a sitting duck easy to control. Like what if we've been lied to for years before we were even born? Born into a society in which we never stood a chance because this had been played out for years already and everyone was already screwed. And what if when they said freedom, they meant slavery? And choice, agonizing regret. And worst of all what if it was all on purpose, these bastards cheering us to do it, do it, do it, telling us it's freedom and sexual liberty and expression, bullshit, knowing, but knowing, they knew, that's what I'm saying, that that's how'd they trap us in all their sick and twisted, deranged, absolutely deranged, schemes."

"I have no idea what you're talking about," he says.

Now Margaux looks at him and says nothing.

"Please," he says, a final time. "Just please put me out of misery. Just one time. Let's just be together once. You can throw me off a cliff, throw me to sharks afterwards. Just once. Just one time."

Margaux exhales. "I have to go." And then, and from where this came, she had no idea, for it took her completely by surprise. Almost as if then, at that moment, it was not her, but a stranger, reciting the words.

"God bless you."

Margaux leaves *Two Mallards Motel* and heads for St. Edith Stein's. It's sometime past midnight. She has to go. She feels compelled, pushed ahead, pushed like some crab or turtle caught in the tide floating about the waves, a powerful surf, and soon she and the final wave are going to be breaking onto the beach. She goes to the front doors, as if expecting them to be open, and pushes. They are; open. She steps inside and I feel as though now, here, I, Margaux Himmel, am me, myself, and maybe for the first time ever.

I believe, Lord, help my disbelief.

Grace, I don't know, is that what it's called? When God gives you what you need the moment you need it. When God, who has been there all along, you denying He was, decides to allow the wool to be lifted from your eyes and you can feel that you have been healed. I know I have been healed. I believe.

". . . . I need to be baptized now."

It works. I don't know why. It works. I ran up to him. I tapped him on the shoulder. This man, this priest, is that what he's called, a priest? Maybe my face said I'm begging. It works. I don't know. He doesn't ask me any more questions. He motions for me to follow him. . . .

—*Credis et in Spiritum sanctum, sanctam Ecclesiam catholicam, Sanctorum communionem, remissionem peccatorum, carnis resurrectionem, et vitam æternam?*

I look down and read off the card I was handed before.

—*Credo.*

—*Margaux, vis baptizari?*

—*Volo.*

He then pours water on my head, three times, each time after naming One Person of the Holy Trinity, each God, each equally God, together and united, Three Persons in One God.

—*Margaux, ego te baptizo in nomine ✚ Patris, et Filii, ✚, et Spiritus ✚ Sancti.*

Z.

"Can I sit here?," I ask Father Anthony, it now sometime closer to morning than night. "Can I sit here and read?"

"Stay as long as you like," he replies.

. . . .

In some feeling near "ecstasy," I don't know how else to describe it, I more glide than walk back to the benches, the "pews." I sit down and grab a Bible and open it randomly and place my finger down and begin to read.

The Gospel according to Saint Luke, chapter 23, my thumb on another, smaller, number. 28. I read aloud.

I continue on into Chapter 24. I flip the pages forward and see this is the last chapter of this section. I will finish this section, then choose something else. I'll do this all night. I'll sleep here, I don't care, I am so happy. I'll do this all night.

Praise God, I am happy.

And on the first day of the week, very early in the morning, they came to the sepulchre, bringing the spices which they had prepared.

> **2** And they found the stone rolled back from the sepulchre.
>
> **3** And going in, they found not the body of the Lord Jesus.
>
> **4** And it came to pass, as they were astonished in their mind at this, behold, two men stood by them, in shining apparel.
>
> **5** And as they were afraid, and bowed down their countenance towards the ground, they said unto them: Why seek you the living with the dead?
>
> **6** He is not here, but is risen. Remember how he spoke unto you, when he was in Galilee,
>
> **7** Saying: The Son of man must be delivered into the hands of sinful men, and be crucified, and the third day rise again.
>
> **8** And they remembered his words.
>
> **9** And going back from the sepulchre, they told all these things—

. . . 2:26.23 a.m.

A.

The weather this time of year, this time of day, is hot, humid-hot and sticky. A rainstorm has not long passed. One of those pop-up thunderstorms that fold just as quickly, the fragments of which afterwards cling like tree sap to all visible down below, out a window being steadily heated so the viewers inside the room feel like ants on the subject end of a magnifying glass.

It is nearly four o'clock in the afternoon. The temperature hovers around 100. The rain droplets on the trees, the puddles on the sidewalk, the muddy puddles many of them having absorbed a fair share of a horde of passersby's shoes, stick to the shoes, the sidewalk, the lower parts of pants. The city has become a morass of butter and molasses.

".... Wednesday, June 28, 2064," Jon-Kirk Bellows reads aloud off some screen he has picked up off the table around which five of them, co-workers, sit. "Why do we add the year, still? This is our paper. Why do we have to add the year? Is there any person in this country that doesn't know what year it is? The *Post* doesn't do this, why do we?"

"Why does this bother you?" Melvin asks.

Jon-Kirk removes his glasses. He rubs his eyes. "It's the little details that matter. People have been trying to make clean breaks from the past since the French Revolution. It's always some baby back beta bitch who wimps out and mucks it up for the lot. You get some momentum, you start cracking the eggs for the omelet, and then someone somewhere gets nostalgic. A bit of this tradition here, just a tiny bit, then, well, soon people want more and so more concessions are made and nothing gets done. It happened in 1848, happened after the Civil War, it always happens. Even now, even with all the progress we've made these past decades, I'm scared it'll happen again. And when it does, we'll lose everything."

"I don't understand what's wrong with listing the year," Melvin says.

"Maybe next we'll want to put *A. D.* in front of the year, huh? It's all about the little details."

"Margaux," Melvin says. "What do you think?"

"About the year?"

He nods.

"I don't care."

"Look, look at this" Jon-Kirk says, smacking the screen. " '150 years ago a Single Shooter Altered the Course of History and Ushered in the Modern World.' That's the headline of today's paper. This sappy, wistful reminiscence of times gone by. And then people wonder when the masses pine for it. You read and damnit if you don't start feeling some kind of human connection with Franz Ferdinand and Sophie and then, after that, it's hardly a stretch to start feeling something for the Habsburgs, for monarchy, for ages of 'faith' and 'patriotism' and all that nonsense. The funny thing is all these idiots have no idea they were already then neck deep in the post-Nietzschean full abandonment of God, of truth, of meaning. But perception is reality. We're contributing to the problem, that's what I'm saying."

B.

Because of the government's tireless promotion of public virtues like asexuality, bestiality, pillow partner holographic polygamy and the very popular "robotic hook-up scene"—the best feature therein being A. I.-A. I., "Atomic Insemination (by) Artificial Intelligence"—the American population, which once numbered close to 500 million people, has fallen to 160 million. It's something all Americans can be proud of. Finally, the collective genius and energy of America had been focused on the singular goal of Mother Earth's carrying capacity health.

The President is very happy with the work his cabinet has done in encouraging "Patriotic Purging," the voluntary sometimes slightly coercive campaign which asks Americans over the age of seventy, and anyone else who might be disabled or bored of life, to euthanize themselves out of "love for the country and love for the planet, our common home." It is a very simple and painless DIY process that can be accomplished in less than a few minutes. Impossible to miss red booths, somewhat similar to the public phone booths of yesteryear, can be found on the street corners of most major cities in America. There's one right down below where Margaux was looking before. It's wet from the rainstorm too. Purge-Heroes enter the booth, present their wrist for digital scanning, select their preferred Bye-Bye World playlist, and then choose the inscription they want on the 100% Biodegradable medal that will be sent to their families thanking them for their service.

One of Margaux's friends chose "I hate you people with every fiber of my being." It still makes Margaux laugh, how witty it was. This friend, Tim, he and Margaux went to college together and tried what used to be called "dating." They found themselves to be "incompatible" from five minutes into the first meal. Instead of trying to pursue anything serious they decided to meet up every once in a while to have sex. That didn't work either. And when Margaux told Tim one night that she thought they should stop, and that she had been seeing and having sex with other people, Tim became something like "crestfallen." The look was all over his face. He looked sad. Then, maybe two months after that, the old Tim was back, bounce in his step and an unmistakable pep in his voice when he explained to her that despite being thirty-two years old he felt ready to make the ultimate sacrifice for the planet. And so he stepped into one of those booths and picked his music and pressed the button that, instantly and completely, fired the frequency necessary to turn his former whole self into a mush-like departicalized puddle of gooey "stuff." Margaux, most people for that matter, doesn't like thinking about the details inside the booth. Negative thoughts make for bad vibes. She is grateful that when the button is pushed the booth blares the Bye-Bye music very loud and that one cannot see inside.

. . . .

Margaux nods.

She is good at her job. (And, by popular consensus, good looking too. She's used to being called attractive. One trashy magazine recently ranked her # 1 in their "Most Smokin' Media Mommas—2063."[2]) Technically an investigative reporter, and certainly she considers herself a professional journalist with high standards and a respect for norms and procedures, she is, in the truest sense

---

2   Will Brad and Kent Jockenjoomer, eds. "Most Smokin Media Mommas—2063: Our much anticipated list. Margaux retains her title!" *GB Triple F Magazine: Girls, Babes, Foxes, Floozies, Flirt*, XVI, Nov, 2063, 48–62.

of true, a roving interviewer who is paid, handsomely, to go from place to place and put the correct spin on a story. She flies into town, locates the target, then commences the pre-arranged skit see schtick. It's basically the same spin every time, the same approach and framing. Only the characters change.

Her most recent job was at some nuclear power plant in western Michigan where a unionization effort had come dangerously close to winning concessions, perhaps even fair wages for the workers. The company CEO and his shareholders called John-Kirk looking for some help. The would-be union leader was proving to be as popular as he was good; good at organizing, good at speaking, good at displacing the local-oligarchs' unearned therefore not rightfully theirs money from their pockets into the proper pockets, that's what it came down to.

Margaux got the job done in one interview. Opening with fabricated common ground about herself being the daughter of a carpenter to disarm and disarm she does so terribly well, she led him, gently therefore unawares, down a road from explaining his position clearly and convincingly to soon not being sure whether he supported this one outcome that was sure to hurt workers, not sure whether he had even thought about this other potential pitfall, and definitely not able to explain what he would do when X would inevitably occur as a result of the Y and Z he had supposedly been promoting. He had no idea what she meant by $Y+Z=X$. He was actually quite sure that not only did Y plus Z not equal X but that he had never mentioned Y, Z, or X, separately or in tandem, and this because, if forced to admit it he would, he had no idea what those terms meant anyways.

He really had no idea what she was talking about. And that was the point.

When she closed by accusing him, in rapid succession and without time to think let alone respond, of being...

C.

Margaux's coffee is a hot coffee despite it being summertime. Amber keeps sipping.

"No," Margaux says. "What do you mean?"

"You don't get it, do you?" Amber says, hands extended, palms open and out.

"Get what?"

"What I'm saying."

"*What* are you saying?"

Amber lets out a disgruntled half-exhale, through the nose, mouth closed, and slumps back into her seat.

"That I don't know what to make, like, make mean, find, uh, the like meaning in that, in that, like, uh," she grabs her own cheeks, grabs her face two-handed, and gnashes her teeth in exasperation. "See?"

"See what?" Margaux says.

Amber says nothing. At that very moment a burst of pulsating, electronic music cuts through the air. Another American hero has been Patriotically Purged. The patrons at the café, Amber included, offer a brief round of applause.

"He's told me about it, about marriage, Margaux."

Now Margaux sits back. She starts laughing.

"What?"

"He's 'told me about marriage.' What does that even mean?"

"That I think, like, like that he wants to do marriage with me."

Margaux scoffs.

"What?"

"This is not,'"Margaux says, "this is not, an 'issue,' it's not a 'thing.' I'm sorry, this is stupid. You're worked up over nothing. You can't marry, you're not allowed—...they, we don't do that anymore and for good reason, Amber. I'm sorry, I'm just, I can't believe you're torn up about this. But...let me help...you want my advice?"

Amber nods.

"Marriage is slavery. Back then, even 'good marriages' were bad, actually even worse because they led to families and then that's slavery for two multiplied by infinity. Kids left to be raised by their parents, within these marriage-based families, was hell on earth. It's not *so much* better now, it's simply *good*, or *not awful*, for the first time ever. There's a reason for the high school love camps. It's science. The more partners you have, and the earlier you start, the freer and happier you'll be. If you really want my advice, get out now, drop this guy before he causes you any more stress."

"I don't know," Amber says.

"Don't know what?" Margaux says.

"I don't know. I agree with you. I just can't shake it, though."

"Shake what?"

"The things this guy has told me."

"What?"

"He'll be like," Amber pauses to pop a Werther's original caramel into her mouth, "Like, and I don't mean about the marriage stuff, but about sex, like he said that the government wants people to have a bunch of sex with a bunch of different people because they're easy to control that way. Like, he said that it was a really sick and twisted trick they play on us, like we're puppets on a string, those are the exact words he used. But that they, the government, knew what they were doing all along. That they pretended that the love camps, and the Everyone-with-Everyone dating initiatives, and the Anonymous Hook-Up Hee-Haw Fairs were good for us, that they made us free, but, actually, we became like totally enslaved; to ourselves, to others, to them, above all. He said that the more people you have sex with the more likely you are to become what he called, a, a sheep, a robot, like something about how giving away something so personal like sexual stuff meant you basically cared about nothing and would give up anything to anyone, especially your free will and sense of freedom, period, and so this was exactly the type of people who the government needed to have as citizens. To like control them, us, to control us, completely."

"So what's it been like for you two, though?" Margaux asks.

"What?"

"Sex."

"We haven't done it. That's what I meant when I was saying before about the whole, the marriage—

"You're kidding."

"What? No."

"You're not being serious," Margaux says. "Really? You haven't had sex with Steve?"

"No," Amber says.

"Okay," Margaux says, fiddling with her now empty coffee cup. "My last piece of advice is the same as before: get out, stop seeing him. Forget him. The guy's a complete idiot."

D.

It's late September. Dry, fine, but well into the 90s and it feels very hot and the sun is shining brightly, oppressively, despite it being late in the evening near twilight. Margaux is in Georgetown; the neighborhood, the school. Georgetown, like all places and now forever it seems, does not do air conditioning. They care and they let you know they care and if you do not care they let you know this makes you a bad person.

It's an off day from work but she's in a setting—the whole janky preamble of people shuffling and skipping about but to nowhere, to this place then back to the initial spot and around again under the hum of people talking in a medium voice but about nothing and when does it get underway anyways?—that feels familiar, as if on assignment. A story she will actually be covering is the David Crawford saga, two weeks from now in New Bavaria. It will be her first trip to New Bavaria, privately or professionally, and whether that's exciting or not it's certainly not the quotidian janky hum. A week before that, she'll sit down with the president for an exclusive, primetime interview.

Margaux's sister, a professor of international relations at the Catholic University of America,[3] invited her to come. *Come listen*

---

3   The overtly *Roman* Catholic University of America. A fact that has caused no shortage of headaches for the ACC ecclesial hierarchy and their affiliated academic minions and other assorted sycophants. That the best, bar none, period, "Catholic" school in America is one keeping to the "traditions" gets their goat, so to speak. CUA is so good, academically speaking, that more than half of the faculty are self-proclaimed "convinced atheists and/or pure voidists" and yet, because CUA sets the rules and *our house our rules don't like it you can leave*, attend the required weekly campus wide Mass on Friday and on Sundays and make sure to make their 10-minute weekly "holy hour" of Eucharistic Adoration in front of the exposed Blessed Sacrament. That they, the non-believing faculty, don't believe means nothing to the CUA people. This is an evangelical mission to them, the CUA people. Bring the horse to water, God will do the rest; they say things like that. What is sure is that the lines of demarcation have long been drawn deep in the sand. As liberal Catholicism became more and more liberal unto the ACC split

to the talk, then we'll grab dinner. It's on me, your big sis, etc, etc. Big sis is currently in the water closet, or elsewhere, but not in the empty seat next to Margaux.

Margaux checks the time. She checks the program and reads the title silently to herself.

> *Our Past Half-Century: Brief Reflections and Intellectual Discourse and Dissent from the Bright Dawn through the Time of Troubles unto the Now, 2014–2064.*

. . . .

What Margaux did find interesting was the moderator's opening summation of the past fifty years of historical events. She had heard these names and places and happenings countless times before. This should have been the boring part. But hearing it so concisely, one thing after the other and within the paucity of ten allotted minutes not a second more, she found almost exhilarating.

. . . .

About the 2020s, a decade more or less synonymous with the "American Time of Troubles." A dark period in American history that was without question the "low point" and/or "nadir" of the "American experiment" to date.

About how the Time of Troubles ended with the Russo-Chinese Confederation annexing California plus all of Oregon and Washington and parts of Nevada and in such a painless matter that despite causing quite a ruckus in terms of opinion, public and private, it was nearly identical, as historical comparisons go, to Austria-Hungary's annexation of Bosnia-Herzegovina in 1908; people, principalities, and state-powers were pissed, maybe equally, in 2031 as in 1908. But that didn't mean anybody could do anything about it, then or now.

---

other Catholics, the "traditionalists" and simply those not on the "other side," decided this was a strange, maybe kind of welcome, liberation to go whole hog and dial it back to the Middle Ages concerning opposition even rigid middle fingers to Masonic/Enlightenment/post French and American Revolution/Marxist hyphen Bolshevik hyphen Leninist/ plus 19th century humanist and positivist lip service to the "separation of church and state" and private religion and all that. And CUA makes all people at their school do these things. If they don't like it they, the atheists, can leave. Margaux's sister is one of these people.

About all the dominos that fell following the annexation of Russian California.

About how in 2033 Canada invaded Maine from a four-pronged attack out of Sherbrooke, Quebec and how this was really the great "shock," for everyone always expected the hated Russians and also hated China but Canada, Canada? Not just an old ally, an ally regaled, worldwide, for a friendliness bordering on spineless passivity never wanting to offend, encumber or harass, even unintentionally. The Canadian forces took all of Maine in three weeks (and with less than four hundred combined casualties), two weeks afterwards occupying Vermont and New Hampshire from their former border down to a rough parallel line from Conway in the east to Middlebury in the west. They did it all "old-school"; no drones, no missiles, no heavy explosives of any kind, just eight squadrons of stormtroopers taking town by town.

When the American president of the time decided that enough was enough, and that while "aggression against Maine, New Hampshire and Vermont" was one thing, the "buck stops in New York State," and so deployed half of the U. S. Army to Ticonderoga and Port Henry and threatened to "nuke the living piss out of Ottawa and Montreal." The Canadians backed down.

The troops withdrew back across the old border. The Canadian PM issued a live TV apology. He even offered to give the U. S. parts of New Brunswick as compensation for "our unprovoked, wholly inappropriate actions blindly undertaken because of the corrupting influence of Russian actors in California." Not to be outdone in generosity, the American president thanked his counterpart and told him that while Canadian troops must agree to never again invade either New Hampshire or Vermont so as to 'threaten New York state' they were free to keep Maine and he would see to it that the forthcoming peace treaty would list this prerogative first before all other considerations. Maine is today part of Canada. The two month "Canadian-American War" is colloquially referred to as the "Shitshow War" and the Treaty of Edmundson that concluded it the "America licking Canada's boots' ass Treaty."

About how two years later Canada and Mexico united to become the Affiliated North American Republic.

About how and why the European Union dissolved in 2049.

About New Bavaria, rather the "New Bavarian problem."

About how in the year 2050 the former U. S. states of Louisiana, Arkansas, Tennessee, Mississippi and Alabama plus the Florida panhandle east to Live Oak then straight down south to Haines City, and the South Carolina piedmont region, home to the magnificent Clemson-town and its Clemson University, seceded from the Union without a shot or a single Fort Sumter reference loosed to form the "confederated nation state of New Bavaria."

About how New Bavaria is not something like, or kind of like, a Roman Catholic theocracy but simply a Roman Catholic theocracy.

About how New Bavarian claims that they are not a Catholic theocracy but that they have a constitutional monarchy, elections, and that the sovereign does have a little more fiat power than British kings and queens at their most paper tiger but nothing, light years away from, the true autocracy of someone like Tsar Nicholas II, both to the max pre-1905 and a bit subdued by the Duma thereafter, means nothing because they're a Catholic theocracy!

About how people from a century prior might be puzzled even confoundedly mental pretzel meltdown discombobulated by how a Catholic theocracy might have emerged in the lands of the former Confederacy and what was once known as the "Bible Belt" but these one and same people would not understand the social realties of the mid-stream Time of Troubles circa late 2020s when, as if *en masse*, "Protestantism," generally speaking, collapsed controlled demolition style—to the ground, flat, to rubble in 2 seconds tops—and the ex-Protestants either became atheists, or soft-pedaling dogood secularists, or, some of the more liberal minded among them, joined the coincidentally protesting part of the Catholic Church (what would become the "American Catholic Church" in 2044) whereas others joined the Catholic Church and actually believed her doctrines and aimed to live as faithful Catholics faithful to the pope and the magisterium and tradition. Many of these ex-Protestants lived in what used to be called the U. S. South, in the ex-U. S. South's "Bible Belt" now called New Bavaria.

About how New Bavarians almost wholly eschewing modern technology in favor of living a life similar to the Amish of olden days, banning not just self-driving automobiles but ones with any form of GPS, anything external, anything that could track or be tracked, was evidence of their barbarism, not proper detachment unto a simpler way of life. And about how New Bavaria acknowledges no separation of Church and state when it comes to quote unquote moral laws; their social law being based on Catholic principles, and that this, the moderator explained, is not just cause for concern but just cause to regard New Bavaria as a rogue and "terroristic-type" state both an embarrassment and grave offense to every good citizen of the United States of America.

About how what remained of carved out former Florida, along with all of the former state of Georgia, seceded to join the ANAR.

About how Texas defended both New Orleans and Little Rock in the failed U. S. border sieges of '51 and shortly thereafter, having taken up arms against their own government, for they were then still part of the U. S., went full Alamo and returned to their glorious independent decade of 1836-45 and became once more the Republic of Texas.

About how in 2059 the U. S. states of Idaho, Montana and Wyoming formed an "autonomous interior region" called Greater Idaho that, while loyal to, and still fully a part of the United States of America, is still *autonomous* within the *interior* of a country it claims to be integrated into; and how maybe that says it all.

But, ultimately, about how the United States was in 2014 a contiguous, sea to shining sea nation from New York to Los Angeles and from Brownsville up through the amber waves of grain plains to Bismarck, North Dakota and while Americans were far from ideologically unified, far from seeing eye to eye on even some things, they were, at minimum, at least unified politically, strong in the strength found in numbers, for Alaska and Hawaii counted then too, but now, in 2064, Russian California was but the beachhead of more RCC territory out across the Pacific, including Alaska and Hawaii, and Texas was independent, and Maine was part of Canada and Canada was no longer even Canada but something called the ANAR and these two new nations on what used to be the Lower 48 were now joined by a third, a reactionary, overtly religious country, opposed to just about everything the United

States had come to stand for in these well-worn, tried and tired, latter days.

And so just like in the fateful summer of 1914, maybe it *was* better then, better before, back in the past during days gone by. How can a person find the fine line demarcating childish nostalgia from the desire for something truly better, true and good if not *the* true, the good, maybe even the beautiful? It is difficult to say. Maybe the Hapsburgs and their polyglot, multi-ethnic and imperial but soft imperial rule with plenty of rights and privileges to go around for all, was better than what emerged after more than a hundred million people had been wounded, maimed, or killed by artillery shells, guns, and a plague. Maybe in comparison to what came after the Great War what was before was not just better but some time near some kind of place a bit like Eden, fallen though it was; because golden, it was. And maybe something similar had befallen the United States as well.

. . . .

Margaux had fun with her sister. Dinner afterwards was very enjoyable. They get along great, as much authentic best friends as blood relations can be. All the closeness but minus the accumulated annoyances and exhausting sometimes catty competitiveness and small-minded smug spitefulness found unfortunately but naturally in longstanding, hyper-close relationships of whatever stripe but especially in sisters. The food too, it was absolutely delicious.

Afterwards, Margaux's sister surprised her with tickets to the Washington Capital City Symphony's "German night,' a concert featuring a mélange of Mozart, Bach, Haydn and Beethoven. Being an amateur, although not half bad, pianist, Margaux could tell that musically speaking the concert was not just poor quality but bordering on embarrassing. But that was before Margaux's sister, having noticed her pained grimaces as the performance got underway, informed her that each and every musician was an immigrant. Armed with this knowledge, Margaux relaxed. She even joined in the encore-begging standing ovation at the end. She now understood why German night was the hottest ticket in town.

As the two parted ways into the night, Margaux was momentarily startled by the sound of a Patriotic Purge but a few yards to her left. And then, what luck! This most recently minted American hero had picked Margaux's favorite song for their Bye-Bye music. Margaux couldn't help it. No one was on the street besides her, no one was watching. And so she danced, started dancing and couldn't stop, even as the rain began to come down in sheets.

Between Covid and
Me & Humility[1]

OCCURRING DURING THE INTER-WAR period, those twenty years between the First and Second World Wars, the Spanish Civil War is not as well-known as it should be. For many, Picasso's famous painting *Guernica,* commemorating the April 1937 bombing of the same named city, is the sole point of reference. And yet within those three years fratricidal violence between Spaniards reached a fever pitch rarely approached, much of it directed against the Catholic Church. Nearly 7,000 clergymen and women were killed during the conflict, some of them in the most gruesome fashion: disembowelment, castration, being burned alive.

A priest who survived this crucible is the founder of Opus Dei, St. Josemaria Escriva. I once heard a story about Escriva, one of those impressionable stories you hear once and know you will never forget. The priest was walking somewhere in town down some alley, dark or light it was probably narrow, and as he readied to turn left or right he noticed a man approaching him with considerable earnestness, reaching, so it seemed, for a gun. Escriva was frozen in place. The man kept coming closer and closer. And then, out of nowhere, a massive man appeared, imagine, a truly huge man, close to seven feet tall but absolutely ripped, not an ounce of fat on him, one of those people who either by genetics or hard work or both has attained negative 1.1% body fat. And this huge man went at the other man with even greater intent. He scared him off. The would-be assailant turned and ran away. Escriva, we can assume, had still not moved from where he had been standing all along. "Mangy Donkey," the huge man said to the saint, perhaps patting him on the back or squeezing his shoulders. "Many Donkey." Then he too turned and left.

---

1 This article was published in the May 2022 issue of *Catholic Journal.* "Between Covid and Me and Humility."

Escriva, as he recounted the story later, knew immediately. *That was my Guardian Angel.* Escriva was sure this was his because the only time he used the term "mangy donkey" was in prayer, referring to himself; an appellation of humility, he nothing but a mangy donkey before the grandeur of the Divine Lord of the Universe. He did not share this moniker with anyone, not a soul, nor was it written down or accessible by any other form. So here was this man, this donkey, humbling himself daily in prayer, trusting in God, and when help was needed it appeared. And maybe we mangy donkeys don't deserve full unveiling, don't deserve our Guardian Angel to appear and say, "Yeah, by the way, I'm your Guardian Angel. Mark, nice to meet you. I've got like, uh, half an hour before I have to get back. You wanna shoot some hoops?" "Mangy Donkey." It was enough.

I have begun tonight's talk with this story because something similar happened to me recently. Although, for full immediate disclosure, in a reduced significantly scale. What I'm about to recount to you is not my own encounter with my Guardian Angel. Just the kind of unexpected answer to prayer that is timed perfectly because God's timing is perfect.

I contracted Covid right at the beginning of last month, August. I was very blessed, very fortunate compared to the myriad people who have truly suffered during this pandemic. My case was mild, maybe even mild-minus, 2 out of 10. And yet, for someone who is pridefully used to feeling healthy and vigorous all the time, pridefully entitled to not feel under the weather for more than a day, no, scratch that, a few hours, it was, without question, the sickest I have ever been. I had a fever for over a week. I had plenty of congestion, a cough, and debilitating fatigue that nicely coupled with insomnia so one could spend all day and all night in bed but without rest, restlessly awaiting a recovery that kept being delayed by the day. Delayed like Italian trains. When they say, it's coming in five minutes, they mean it's smoking in a ditch on the side of some road while the guys who are supposed to be repairing the train are themselves smoking. I had basically every symptom that is to be expected and a few extra symptoms that perhaps are inappropriate to discuss in polite society.

Well, ok, since you insist, I will share with you one of these latter symptoms, but only because public health authorities consider it extremely rare, even more rare than public health authorities providing accurate information. Now, wait, before anyone gets upset and asks how dare I criticize doctors without having a medical degree myself allow me to remind you that I have the exact same medical degree as one of America's most trusted health advisors, Bill Gates.

I developed the ability to time travel, but only for two days, this malady went as soon as it came, like a mid-July Kansas prairie thunderstorm spitting grapefruit hale but leaving on the wings of a rainbow. I time traveled back to the nineteenth century and found out something interesting about our state. One delegate amongst a select few tasked with naming the place—as it transitioned from territorial status to statehood—wanted to call it "Awakenstaten." The reason being, as this one and same man, LeRoy McBeebob Biddles explained to me, that Idaho people were tired, dog tired worn down all the time. But wait, *were,* he said, because him and his brother, McMozart, had started a small coffee company that had taken off from day one. Idahoans couldn't get enough of the Biddles brothers coffee and so what was once a populace plagued by exhaustion was now turned up alert. "Awake," he said, "ya see? We can drop the whole Idaho territorial thing and move straight into the bright light of progress, we can become the 'Awake State,' Awakenstaten. And double meaning too, awake from the coffee, physically yes, but also awake intellectually, ready to lead America."

It was at that moment that I realized, what a missed opportunity for us, Idaho. For we could have captured a third meaning here, here and now today, had these delegates accepted the Biddles motion and had Idaho become Awakenstaten. We would be today, as Awakenstaten, literally "Woke State." Imagine how much love we'd get from the *New York Times, The Washington Post,* and *CNN,* among others, if these organizations' purveyors of goodspeak truth would greet their audience with "Thanks, Chris. Yes, I'm here live outside the capital in Boise, Awakenstaten . . ."

Unfortunately, the motion for the name change was rejected. More troubling still, the Biddles brothers ran into bunny-hopping heaps of legal issues when it was revealed that they had been selling their supposed "miracle coffee" without the proper licensure and with permission from health/food safety authorities on, quote, "solely an emergency authorization basis." It was indeed an emergency, a pandemic some said, workers falling asleep on the job. That tired workers posed a danger to themselves and to others was, of course, unimportant. Companies were losing loads of piles piled on piles of fat-thick greenbacks restrained by snapping rubber bands money by the day. Something had to be done.

So a few CEOs rubberbanded together and developed a genius plan by which they could force everyone to take something they themselves did not want to take and which could not touch that most special organ in their body, that beating pump of love, their wallets, for they were immune from any legal liability should anything be or become amiss. Some pretty nasty side effects were later linked to secret ingredients McMozart had added but not disclosed. And so it seemed, in hindsight, it wasn't such a good idea for the Idaho territorial government to have mandated the drinking of Biddles brother coffee—one cup a day, no exceptions, no filing for a tea exemption—but that's what they had done. I don't know what happened after that. My time traveling symptom had resolved, I couldn't go back. Sorry.

On day 12, or nine, or whatever of my bout with Covid I called out to God something like, "please, Lord, please help me with this. I'm tired of this. Please let it be over," something like that. That God would soon answer my prayer is only further evidence of His infinite goodness for, to be honest, I was being kind of a whiny baby at this point. My symptoms had been improving, even the Go Cougs WSU Cougar Health Go Cougs people who had called me to confirm my positive PCR test told me that I was out of the contagious phase, out of quarantine necessity as of two days ago. Then they closed the phone call with "Go Cougs." All this should have been received as positive news, but I did not receive it that way.

There I was, the next day, on the campus of Washington State University, having just parked my car, well, in a car that had just been parked, my wife was driving. And there's not a soul on campus because it's the summer and this parking lot is as empty as a ghost town and yet, right next to us, two college kids park and so tightly that I think it's going to take contortionist maneuvers to exit the vehicle without our door slamming into theirs. But's that the mood I'm in, the whiny baby mood, and I want to smash their door with my door, a few times, for good measure. All four of us get out at the same time and I see these people and it's like, great, frat guy and sorority girl from central casting. The guy's even wearing sunglasses, a ripped tank top and a backwards baseball cap. We go to deposit the coins in the parking meter and the girl asks if we wouldn't mind holding a flyer for some apartment complex while she takes a photo and shares it with, whoever, or whomever, of whatever...I mean whatever college people do now. I get it. If I wasn't me and I saw the me that was no longer me, the new me would totally ask the old me if the new me could take a photo of the me that is the subject of this sentence. So we agreed. But I blurted out something super dumb like, "uh, well, uh, do you mind if like, a keep this flyer because, well, I mean, I just like got over Covid or something."

It was at that precise moment, Mangy Donkey pedal to the medal, that this Incognito Aquinas frat boy opened his mouth and proceeded to let spill out spool after spool of what must have been divinely-touched golden wisdom as if on pick up the prescription at the next window, sir, have a nice day now, just what the doctor, the Divine Physician doctor, had ordered for me at that moment. "I had Covid, too," this guy said. 'And it was really tough; a month of really bad chest pain, really feeling down in the dumps, night chills and sweats, but, you know what, I got through it and," smiling at me, at us, "you will too. Don't worry," he said, like he knew I'd been worrying! Then he and his companion walked away.

The next few hours at the office were an honest experience of passing from anxiety to peace, an interior calmness thanks to the words this guy had spoken to me, thanks to God. After that, having returned home and drinking tea while eating oranges outside, my wife opened the door and asked me what was wrong, for I was crying into my oranges as I struggled to eat them. These are tears of joy, I explained to her, and God bless that frat guy, that mangy donkey. For not only was what he had said so comforting and with perfect timing but it was such a great lesson in humility too. The very person who I had falsely judged from first sight, this, as I imagined, dumb and so "cool" and so dumb maybe day drunk rockhead college kid, his words would not have hit me more squarely had they been spoken by my actual Guardian Angel. God be praised, He who uses the weak to humble the strong, or, in my case the idiot. It's not the first time I've been proven to be that, an idiot, and I'm sure it won't be the last.

This one moment led into a long train of reflections on humility and, ultimately, to this, this talk. I watched a YouTube video on the humility of the Blessed Virgin Mary and was struck by the claim that she never, in the entirety of her life, preferred herself to anyone. What a goal to aspire to, even if we, not immaculate and sinless like she, are bound to fail. To always give someone the time of day, to listen to others with genuine intent, maybe just to care, to show someone we care. And then I thought about the ultimate example, not just of humility but of all things, Christ Himself, and how radically humble all His actions were because, and this is the singular important thing, because He did not have to be. Christ is God. God is perfect and so had He come to Earth and displayed that grandeur at each and every turn it would have been appropriate, right and just, because for God to "show off" his divinity would not be false or fake. God being God aligns with truth, the barometer of humility, more on that soon. But you know how God actually acted when He came to Earth. The sole person who did not have to be humble was beyond measure. And so since the one who did not have to be was, we have no choice to but to be ourselves.

But what is humility, anyways? Let's first address what it is not. It is not, as the great preacher Father John Corapi pointed out, tearing oneself down to the lowest factor possible. As we all know, people who do this often are manifesting a weird type of pride, lusting after that moment to declare their utter worthlessness for all to hear. Father Corapi explained this attitude when saying, "Humility is not walking around with your head down saying, 'I'm no good. I'm go good.' You may be no good, but that's not humility."

Humility is the acknowledgement of the truth. It is esteeming things as they are, honestly. A humble, see: honest, statement declares that God is God, the Maker and Sustainer of the Universe, Everything, whereas me, I am nothing but a tiny dot, a contingent being who did not have to be but was brought into being by God's love; and that's the great catch, God loves me, He loves you. That's a humble statement. LA Rams quarterback Matthew Stafford admitting he is good at football is humble. A good baker saying the same about her culinary skills is humble. World class Russian pianist Evgeny Kissin agreeing that he plays the piano well is humble. But Usain Bolt saying he's "not that fast," or Tom Hanks introducing himself as someone whose "hobby is acting," or me saying "I'm not that smart, not that good looking" these are not humble statements. I think you get it. Humility is simply acknowledging the truth, the way things really are.

But let's extend it. For humility is not a destination but a pathway, a road towards caritas, that great two-pronged law and prophets command from Christ to love God above all and your neighbor as yourself. Now I want you to imagine something. Because we're going to put *humility is the acknowledgement of truth* into a semi-mathematical expression. Imagine this: an old school blackboard that's green not black therefore dating itself to circa 1977–1981 and on that green blackboard is a solitary line of white chalk running from left to right. On the far left is written 0–4. On the far right is written X, but an arrow directing one's eyes off the board indicate X cannot be contained to this academic easel hanging on strained screws in some damp first floor classroom of a state university's auxiliary building CC.5.

0–4 ——————————————————————————— X →

0–4 is all of humanity from, what we fallen people, with the eyes of the world, imagine to be the worst and the best among us. 0: people the world would describe as "failures," worse than that perhaps. 4: people who are "successful," "super talented," our "best and brightest," even unto a horrid sometimes blasphemous sycophantic adulation of those with a sports skill, or type of voice, or enormous bank account, as if they were more than human. X, the factor off the chart, off into infinity, beyond our comprehension, is God. And if you look at this 0–4 to X picture with the eyes of faith, with humility, under the clear skies of reality, you notice that there is very little difference between the 0 and the 4. And, in fact, there is *no* difference whatsoever. Everything good comes from God, that's the humble truth, so even a hypothetical Nobel Prize laureate, Olympic gold medalist, Academy Award winning model/actor who speaks thirteen languages fluently can humbly, truthfully, say nothing but "God be praised" for whatever gifts he has been given he is cognizant, if he is in fact humble, that he is no better, not one ounce better, than that man next to him, mentally challenged and confined to a wheelchair from his early years unable to feed or clothe himself or do anything without assistance. We are indeed all of us brothers, all pathetic sinners with nothing of our own to boast but, following the counsel of St. Paul, that Cross of Christ whose Death and Resurrection is our sole hope for deliverance from this vale of tears through which we pass. And God, "X," on this board, He is not, as the lukewarm worldly believers would have it, "9" or "90" or even "900." He is Infinity. His greatness impossible to capture, impossible to describe, yet the sustaining source for all of it, all of us.

Okay then, so how about four things we can all takeaway from this talk to help us live, by the grace of God, more authentically humble, more truthful lives.

1. Humility is the acknowledgement of truth, don't fall off the boat in extremes either way; just the truth, reality, period.
2. Keep the 0–4 to infinity scale in mind for a visual aid relative to 1.
3. Imagine everyone, every single person you meet, is better than you; more intelligent, more interesting, better at even that which in humility you are good at, and holier than you especially, closer to God. Try living this and you might even approach, however dimly, that example set by Our Lady who preferred all people to herself. Finally,
4. Do not take yourself too seriously. We're meant to take God seriously, to have holy fear towards Him and worship

him with devout attentiveness. Take your job and your talents and serving your family seriously; but not yourself. Learn to laugh at yourself, that way when others inevitably laugh at you, you can join in and claim, plausibly, that those people are laughing "with you, not at you." I'd like to imagine that if Bill Gates was here tonight, he'd laugh at the earlier jibe directed his way. I'd then point to him, he doubled over in jovial mirth, and say "Aha, behold a redeeming quality. Also, I guess he's not a robot."

But how can we combine these four points of humility in light of the Covid pandemic? First, I'd argue, let's all stop pretending we know things we do not know. We do not know if the vaccines are safe or dangerous long term; we do not know if there are serious long-term effects from even mild cases of the wild virus; we do not know if the virus escaped from a lab or jumped to humans zoologically; we do not even know who the good and bad guys are in this narrative, we do not know. One day we might know, I'm even confident we will know more of if not the whole story, but that day is not today. So, especially on that last point, why don't we just pray for everyone?

For in praying for everyone we'll be praying for the good guys along with, and perhaps earning all the more merit in doing so, the bad guys, for it is Our Blessed Lord Himself who counsels us to pray for our enemies. Pray for everyone, wish everyone well. How nice, if in the spirit of humility, the unvaccinated stopped slandering the vaccinated with terms like "sheep" and "useful idiot" and "Big Pharma Fauci-Ouchy shill." How nice if the vaccinated stopped treating the unvaccinated as if they were unclean, almost leprosy-like science denying, selfish people bent on harming themselves and others. Is it really that hard to have an attitude like: whether you got the shot or not I wish you nothing but the best, health and well-being. May God bless you. Because if we know that Christ desires unity, fraternal goodwill between people, mutual respect unto love, then who, perchance, is the source of disunion and hatred? If the pandemic is causing you to hate, detest, and look down upon your neighbor, be assured that internal prod is not being pushed by God. If we are to ever emerge from these now eighteen troubled months, we must do it unified, bound by love and compassion for one another, or not at all. We must strive to practice the full spectrum of humility, otherwise we will fail.

I'll leave you with a final story, a small anecdote. It is probably my favorite story about humility and St. Antony of Egypt, the legendary 4th century desert hermit, is the central figure. St. Antony was out one day and crossed paths with Satan. "What are you doing out here?" the saint asked the devil. "I'm busy tempting the brethren, the usual." Soon the devil began to mock him. "You know, Antony. I hear you've developed quite the reputation for fasting. You go days, close to a week without food. I never eat. And, uh, I hear you keep vigil for hours on end. You stay awake night after night trying to pray without ceasing. I never sleep. But, you know what, I have to admit something. You are humble. And I am not. And in the face of that, I am powerless."

Christianity and Conspiracy Theories

I AM A HISTORIAN. MANY HISTORIANS ARE boring. But me, I am a historian and cool. I think, if my research proves correct, I am the only cool historian in human history. I'm also the only male model historian, but, one thing at a time. Former Washington State football coach Mike Leach loves history. He once responded to a question concerning the existence of Big Foot , "I hope there's Big Foot, I doubt there is, not to throw a whole shadow over the rainy forest in Washington where there's already a lot of shadows, uh, ya know, I hope there's Big Foot, I don't think there is, the reason I don't think there is cause we've found bones of dinosaurs and everything else but we haven't found bones, that I've heard of, of Big Foot, it'd be fun if there's Big Foot, I hope there's Big Foot, um, but my guess is there is not."[1] Uncle Rico doppelgänger quarterback Gardner Minshew, who played for Mike Leach and almost won a Heisman trophy, thanks to his penchant for jort and stache sporting and also being good at football, once himself opined, "We've lost two games this year, but the Cougs have never lost a party."

Big Foot and a WSU undefeated party streak are prime fodder for the deepest and most intricate conspiracies, both making for riveting historical reading as well. For who amongst us here could ever put down a factual, historical account of a college party in Pullman. That moment when that one frat guy who looks like every other frat guy ever returns to the keg for the fifth time, red cup in hand, and utters words on par with Shakespeare and Cervantes. "Sup, brah." That time when that guy tries to work up the courage to talk to that girl from that class but fails; again. That one toilet, for which even its most ardent supporters in the

---

1   https://www.nbcsports.com/northwest/washington-state-cougars/lets-remember-some-craziest-things-mike-leach-said-while-wsu

design team that brought it to market and final installation, could have never imagined would have the wherewithal to withstand being vomited into so many times.

What I'm getting at is, I'm going to be telling you a lot about history tonight, and then a brief history of conspiracies as they appear in real historical time, our historical time, and then conclude by asking you "so what" and "so what should we do?" I'm going to tell you a few different histories, in fact, actually variations of the same story, the story being the history of the United States of America since the Second World War by way of four lenses; in order:

1. Just the chronological facts
2. The providential interpretation
3. Oil and Imperialism talk
4. The Granddaddy of all Conspiracies

1. Just the chronological facts. By the end of 1945, the Americans had defeated both Nazi Germany and Imperial Japan, ushering in, on the wings of the atomic age, the soon to be called "Cold War" which pitted a Western and capitalistic and individualistic value system against the collective communism of the East. While the Iron Curtain descended over Eastern Europe, the American "Baby Boom" propelled the post-war generation into a hereto unheard of decade of prosperity, the Levittown lemonade stand picket fence family homes reachable by an Interstate system surpassing even the Roman Roads themselves. The 60s brought much social strife, racial and between the sexes, as well as the overturning of long-standing mores concerning family and sexuality and drug use and being publicly naked in the afternoon on New York farms turned music festival grounds, along with the start of a disastrous war carried over into the next decade. But, hey, we did put a man on the moon. (I mean, we....we did, right?). America seemed to be winning the economic-ideological fight against their sole superpower rival, as stocked shelves and money to fill stockings at Christmastime attested to. When the Berlin Wall fell in 1989 it was the final sign of a decisive American triumph that had begun the moment Ronald Reagan had taken office; "Morning Again in America," Yuppies and deregulated Wall Street money, muscular international diplomacy personified in that famous phrase, "Mr. Gorbachev, tear down this wall."

Little wonder that following the collapse of the USSR in 1991 the historian Francis Fukuyama asked if this signaled the *end* of history?[2] With communism now joining the historical dumpheap of failed systems, was it not reasonable to assume that American liberal democracy, where everyone was free to binge watch as many episodes of *Friends* as they wanted while wearing Levi jeans and eating McDonalds and drinking Coca Cola, would be all of the end all be all until the end? Certainly Fukuyama acolytes were disappointed by the events of September 2001 and the subsequent two decade war in the Middle East after the 90s seemed to promise, at least implicitly, the final realization of Woodrow Wilson's, or maybe more precisely Immanuel Kant's, perpetual peace. And it wasn't that long ago, certainly before this thing we are currently living through, that Americans could say, without sarcasm, that the "American way" had conquered the world. But now, in the year of Our Lord, 2021, we look out and see so much of the internal divisions at home and the rise of autocracy and theocracy and challenges to our hegemony abroad and it gives us pause. How long can we keep this going?

2. The second interpretation of 1945–2021, **the providential one**, is a variant on the just taken you through timeline with one added factor, and an ultimate one, namely, that God has specially blessed these U. S. of A. and, upon us, God willing, that blessing will ever remain. It's right there in one of our most iconic songs: "For purple mountain majesties above the fruited plain! America! America! God shed His grace on thee." Presidents from JFK to both Bushes to Obama to Trump have used a singular phrase, "shining city on a hill," to describe America and its quasi-religious mission to spread freedom and liberty across the globe.

So, according to this reading of recent history, the Greatest Generation's victory over Nazism paired well with the atomic dispatchment of the Japanese, the latter methodology not in the slightest bit problematic, morally speaking. The Cold War only confirmed America's providential blessing for while our atheistic

---

2   Francis Fukuyama, *The End of History and the Last Man* (New York: Free Press, 1992).

opponents openly vaunted their opposition to religion, trampling on the rights of their subjects under cold, steel boots, we had prayer even in public schools and "In God we Trust" on our money and our biggest TV star a Catholic bishop. That the Eisenhower years were indeed so prosperous was only more evidence that God was smiling down upon us. And, sure, the 60s and 70s were kind of forgettable, and highly problematic. Ask anyone who lived through these times, I mean, if they can remember them, but the 60s were the decades of Civil Rights, right? This generation's great triumph for equality as the Emancipation Proclamation had been 100 years prior. A great, almost religious-like crusade because that's what it means to be American: to always be striving for betterment, for one, for all. And is that not the lesson of the 1980s? That America, sponsored, if you like, by Heaven, won, overcame a decrepit and corrupt and morally bankrupt system pre-destined to fail. And Fukuyama is right, by the way, and the glory of the 1990s is therefore in no way diminished, FYI, by the need of ever-increasing interventionism in geopolitics following 9/11 just as there was nothing bad about U. S. involvement in Vietnam. In both cases, American actions were wholly justified and even theologically sound. For God having personally blessed this land what can remain but a sacred duty for America to spread its ways to all the world?

3. The third interpretation—Oil and Imperialism talk—is as cynical and negative as the previous one is positive see fawning. According to this school of thought, America committed a crime against humanity in dropping atomic weapons on two Japanese cities, made all the more abhorrent by the real reason behind it, as a warning shot to the Soviets. And what was our spiff with the Soviets about? Money, power, trade routes and control of the world economy. We went to war in Korea and Vietnam not for ideological reasons but to make sure we would be able to dictate economic realities in the Pacific regional sphere. We removed a democratically elected leader in Iran, Mohammed Mossadegh, and replaced him with a puppet, the Shah, because we can control puppets, and make them divert their resources into the proper pockets. That's why from Mossadegh to Salvador Allende and to more recent examples like Sadaam Hussein, Gaddafi, and Bashar

al-Assad, we get involved. And it's often a bait and switch shell game, claiming, publicly, that it's for moral reasons, while the true motivations lie below the surface, revolving around economic enrichment or better geopolitical positioning. And so 9/11, tragic though it was, became the perfect pretext for endless wars in a region we were all too happy to drop anchor, offering strategic and monetary rewards aplenty with the perfect alibi of being there to "spread democracy" and "fight evil" ever at the ready.

So there you have it, three possible interpretations of the past seventy-five years. The fourth one I'll get to soon. But, as it deals heavily with extraterrestrials, it would only be fair for me to now pause, albeit briefly, and recount to you a recent experience a close friend of mine, who will remain unnamed, had with aliens. Look, let's cut to the chase, he was abducted. And, he told me about it. So I'm here to tell his story because what are friends for?

He got abducted in what I guess you could call the "standard way," was out for a midnight walk on the gravely underfoot crunch and pop of the Old Moscow-Pullman Highway, that glorious road right turn away from the Kibbie Dome just right outside our doorways here. That road begging for a mineral hot spring by the side of it, a bench built under which towels are properly folded, with a beer tap built into the bench, clean glasses by the towels, the whole thing affording a clean look at so much of what the Palouse has to offer the ultimate offer being why don't you stop on by, drop on into that 105 degree water, allow us to pour you a cold one while you focus on exhaling slowly and smiling as contently as you can. A few beams of bright light illuminated downwards onto his head from a cylindrical shaped flying disk and they beamed him up onboard. There was only one alien there and his name was Munchie. He looked like, well, an alien, you know, the eyes and the weird head, that's what my friend told me anyways.

Munchie asked my friend, "would you like to get probed?" My friend said no. Munchie then asked him if he had any questions "before I release you." "Release me?," my friend asked, "I just got here." Munchie then explained that 99% of an alien abduction is the probing and post-probing procedural protocol. "Okay," my friend said, "yeah, yeah I got some questions. Can you guys teleport?" Munchie explained that my friend would have to clarify who *you guys* were exactly? "You know, man, you, aliens." Munchie said that there were many types of aliens and that one had to be more specific and, above all, that the term "aliens" was highly offensive, a buzzword of bigotry back home, and that my friend should never use it. "What should I call you then?" "Well we identify as Non Carbon Argon Based Biomechanical Applied Biospherical Androstenedione Backed Android Billed Anthropomorphic Beings. It's a real simple acronym: NCA-BeeBee'ay'Bee—AB, AB, AB. But, above all," Munchie said, "it's about respect, it's about common decency." Munchie then explained that the Swedish pop group ABBA was listed as a hate group on his home planet because their use of the letters A and B in their own name was considered an intentional affront to his people, like they were mocking them.

At this point my friend was pretty pissed and didn't care if his question would ever be answered. But Munchie had a question for him. "How does a male type of a particular species win the special affections of a female type of the one and same species?" My friend responded that he had no idea because he was afraid to talk to women. "Do you mind I run something by you," Munchie asked, quickly adding that "run something by you" was his favorite Earth-being saying slash idiomatic expression and it had taken him years to understand how to use it in the proper context but he was now thrilled that it had finally clicked for him and so used it at every opportunity.

"Sure," my friend said, "shoot." Munchie immediately pulled out some-kind of laser gun that looked like a toy but, my friend imagined, could probably turn one's cell membranes inside-out and so this marked the first time of the whole encounter that he felt genuinely terrified. Munchie put the gun away, laughing, saying that he was just joking and understood what my friend had meant by "shoot" but wanted to "Grendel" him. "Grendel?" my friend asked, perplexed, 'the creature from Beowulf, ah … the troll from Beowulf, you wanted to troll me." Exactly, Munchie confirmed, quite pleased with himself. "So look," Munchie said, "there's this female, a pondskipper, we call them, the female NCA-BeeBee'ay'Bee—AB, AB, Abs. Her name is Moon-Comet and I just, I'm for certain deep in the emotionals when it comes to her. But the sparkray between us is unrequited if not absent altogether. I'm saying I don't know if in my possession is that which pondskippers want. I mean, pondskippers want garabageeaters with skills, you know? Time traveling skills, anti-gravity skills, galaxy hopping skills. A pondskipper like Moon-Comet she's probably only interested in garbageeaters who drive spaceships really fast or can sing really well. And that's why I'm going to sing a song for her to try and win her undivided attention. Of all the many facets of Earth 'pop culture' as you call it the most romantically charged, by far, in my opinion, is the old *Chillis* theme song centered around consumers demanding more baby back ribs. So, what do you think?'

"You're, you're gonna sing the *Chillis* theme song to this girl you like, and because of this she'll fall in love with you?"

"Yes, exactly."

"You're going to sing, 'I want my baby back, baby back, baby back, I want my baby back, baby back, baby back, *Chillis,* baby back ribs, barbeque sauce' to this girl you like?"

"Yes, what do you think? Is this a technique you yourself might employ?"

"No."

My friend says the next thing he remembers is waking up back on the Old Moscow Pullman Highway wearing a literal 1950s style dunce cap surrounded by what must have been huncreds of empty cans of Miller and Natural Lite but having to explain to the four police officers on the scene why he was fiercely clutching yet another receptacle, a mason jar, with a sharpie marked question scribbled on the front of highly offensive, unrepeable content and why, to top it all off, he was out here, in the middle of the night, on this road, naked. You see, it was all one last troll from across the stars from Munchie, he was still quite bitter at my friend's lack of help with Moon-Comet.

Aliens and UFOs are an integral part of our fourth, outlier, timeline of the night, the conspiratorial one. And conspiracies are indeed like Pringles chips, once you pop ya just can't stop, so we won't. According to this timeline, post-War America's greatest "other" was not the Soviet Union but extraterrestrial others from another dimension. We all know about the alien arrival at Roswell, New Mexico in 1947. You've heard of Area 51. But less is known about the meeting extraterrestrials had with President Dwight D. Eisenhower in the early 1950s, a top-secret test group that included non-military personnel including a Catholic archbishop—to see how the public might react to actual disclosure—and, suffice to say, it went not good. That the invitees were shocked down to *my mouth is open and I'm trying to expel sounds but silent I remain* is perhaps an understatement. And so those in the know here we're basically like "yeah, we're never admitting anything about this to normal people, ever."

The 1960s closed by us not going to the moon. It was faked. Or, if it was real, it was once again some kind of New World Order plus aliens thing; trying to build a new reality, a new civilization away from the Earth once the Earth no longer exists or has been so damaged and ravaged by whatever that they need to find refuge elsewhere. "They," the New World Order, something we can be assured does exist owing to the media and "experts" assuring us that it does not. The New World Order, a trans-national cabal of the super-rich and the super old familied and the super unelected hence the totally un-recallable and un-firable and un-accountable who spend their time—notice I didn't say *free* time because these people have nothing but *free* time—plotting and scheming, scheming and plotting.

The New World Order, not really a singular group but a loose collective of the world's richest bankers and most powerful politicians and most influential media members who meet a few times a year in some creepy castle in some dark forest somewhere or miles below the Denver Airport to do whatever they do there, have planned and orchestrated countless wars, false flag operations, rigged elections, assassinations, stock market plummets, even managed the responses to pandemics aplenty. The goal is always the same, and it's a two-fold goal: enrich themselves while impoverishing the people and, above all, consolidate more power and influence into their hands at the expense of the many. The reasons go something like this: ever since Thomas Malthus' 1798 book *An Essay on the Principle of Population* the elite have been obsessed with the idea that more and more of the serf-undesirable underclass will be born and blight the earth stealing the precious few resources that they, being the cream of society's crop, should have the right to use and abuse as they see fit.

All this first reached a fever pitch with the eugenics movement of the early 20th century before falling out of fashion, for obvious reasons, with the rise of the Nazi party. So much of New World Order propaganda can be reduced to wanting "not them," us, to be as few as possible so "they" can have it all and more abundantly than ever. So, I ask you, do glossy magazines run headlines like "when having it all means not having kids" because they really believe this or because they want less of the common people around? Do they support abortion so passionately because they believe in "reproductive rights" or because they want less of the common people around? Do they attack the traditional family because they hate families or hate children or because they want less of the common people around? They love kids, notice how many of these people have five, six, even seven children. They just don't want you having children. Do they support contraception so assiduously, and sterile relationships so stridently, because they are fighting for "rights" and "freedom" or because they want less of the common people around?

Let's take a look at what has been termed the "blueprint of the New World Order," the Georgia Guidestones, an American Stonehenge hiding in plain sight on a hilltop in Elbert County not too far from the South Carolina Piedmont. The Georgia Guidestones are composed of six granite slabs weighing a quarter of a million pounds in sum. They were funded and built by a group of anonymous donors—not suspicious at all—who, in 1980, built what they envisioned to be a tripartite "compass, calendar and clock' structure that could 'withstand catastrophic events"—totally normal so far—dedicated to the initiation of a new "Age of Reason" proclaimed in stone in a variety of languages including Babylonian, Ancient Egyptian, Hebrew and Swahili, you know, it's basically a standard, run of the mill type project.

Opinions on the Georgia Guidestones—owing to their advocacy for one world government and new age religious ideas—range from seeing them as nerdy and weird to being, quite literally, the ten commandments of the Antichrist.

Here are points two through ten, verbatim, as they appear on the stones.

2. Guide reproduction wisely—improving fitness and diversity.
3. Unite humanity with a living new language.
4. Rule passion—faith—tradition—and all things with tempered reason.
5. Protect people and nations with fair laws and just courts.
6. Let all nations rule internally resolving external disputes in a world court.
7. Avoid petty laws and useless officials.
8. Balance personal rights with social duties.
9. Prize truth—beauty—love—seeking harmony with the infinite.
10. Be not a cancer on the Earth—Leave room for nature— Leave room for nature.

You'll notice I started at number two. Here's number one, the first inscription on the Georgia Guidestones, verbatim: *Maintain humanity under 500,000,000 in perpetual balance with nature.* There are currently 7.9 billion people on Earth. To "maintain humanity" at or under 500 million means to reduce the world's population by 84.2 percent. How, exactly, do you just get rid of seven billion, four hundred million people? Because it seems even nearly an endless amount of contraceptives, abortions, sterile relationships, and wars would come nowhere close.

And so, according to this timeline, there is no "just the chronological facts" and there is no "good" America or "bad" America. There is only the behind the scenes will to power of a group of people who, like the devil, play their greatest trick in getting everyone to deny their existence therefore ensuring their unchecked and unregulated ability to do as they please, doing as they please meaning starting and ending wars on a whim, hijacking causes on the left and the right, all the better if it looks bi-partisan, and all for an overall goal to reduce as many of us using whatever excuse is most fashionable at the time—perhaps today it's public health, the planet, climate change—so when the dust settles they will have more; more power, more resources, more of whatever they want, to do as they want whenever they want. They will have more and you will have less and there will be less of you, all of you, and therefore more of them, at least proportionately. And if you, at this moment, are wondering where exactly the aliens fit into all this nonsense it's usually that the aliens are the masters of the New World Order Masters of the World, or that the New World Order people are actually aliens themselves, or that the NWO and the aliens are something like allies and equals and have some kind of agreement to keep all this business out of public view and since that has largely succeeded and the common person is none the wiser, and really considers "aliens" a heaping pile of B. S. anyways, it just further confirms how intelligent, and how stupid, they and we are, respectively speaking.

But how should Catholics, Christians of all backgrounds, react to, approach, this?

Above all—number one, you could say—take comfort in Our Lord's words in the sixteenth chapter of St. John's Gospel: "Take courage, I have conquered the world." Our faith teaches us to say "Jesus, I trust in You" and to "be not afraid," as St. John Paul the Great often reminded us. We Christians, we know how the story ends. Christ the King who won the battle once and for all on Calvary will come again in His glory to judge the living and the dead. Christ wins, and the victory is not just assured but already secured. So, first and above all, be at peace, be tranquil, be faithful knowing that no matter what may come God is in control and that nothing, not a single past-ripe leaf more goldenly yellow that the thickest Hefeweizen you've seen then smelled then smiled then sipped falling from a forgotten tree deep in the River of No Return Wilderness, does so without his permission.

Second, avoid the oldest heresy in the book, Gnosticism. Christ preached openly, the saving message of His Gospel is available and understandable to all. If ever someone comes to you promising secret formulas for special enlightenment which will enable you to reach alternate planes of consciousness beyond the matrix itself blah, blah, etc, blah, just turn and sprint as fast as you can in the opposite direction, even head down and eyes closed, unless directly behind you is a brick wall, for in that case make sure it's head up and eyes open. That's one of the defining features of all conspiracy theories, that here's something secret and hidden that only those with special powers, or something, can comprehend. And so this often makes something which is complete B. S. and dumber than stupid insanely cringe, too. But it can be dangerous as well, for those who get sucked in and become "true believers." Everything worth knowing, and I mean for the ultimate question of your own salvation, is out in the open and accessible to all people: Love God above all and your neighbor as yourself; the Ten Commandments; believe in Christ and be Baptized; repent of your sins; receive the Eucharist; do unto others as you would have them do unto you.

Okay, so one and two, excellent, faith and trust in Christ leading to authentic tranquility plus a nice vaccine, if you will, against Gnosticism. But, in conclusion, I would add the necessary components of being "innocent like doves and sly like serpents" and being humble, humility, as you all know from our September lecture, being nothing more or less than the acknowledgement of truth. Yes, we know how the story ends. Yes, Christ wins. But don't be naive and therefore assume that the evil of the world is overrated or that no one would ever sit around with other evil-minded people plotting things that might bring destruction to many for the benefit of the few. As St. Paul told us, we fight principalities and powers. Spiritual warfare is real. And so while many, maybe the vast majority, of "conspiracy theories" are complete garbage and wholly false, it is certainly true that some are not and that one of the oldest ones is really not a conspiracy at all. The devil hates you. He wants you damned, sent to hell with him and the demons. And it matters not little but not at all the means by which he tries to accomplish his plans. So, be watchful, as the Bible tells us, and cling to Christ, His Church, the Blessed Mother and the whole communion of Saints. For we live in perilous times and must remain innocent and holy but not stupid, not intentionally blind.

Divine Mercy, indeed.

Jesus, I trust in You.

Label Catholics

LABELS ARE A CONSPICUOUS AND SER-viceable part of everyday life. Strolling aimlessly through Co-Op aisles near twilight in summer, the streets outside calm, devoid of autumn's buzzing hive, the air devoid of even slight breezes, and nothing through those large panes but a indigo backdrop to an orange-tinted sunset viewed best from the Old Moscow-Pullman Highway, you yourself breezing along dropping fruit into your handcart fighting fruit flies flying towards the freezer section where with one fell swoop you can stop, slide open the frosted door, and pick up a container of organic mint chocolate chip ice cream for inspection. Precious label, what a treasure trove of secrets you divulge at first glance full information: milk, but of course, and chocolate chips too, but don't forget about the xanthan gum, the locust bean gum, the cane sugar, the cocoa butter, all of it churning your spoon, and then your stomach, to the tune of 9 grams saturated fat, 35 milligrams of cholesterol and nineteen grams of sugar. And that's just per suggested serving size, but who can follow such a puritanical imposition? Labels, what technology, and right there in the palm of your hand. You love this stuff, the ice cream, but not even the 69 milligrams of calcium or the 97 milligrams of potassium or the 3 grams of protein are enough to move the container from the freezer to the checkout line. You put it back. Then you put your mask back up over your nose and mouth because one of the Co-Op employees glares at you like you just backed over his pet with a bulldozer after first strapping said pet with a plastic explosive the explosive exploding as the pet was crushed like plastic. *Okay, dude, wow, got it, chill...it's back on.* See, the mask is like a label, too. It says, without a spoken word, that you...actually, never mind. What is on my mind is another label, a name tag, yeah, name tags are labels too, that the very reprimanding party was wearing which left me... perplexed. It read: R. Bipples Jay Paintporfolio. Should people like this being giving advice about anything?

We like labels. We make use of labels all the time. How else would you know that athlete's foot cream removes itching, burning, crackling, scaling *and discomfort*, if not for labels? How else would you know that 100% sodium bicarbonate, known amongst its friends as Baking Soda, not to be confused with hearty partying frat bro Michael Sodaris, aka "Baked Soda," can be dissolved 1 or 2 cups into a warm bath for a 30 minute soak, if not for labels? And how, I ask you, would you be aware of football coach, and now second time *Hippo Lecture* subject, Mike Leach and his most memorable quotes without the search engine label telling you you're in the right place to type and find. "I think the most important thing is confidence," he once opined. "A lot of people think they're confident, but if you think about it, most people aren't." "If you get into a fight, don't take your helmet off," he once told his players. "We're looking for smart football players, not dumb ones." And who could ever leave out the following gem from his time as WSU head coach concerning dating advice aimed at young men on the Palouse trying to find that most special girl. "First take her to CDs Pit House BBQ in Moscow...if she will get her hands dirty with some great BBQ, you will know you are on the right track."[1]

And so we like labels. But there is a place where labels are not just inappropriate but ineffectual to the point of hands up, palms out, discombobulated befuddlement. Labels are bad when it comes to Catholicism. And "label Catholics," those of us who celebrate being labeled a *blank* Catholic are losers and should be publicly called out. I hope when they order ice cream in the summer the scoops on their cone fall off onto the pavement before they can eat them. There is no such thing as a *liberal, conservative, modern, traditionalist, pre or post-Vatican II, black, white, social justice, environmental, American, Asian, European, African* Catholic. Now, okay, there is a based and redpilled 3% body fat 700 pound deadlifting farmer and beekeeper Catholic, but let's save that for some other day. You are either a Catholic or you are not a Catholic. You either accept the full measure of what Holy Mother Church proposes for our belief

---

1   Holly Anderson, "Highlight's From Mike Leach's AMA," *Sports Illustrated*, May 8, 2012.

and, may God help you, strive daily to live out this most blissful adventure or you do not, the do not usually code for I disagree with this, I disagree with that, I disagree with the pope, I disagree with the guy who disagrees with the pope, and, wait, actually hold on, oh, my stomach, it's, it's feeling a bit disagreeable as well, oh, wait, sorry, bye. Do you think anyone has the slightest shred of sympathy for you, sprinting off to the bathroom for some heart-to-heart conversations with the toilet in light of your I disagree, I disagree, I disagree "Label" Catholicism? No, you deserve it. Also, you sound like a Protestant. Sorry, I didn't mean to use profanity.

Label Catholics. Don't be one. Don't be a label Catholic. Put honey and milk in your coffee in lieu of artificial sweetener? Do. Be a label Catholic? Don't. Hunt whale sharks from a helicopter with a spear? Don't. But be a label Catholic? Also no. High school scenario: you're a sophomore guy and kinda geeky and a bit lacking in self-confidence, like Mike Leach explained, but then, out of the blue, a really pretty senior girl who's got a great personality and also volunteers at the local animal shelter, where she fixes puppies' hurt paws but really their hearts, asks you to go to the Fall Harvest Festival dance, should you say yes? Yes, go with her. Also, now you're a legend. But then you find out she started a charity called "Dates for the Needy: Nerds are People too." This complicates matters, and probably deflates the balloon of your recently swollen ego substantially. Just don't be a label Catholic, that's what I'm getting at here.

So who are our targets, rather the stars of our show? In the order we'll discuss them: Environmental Catholics, Conservative Catholics, Liberal Catholics, pre-Vatican II Catholics, Vatican II Catholics. Five out of probably 50 if not 500 possibilities. We just don't have the time, and I the energy, to cover them all. Also, boo! Did I scare you? Sorry if I did. Also, I honestly hope the conspiracy theory where the government recruits a bunch of badgers and augments them robotically to become people-smart and the size of a moose isn't true.

Environmental Catholics. For you, the Book of Genesis and St. Francis of Assisi, do not go far enough. To be a steward of the earth, responsibly using its resources and gifts, working for cleaner water and air for all, is not enough. No, like all heresies and the labels that signify them, you must go to the extreme and without compromise. And so we can hear *environmental* Catholicism in articles like one by playwright Dorothy Fortenberry entitled, "Latin Mass, women priests, celibacy? Climate Change will make all the church's arguments pointless." Climate change, Ms. Fortenberry argues, is far and away the most important issue Catholics should be concerned with. She literally says, "I will submit to you that climate change is the most important thing you could possibly care about … If you are concerned by … de-humanized sexuality, you should be concerned about climate change. If the pace of modern life feels frenetic … the tone of discussion feels unforgiving and opportunistic, you should be concerned about climate change. I have my opinions … about the Latin Mass … clerical celibacy … women priests … gay marriage … [but these don't matter] because climate change is going to render all these other arguments preposterous."[2]

No, you know, Dorothy, sorry, I've a feeling you're not in Kansas anymore when it comes to rational argument. So, following what you said, the next time I flip someone off in traffic, that "tone of discussion" you mentioned, I can just blame climate change? I can blame climate change for all the gross sexualization of our culture that's been rotting away the core of our common morality for decades now? Like, well, you know my promiscuous friend who hooked up with everyone in college and left a sorry trail of broken hearts in his wake, broken promises and just overall degradation of what it means to be human, it's not really his fault, climate change made him do it. And so when over the next century the planet heats up a few degrees we're supposed to take seriously the proposition that the Church is going to say something like "clerical celibacy used to be x, y, and z, but you know, nothing changes theology like the weather so, guess we gotta throw everything out the window, fellas."

It's absurd, it's label Catholicism. Even if the average daily temperature is 150 degrees and you melt if you step outside and

____

2 Dorothy Fortenberry, "Latin Mass, Women Priests, Celibacy? Climate Change Will Make all the Church's Arguments Pointless," *America Magazine*, October 27, 2021.

there is no fresh water left and so on and so forth, this Earth is not your true and final destination. You are going to die and you must above all seek salvation, seek Heaven, therefore maybe the dire circumstances Fortenberry describes would actually make the questions she claims will become irrelevant more relevant as your chances of dying sooner, and standing before God, will have exponentially increased. You've got to have your soul all the more in order and quicker too. I'm all about taking care of the Earth and loving our planet so as to leave it beautiful for future generations. But never at the expense of what Our Lord has commanded: Seek first the Kingdom of God.

Perhaps most gross of all is the near-adulation environmental Catholics heap on Swedish climate activist Greta Thunberg. Jesuit priest Father Thomas Reese, in an article entitled "Great Thunberg, a prophet for Advent" asks as a "member of the boomer generation"—which obviously begs the knee jerk meme reaction, "ok, boomer"—"as a member of the boomer generation, I wonder, 'Are we stupid or are we evil?' Future generations will have to live in the world we ruined." Claiming that Greta Thunberg is "an Advent prophet giving us hope but challenging us to prepare the way of the Lord," Fr Reese cites the following Thunberg quote in support of his claim; the hope she gives. "I want you to panic... I want you to feel the fear I feel every day. And then I want you to act. I want you to behave like our house is on fire. Because it is." Yep, nothing signals the coming Christmas season quite like that. So too another Thunberg quote from the same article, where, if you listen closely enough, you can almost hear children laughing while they sled and skate on frozen ponds under the soothing melodies of Christmas carols. "You have stolen my dreams and my childhood with your empty words... how dare you!"[3]

No, sorry, Greta, I'm pretty sure it was you, or your parents, or your "team," whoever that is, that made the decision for you to stop attending school—you know, like normal kids, school, where dreams are born and childhood is lived in large measure—to "strike for the climate" and subsequently receive international media and

---

3   Thomas Reese, SJ, "Great Thunberg, a Prophet for Advent." *NCR Online,* Dec 17, 2019.

monetary support so you could travel the world doing your best 62-year old librarian scolding Johnny and his friends for talking too loud impression. Definitely no contradiction in being against carbon emissions yet having an enormous personal carbon footprint from all that flying around the globe. And try telling some poor kid in Africa or the Middle East, who's childhood and dreams were actually stolen by war and famine, that you, who crisscross the continents like a movie star, wait, excuse me, a "prophet," are the victim here.

Ok, Zoomer.

But, fear not, this does not stop even non-Catholics from trafficking in environmental Catholicism when it comes to Thunberg. You see, even despite all of the previous information, all the contradictions and headscratchers, Thunberg being a prophet of climate change means that facts or logic doesn't matter. I really think President Brandon, I mean Biden, said it best when he explained, "We choose truth over facts."[4] And the truth here, like former Archbishop of Canterbury, Rowan Williams, made known is that "God has raised up a prophet in Greta Thunberg in a way that no one could predict. She has said things that no one else could have said." And just know that if you object to environmental Catholicism from, let's say, a "traditional" base, meaning, simply, Catholicism is what Catholicism is and we cannot allow any issue, no matter how important, to supersede the ultimate meaning of the faith: that it is about the Death and Resurrection of Our Lord and Savior, Jesus Christ, about salvation, be prepared for pushback from environmental Catholics. A twitter user who will remain anonymous, but one with a blue planet emoji following her handle, and with the word climate literally in that handle has said something to the effect that "traditional Catholic" on Twitter" is code/equivalent to/synonymous with "white supremacist."

Conservative Catholics. Maybe I should call you *Trump* Catholics. Now, look, I understand, trust me, we all have our heroes. And society needs people to look up to and serve as role models. Who hasn't read Therese of Liseux's *The Story of a Soul* and tried to live

---

4   https://www.youtube.com/watch?v=15RjcRJ3Z70

her little way doing all, even the smallest tasks, with extraordinary love? Who hasn't encountered Pier Giorgio Frassati and thought, I, a young person in the world, would like to sanctify my little circle of influence as he did? And who hasn't looked at the example of Donald Trump—from his insatiable lust for money, his quotes on women, about women's body parts, the gold toilets in Trump tower, and his heart warming comments about Christians: "Can you believe that bullshit," Trump said following a laying on the hands prayer session with Evangelicals. "Can you believe that people believe that bullshit?"[5]—and not thought, that's the guy, that's the Christian candidate I've been waiting for all my life.

Christ tells us to welcome the foreigner and the downtrodden and that the way we treat the less fortunate will be held up as the metric of how we treated him. Trump, whose father apparently instilled in him the Christian optic that life is a Darwinian contest between "killers and losers," apparently had the following musings on border security. Now, before I give you the quote, let me say that I am all in favor of border security, that I support a country's border and that we certainly cannot, in the vein of some misappropriated perversion of charity, go full open borders and invite whoever, literally everyone the world over into our country. That too is not Christian, for an authentically Christian view on immigration is not just about welcoming the stranger, it is, but also about striving to protect the safety and security of a nation's citizens, this including not undercutting their livelihoods by forcibly importing a cheap labor force to be exploited, and, it, a Christian view on immigration, also demands responsibilities of the immigrant, of respecting the norms and laws of the host country.

All that being true, I want to present you with a Trump quote and ask you to compare it to, for example, Christ's words in Matthew 25: *I was hungry and you gave me food, I was thirsty and you gave me drink, a stranger and you welcomed me, naked and you clothed me,* and, ask yourself, does this sound like the words of a truly Christian politician?

---

5   McKay Coppins, "Trump Secretly Mocks His Christian Supporters," *The Atlantic*, September 29, 2020.

Privately, the president had often talked about fortifying a border wall with a water-filled trench, stocked with snakes or alligators, prompting aides to seek a cost estimate. He wanted the wall electrified, with spikes on top that could pierce human flesh. After publicly suggesting that soldiers shoot migrants if they threw rocks, the president backed off when his staff told him that was illegal. But later in a meeting, aides recalled, he suggested that they shoot migrants in the legs to slow them down. That's not allowed either, they told him.[6]

I respect if you support Trump, maybe voted for Trump, because of his defense of life—a position, which irrespective of whether it's heartfelt or not, meaning if he actually believes it or not, and with that I obviously cannot judge or say, only God can—something that has been, truly, Catholic. Donald Trump's *presidential* pro-life record and his appointment of pro-life judges is commendable. But if you are a label Catholic, conservative turned Trump Catholic, who views Trump as a *fully* and *authentically* Christian politician I would have to object. If you can't tell if a candidate is sincere in their faith or just using it opportunistically to garner support and votes, which is probably the literal definition of what it means to be a politician, say or do whatever gets you elected, then there's a good chance it's the if it walks like a duck, talks like a duck paradigm.

I'll leave conservative slash Trump label Catholics with a personal anecdote from my in-laws kitchen in Nampa, Idaho. We, my in-laws and my wife and myself, were gathered there after Mass and talking to two guests, parishioners and daily Mass goers too, the woman of this two guest couple very much into Trump Catholicism. After going on and on about all the wonderful things Trump was doing for Catholics, and for the restoration of quote American values, she said, and I forget which term she employed exactly, that Trump was either a "new King David" or the "successor to King David." It was at that moment, immediately, that I was like, in the safe space of my inner voice kept on mute, "alright, I'm gonna leave now."

---

6   Eugene Scott, "Trump's most insulting—and violent—language is often reserved for immigrants." *Washington Post*, October 2, 2019.

Liberal Catholics. I think I've already given them enough ink in the earlier environmental section but I'll say briefly that the problem with liberal label Catholics, as I see it, is that, like the environmental label Catholics, they take their favorite pet issue and raise it not just above all others but above the faith itself. It's probably too simplistic as comparisons go, but I think label Catholics on the right are susceptible to error by way of cult of personality, elevating people, like Trump, or maybe a media personality like Michael Voris, I am a *Church Militant.com* label Catholic! Or, just look at the breakaway SSPX, named in honor of a guy who truly was an absolute boss pope, Pope St. Pius X, but whose memory has been muddied and scuffed up by association with this rightwing, anti-Vatican II label Catholicism. Label Catholics on the right gravitate towards exaggerating a person. Label, liberal Catholics of the left exaggerate and so obsess upon singular issues such as priestly celibacy, feminism and the Church, racism slash anti-racism.

And we see much of this—upholding certain, highly selective, issues as preeminently important—in the general outlook, see: favorable coverage, of arguably the most famous Catholic in America today, President Joe Biden. I'll say the following about Biden and all of it is sincere. It's cool that we have a Catholic president. Biden does seem like a reasonably nice guy, someone you'd want to have a beer and catch up with. It's awesome that he attends Mass and carries a rosary in his pocket. It's also true that it's absolutely scandalous and embarrassing how frequently his public positions and actions, most especially on abortion, fly in direct opposition to the Catholic faith he claims to practice devoutly and insists formed his thinking.

When Mario Cuomo invented the *I'm personally opposed but* doublespeak in 1984 at Notre Dame (perhaps the year most appropriate owing to the term's fundamentally Orwellian sly dishonesty) it was B. S. It is still B. S. today. Would any politician say, "I'm personally opposed to slavery but, you know, I'm going to do all I can to vote for laws that enshrine it. Don't want to be imposing my Catholic beliefs on others." (?). But this is exactly where Biden et al. stand on abortion. It's just another variant of label

Catholicism, meaning it's not Catholicism. But these liberal label Catholics fall over themselves making excuses for Biden, arguing that because we see him at Mass and that he carries a rosary (the pertinent questions, of course, are does he *pray* the Rosary, is he in a state of grace to receive the Holy Eucharist at Mass? [God alone can say and judge]) and, most especially, that he supports their own personal label Catholic issue, all is forgiven. For some of these liberal label Catholics it is not love—sorry, St. Paul—but support for the UN's sustainable development goals that covers a multitude of sins and serves as evidence that these Catholic politicians are in fact *devout* Catholics.[7]

I'll direct you to a recent article by journalist Michael Sean Winters—author of the book *Left at the Altar: How the Democrats Lost the Catholics and How the Catholics can Save the Democrats*—entitled "In 2021, it became obvious the US bishops and the pope are singing from different hymnals."[8] This piece appeared in the *National Catholic Reporter*, a journal subtitled 'the independent news source' but that is, at least so it seems, further to the left than Bernie Sanders in Moscow, Russia being gifted a first edition of Marx's *Das Kapital* by AOC while Fidel Castro sings the Internationale *a cappela*. A photographic negative of *The National Catholic Reporter* would be a periodical entitled *Donald Trump Catholic Patriot King David Bald Eagle Catholic Build That Wall Magazine: The Independent News Source*.

I'm going to read to you a few citations from Winters' article to illustrate the points I made above and earlier concerning President Biden. Bemoaning that his magazine had named LA Archbishop Jose Gomez its "Catholic Newsmaker of the Year" Winters complains of the bishops conference's "catastrophically narrow focus on President Joe Biden's support for legal abortion." The bishops should instead promote Biden "articulat[ing] the importance Catholic social teaching has had on his political views."[9]

---

7 Margaret Fosmoe, "Mario Cuomo Speech at Notre Dame Focused on Abortion," *South Bend Tribune*, January 2, 2015.
8 Michael Sean Winters, "In 2021, it became obvious the US bishops and the pope are singing from different hymnals," *NCR Online*, Dec 29, 2021.
9 Ibid.

In other news, it's too bad that when you put a block of ice into a hot tub the hot water melts the ice. Instead, we should talk about how ice has argued that hot water makes it even harder and more solidly frozen. The "drawn out squabble," as Winters frames the bishops' meeting, "showed a conference…torn between the lousy theology of the culture warriors who think Biden and other pro-choice politicians should be denied Communion and the otherwise universal practice of the church that distinguishes between lawmaking about an evil action and the performance of the evil action itself." Oh, got it. So Catholic politicians can support any law, no matter how evil, no matter that this support will lead to real evils in the real world, so long as they claim that they don't actually, you know, support it. And here I have to agree with Winters. I bet if I walked up to someone and punched them in the face they'd be upset. But if I told them first that I'm personally opposed to violence *and then* punched them in the face, we'd be good, no harm, no foul. And this second punch, post personal objections, wouldn't even hurt. Because it's the thought that counts. Good intentions, as every grandmother will remind you, pave the road to Heaven.[10]

Winters continues along this liberal label Catholic path throughout the article, because, of course. Anyone who likes anything "on the right" is displaying symptoms of a "schismatic tendency." It's good Pope Francis issued *Traditiones Custodes* because the "ideological movement had abused the concessions that had been granted." Winters doesn't specify what these abuses were or are, so I'll have to do some guesswork. 1970s style architecture and moan-whine folk hymns paired with parishioners wearing basketball shorts, or some hardly dressed at all, is good, but liking Gothic cathedrals and Gregorian Chant and the use of a common language that actually unified all Catholics the world over is bad, an abuse. Okay.

Maybe he doesn't specify because the only thing suffering abuse here is the ego of liberal label Catholics who don't understand why no one likes their music and hand holding and greeting the person next to you before Mass for forty minutes in comparison

---

10   Ibid.

to so much richness in the tradition writ large, stretching back over millennia. Winters mentions the removal of Cardinal Robert Sarah—in my opinion, the greatest churchman alive today, p.s.[11]—from his position as Prefect of the Congregation for Divine Worship and the Sacraments as if it's a good thing.[12] But maybe it's all as nonsensical as the following two tweets lay bare. Responding to a man claiming, "I was once called a white nationalist because I supported a more traditional Church. The irony is I'm a light brown skinned Mexican-American." Another twitter user wrote, "Future headline: Cardinal Sarah becomes first White Supremacist Pope." I have a feeling that Cardinal Sarah being a black man from Africa would matter little to nothing to some liberal label Catholics who, drowning in the swamp of identity politics, would no doubt wholeheartedly, and without second thought, endorse such a characterization.[13]

On the final two categories—pre-Vatican II label Catholics and post Vatican II label Catholics—two that I'm going to combine into one, I'm going to say the least. Both are so annoying, period. Both make a label out of Vatican II. Instead of properly esteeming it without overdoing it, they go overboard, they go full overkill unto buzzkill, as much as if the guy who arrived back from a joy ride on your motorcycle not only fails to park it in the designated spot but accelerates over the curb and then really kicks it into high gear going full speed catapult-like airborne over the rim of the Grand Canyon and then down and down and all the while you're just standing there, hands out puzzled by, like, why didn't he just park and dismount? And now our whole vacation is ruined, too.

These people, pre and post Vatican II label Catholics, why don't they park and dismount meaning shut up already? They act like Vatican II is the only Council in Church history, like it's the most important event in Church history. The pre-Vatican II label Catholics seeing in it everything wrong, corrupt and conspiratorial,

---

11   Could he be any more based?

12   Winters, "In 2021, it became obvious the US bishops and the pope are singing from different hymnals."

13   https://twitter.com/search?q=Cardinal%20Sarah%20white%20supremacist&src=typed_query

the post Vatican II label Catholics seeing in it the birth of a new Church, or some kind of nonsense like that, while simultaneously regarding everything that happened before the 1960s as bad or useless or irrelevant. Both of these label Catholics need to stop because all label Catholics need to stop. Label Catholicism? It's bad, I hope you've gotten at least that by this point in the talk. And I can't think of any better way to sum up the label Catholicism of this last, pre and post Vatican II category, than by an interview I recently watched of a famous Catholic internet personality who will remain anonymous because the story is so embarrassing. He referred to himself, this guy who specializes in the pre and post Vatican II label Catholic debate, as the "bad boy of Catholicism." The host almost lost it, almost died of laughter on the spot but somehow kept it together. I almost called a hospital to report severe injuries to my cringe muscles. Look, don't be a label Catholic. It has substance abuse-like negative effects to your brain and common sense, one of the worst symptoms being non-sarcastically labeling yourself a Catholic bad boy.

So I've now taken you through a few labels, you've seen both the overreach and the deficiency, but, you may rightfully ask, what does a non-label Catholic just Catholic look like, what are his beliefs and general way of being? There happens to be such a person in our midst, in our town, in fact, and he works at the Moscow Co-op. R. Bipples Jay Paintporfolio. Is he originally from Atlantic, Cass County, Iowa and the aforementioned based and redpilled 3% body fat 700 pound deadlifting farmer and beekeeper Catholic? You already know. But so why is he working at the Co-op, if he's a farmer slash beekeeper? Wait, farmer and beekeeper, and he cares about wearing masks? To all that I'll say, maybe if you spent more time minding your own business and reading and working out you'd be even half the physical, intellectual and philosophical specimen he is. And that would be really something, let me tell you. No, it's not too late to add some New Year's Resolutions.

Paintporfolio is a *just Catholic* Catholic. He hates labels so much he hires people to remove them from his clothing. He also hires people to photograph him and post the photos on Instagram and he hires other people to buy bots to make it look like he has way more followers than he really does. Look, I didn't say he was perfect, okay? He has 2.6 million followers on Instagram. He's a *just Catholic* Catholic because while caring about the environment he doesn't worship it, he worships God. He hates the political left and right with equal fervor; they suck, all of them, and knowing this he can and will turn to the men and women of his faith for advice and inspiration but to politicians for comedy alone. He accepts Vatican II like he accepts all the Church councils. He accepts everything the Church founded by Jesus Christ tells him to accept. He likewise rejects what the Church rejects. He's just a Catholic, understand?, and so he doesn't think it's anything special that he believes life begins at conception, or that marriage and the family are society's essential building blocks, or that true love is both the emotional response and the conformity with truth and always at the same time because, why is common sense special? And it's kind of like this with everything for this label less Catholic, kind of like St. Augustine's motto to "love God and then do whatever you want," which I'll add to in light of Paintportfolio and all those striving to be like him, "just be a Catholic, live the Catholic faith in its fullness but without additions, subtractions, or exaggerations, and then do whatever you want."

Catholicism, Cults, Fake and Real Religion

H E HAD COME TO ANTARCTICA WITHOUT a permit; Alabaster Alabama Pie Davis III.

An Australian bush pilot born to a Scottish father and Swedish mother in the suburbs of Helsinki had dropped him off dropping him out of the helicopter he had piloted past all those checkpoints. Parachute deployed, Alabama Pie drifted downwards towards the snow. It was a soft landing. The pilot quickly disappeared back across the horizon. If you're wondering how he was Australian exactly, the pilot, considering his Scottish and Swedish parents, and that he was born in Finland, the answer is that he *said* he was Australian. Some people think reality works that way.

The air temperature was several degrees below freezing. It was windy but the sun was shining and the skies were clear. No clouds; for him it was near no clothes. Alabama Pie was wearing swimming trunks. His feet, bare on the snow and ice, this too was not the problem common sense would assume. He was born with a condition. He could be exposed to extreme cold without issue. It was a gift, one with which his grandfather claimed young Pie had "defied the natural laws of the universe." "It runs in the family, boy," the grandfather explained, for he had been blessed with such a gift himself, the ability to defy gravity, to fly, and so getting up out of his rocking chair one afternoon he took off full speed up the stairs of the family's three story house to demonstrate from the roof. The funeral was well attended and gave the family much comfort.

Alabama Pie walked ahead with the determination of a man who knew what he wanted and where he was going. And so he soon arrived. There he was and there it was, just like those in the know said it would be: a book, an important one. He picked it up, sat down in the snow, opened and read.

Catholicism, Cults, Fake and Real Religion

Alabama Pie read the title aloud three more times. Then he yelled it a fourth. There was no one here;not for hundreds if not thousands of miles. He could be as loud as he wanted to be. An interesting side story concerns the presence of a dug out, makeshift hot tub a few hundred feet from where he found the book. Talk about the rich getting richer. Here's a guy who can sit undressed in snow and not feel or suffer a thing. And here's a guy who gets to enjoy 106 degrees on a nice, handcrafted bench with pruny toes tracing the floor of a well-pebbled pool bottom, puffing steady breaths of contentment out into the Arctic air. And so he sat in the warm water and read this book and this is the story of that.

> Christianity is True. Catholicism is universal Christianity. It is the Truth. Jesus Christ, True God and True Man, is the Messiah, the Savior of the World. He is God. God is the author of Catholicism. A cult is a system of collective veneration and devotion. The question is simply whether the object of veneration is true or false. Catholicism, the Church against which the gates of hell shall not prevail, is the true and unique and therefore good cult because it's been founded by the True, Unique, and Good God. All other cults, mockeries and blasphemous counterfeits, are those of whom Our Lord Himself said, 'Watch out that no one deceives you. For many will come in my name claiming, "I am the Christ" and will deceive many.' There is only one Christ, one Church, one true religious cult. All other cults are false, some are evil. I hope you, the reader, will gain some wisdom from these pages.

This declaration, which was written on the second page, was also written verbatim, all 159 words of it, on pages three through thirteen. Perhaps to hammer home the point, thought Alabama Pie. No author was specified outside of a "humble Benedictine monk." Page fourteen listed a table of contents.

0. Pre-Christian darkness, nonetheless Logos shines through
33. The Event
1. Do and Ti and NXIVM
2. Ecumenical Fallacies

Alabama Pie read these out loud too. Four chapters in the book. And yet it was a massive book. It appeared to be tens of thousands of pages in length.

He turned the page and began at the top.

0. Pre-Christian darkness,
nonetheless Logos shines through

It did not have to be this way. It was supposed to be all ours. Imagine: instantaneous wisdom and goodness and purity and simple wholeness, organic unity mirroring the one from whose hands we had been fashioned. But the tree and the fruit and the people and the choices. And so we were banished, as much from the lush garden as from the green pastures of simple truth, and so we were sent off to grope wet walls in dark caves chained to them trying to discern reality from shadows projected by ghosts as hollow as we had become. And so all the cults that never should have existed were thus created, by us, by our sin. And so all this pre-Christian darkness was, whether driven by love or by fear or by lust or by tribalism nothing more than confusion exponentially multiplied into a system of false hope, that having jettisoned the pre-fall birthright of clarity, we, by way of our cults, might somehow stumble back upon glimpses of the divine reality. But no, it was nothing but darkness in this time of pre-Christian darkness, until, "Do not approach. Take your sandals off your feet, for the place where you are standing is holy ground ... Moses said to God, 'If I come to the children of Israel and say to them 'The God of your ancestors sent me to you but they say to me, 'What is his name?' What should I say to them? God said to Moses, 'I am who Am.'"

33. The Event

argued this: that the initial clarity that came out of the post fall darkness when God spoke to Moses and revealed Himself to be the sole Lord and God of all and by his very nature of essential existence, He the unique non-Contingent Being, was brought to fruition in the Incarnation, the earthly ministry, and the Death and Resurrection of Jesus Christ. And so at that point, fake cults were declared over forever, and lukewarm ignorance feigned . . . no longer possible. It was now yes or no. A yes, a back to the beginning full yes to God, to God's plan, to the way, the Truth, the life, or the original fallen angel choice of a full no, and *I will not serve* deeper descent into self-made cults of the most horrifying falsehoods.

Alabama Pie read the G. K. Chesterton parts quoted in this chapter out loud.

This sketch of human story began in a cave; the cave which popular science associates with the caveman and in which practical discovery has really found archaic drawings of animals. The second half of human history, which was like a new creation of the world, also begins in a cave. . . . It was here that a homeless couple had crept underground with the cattle when the doors of the crowded caravanserai had been shut in their faces; and it was here, ...in a cellar under the very floor of the world, that Jesus Christ was born. But in that second creation there was indeed something symbolical in the roots of the primeval rock or the horns of the prehistoric herd. God also was a Cave-Man, and had traced strange shapes of creatures, curiously colored, upon the wall of the world; but the pictures that he made had come to life. A mass of legend and literature, which increases and will never end, has repeated and rung the changes on that single paradox: that the hands that had made the sun and stars were too small to reach the huge heads of cattle. Upon this paradox, we might say upon this jest, all the literature of our faith is founded[1]

---

1   G. K. Chesterton, *The Everlasting Man* (London: Hodder & Stoughton Limited, 1925), 195-6.

Right in the middle of all these things stands up an enormous exception. It is quite unlike anything else.... It is nothing less than the loud assertion that this mysterious maker of the world has visited his world in person ... about whom the thinkers make theories and the mythologists hand down myths; the Man Who Made the World ... It is the one great startling statement man has made since he spoke his first articulate word, instead of barking like a dog. Its unique character can be used as an argument against it as well as for it. It would be easy to concentrate one it as a case of isolated insanity; but it makes nothing but dust of comparative religion.... But what gods are supposed to be, what the priests are commissioned to say, is not a sensational secret like what those running messengers of the Gospel had to say. Nobody except those messengers has any Gospel; nobody else has any good news; for the simple reason that nobody else has any news.... We might sometimes fancy that the Church grows younger as the world grows old. For it was the soul of Christendom that came forth from the incredible Christ; and the soul of it was common sense. Though we dared not look on His face we could look on His fruits; and by His fruits we should know Him. The fruits are solid and the fruitfulness is much more than a metaphor; and nowhere in this sad world are boys happier in appletrees, or men more equal chorus singing as they tread the vine, than under the fixed flash of this instant and intolerant enlightenment; the lightning made eternal as the light.[2]

Christ and the true religious cult or rejection of Christ, false cults, more darkness, more death, more meaningless. Not without reason did St. John say, "And this is the judgment: because the light is come into the world, and men loved darkness rather than the light: for their works were evil." Despite the full revelation of what Christ had come to reveal, and had revealed, people still preferred their fake cults, this monk explained. None so much, and least so it seemed, as the Gnosticism inherent if not essential to most false, bad, evil cults. Christ came and preached openly so

---

2 Chesterton, *The Everlasting Man*, 311–315.

both the most intelligent and the most challenged might hear and understand and repent and be saved. These gnostic guys, all of them, from the Manicheans to the Masons to the Illuminati, they're all the same in that they reject the open air for secret codes and secret meanings and hidden knowledge. It's always the opposite of Catholicism, Catholicism the saving truth opened wide open with invitations for all, reduced, into closed, closeted invitations for the select few. And if not Gnosticism, then the other dominant way fake cults present is in open, anti-Christ-like aping of the singular Truth. "Watch out that no one deceives you. For many will come in my name, claiming, 'I am the Christ,' and will deceive many."

With that the monk ended the chapter, explaining that the next one was going to focus on quote "in depth detail" of modern cults. And that while he could have chosen so many—and why not Jim Jones, he asked, why not David Koresh?—he was going to dedicate it exclusively to two, both examples of the "height of culthood" at the apex of "American decadent decline."

This next chapter,

1. Do and Ti and NXIVM

was 11,226 pages long. While Alabama Pie read every word of it he decided to make an abridged version of his findings for public consumption.

Sometime in the 1970s a man and woman who went by Do and Ti, not their actual names, started posting flyers that read "UFO's in the area. Why they are here. Who they have come for. When they will land." Early followers of the cult recalled being mesmerized by the chemistry between Do and Ti and their combined effect on those gathered. Many of these first followers soon became permanent members, tracing around the American West with little money and hardly a discernable purpose outside of waiting for the extraterrestrial rapture.

And, funny though that might sound, that was the promise. Do and Ti were both aliens and the self-proclaimed two witnesses of St. John's Apocalypse. "I will commission my two witnesses," Revelation 11:3 reads, "to prophecy for those twelve hundred and sixty days . . . [continuing further in the chapter that] anyone wanting to harm them is sure to be slain. They have the power to close up the sky so that no rain can fall during the time of their prophesying. They also have the power to turn water into blood and to afflict the earth with any plague as often as they wish." The monk noted that one scholar of American religion said the "theology" of this group "was primarily rooted in Evangelicalism, but with New Age elements, and a hermeneutic interpretation of the Bible read through the lens of extraterrestrial contact."

Think back to what I wrote earlier, the monk noted. People know that Christianity is true and so false cults still try to associate themselves with the Truth, to God, to the only real, holy cult. Do and Ti could not simply claim to be aliens, rather, to achieve any legitimacy, they had to be aliens who were also end times, Church sanctioned prophets. Things did not end well for Heaven's Gate, as this cult soon became known. Progressing from lesser, just weird quirks, like followers taking on a new name that ended in -ody (there's the Baptism or Confirmation aping parody for you); Alan became Alody, Bill, Billody, Carmen, Carmody . . . well, you get it: the group moved to the outright, and very old school, dualistic heretical in denying the dignity of the body claiming their true alien selves were "higher level" spirits trapped inside profitless "vehicles." This is really as old as it gets regarding Christian heresies, right back to the early centuries when all sorts of heretics used the denial of matter and rejection of the body to reject and deny the Incarnation, the Resurrection, and the Real Presence of the Eucharist.

When you deny matter, asserting that your body is little more than a useless vehicle to be discarded on the scrap heap, it takes little leap of the imagination to include castration in your cult practices. And so Heaven's Gate did, many of them rushing to sign up for this sure sign of fidelity to Do and Ti so as to purify themselves for that which the alien-prophets constantly told them to focus on: achieving the next-level. And when the body is bad, when matter is bad, when the spirit needs to be freed from its earthly prison even by all means, suicide, a most un-Christian act in being the ultimate rejection of the matter, of the body, of the flesh that God Himself forever declared good, twice over in both Creation and the Incarnation, suicide begins to seem logical. And that's what Heaven's Gate tragically did. In March of 1997 the group assured they would be teleported into a spaceship trailing the Hale-Bopp comet and dressed in quintessentially cult-like matching outfits, black shirts and pants paired with matching black and white sneakers and armbands reading "Heaven's Gate Away Team," killed themselves in a rented mansion they referred to as "The Monastery." All 39 of the deceased were found with five dollars and seventy-five cents on their persons for, as Mark Twain had apparently once quipped, "that was the price to ride a comet."

The monk explained that the fake understanding of the human body and sexuality as expressed in the castrating cult above in one extreme was matched, in error, on the other end by another cult of basically the same time and place. NXIVM was an externally presenting wholly secular self-help organization that tried, covertly perhaps, to become a counterfeit Catholic church universal in its ceremony, its structure, and, especially, its obedience. Keith Raniere, a businessman who's debatably pyramid-scheme *Consumers Buyline* collapsed into ruin in the 1990s, found his Ti to play partner to him, the Do figure here, a woman named Nancy Salzmann, a neuro-linguistic programmer who practiced hypnotism after an initial career as a nurse. On a side note, Bonnie Nettles, the real name of Heaven's Gate's Ti, was also a nurse by profession. Is there any connection between nursing and founding and then leading a cult? I don't know.

Raniere, known as "Vanguard," and Salzmann, known as "Prefect," would say that NXIVM was a next level marketing company. Come to these weekend seminars and learn to excel at business. Please do ignore the names and titles, that people are awarded beyond-cringe sashes to wear as they make progress, and that Raniere's stature is so high that a whole week of butt-kissing activities was arranged yearly in his honor; "Vanguard-week," V-week. All that mattered were the networking connections and the effect these sessions had on people who, just like in Heaven's Gate, found first impressions grow into heartfelt assurances that they had found "it," the "way" to live.

NXIVM wasn't into aliens, which is certainly a positive. Or maybe it's a negative. Yes, my apologies, it's a negative. The point is that creating a fake papacy around Raniere, minus Christ's promises that the gates of Hell would not prevail, meant they would and that they did. In October of 2020 Raniere was sentenced to 120 years in prison for a wide swath of various sexual offenses. They're too long to detail here, for the sake of time, but it basically came down to this. NXIVM's marketing maybe did help people get better in business but it was above all a gateway drug into the inner sanctums of NXIVM's secret society full blown cult interior where a most horrifying group existed known as DOS—*Dominus Obsequious Sororium*, Latin for, in essence, "Lord/Master of the Obedient Female Companions."

Under the tutelage, if you can call it that, of Alison Mack, an actress famous for her role as Chloe Sullivan in the TV series *Smallville,* scores of women known as "slaves" had to do whatever their "masters" told them; without question, having provided damaging collateral and taking a vow as a condition of entering the group. Mack was the master of the female slaves and her requests ranged from imposed calorie restricted diets to forcing women to brand her and Raniere's initials on their bodies. The ultimate result of DOS, the ultimate command, was, and you probably know where this is going, sexual slavery to Raniere. And so you understand, I presume, why Raniere got 120 years in prison and, just as clearly, why obedience without God, why a fake papacy without the true religion, the true cult, one that demands total obedience but to lies, is always, always, without fail, a bad idea, and bound to fail.

At that Alabama Pie closed the book. That it was getting cold was not an excuse on two fronts: he had that condition and this hot tub, well, whoever designed it designed it well, for the water was as warm as when he had first entered 22 hours ago. What made him close the book was a sight like he had never before seen in his life. A woman, riding a polar bear, carrying a large jug of something in her hand. She rode up to the very edge of the hot tub, dismounted, and petted the beast on its head. It licked her hand, winked, winked at her!, and then bounded away. The woman introduced herself, told Alabama Pie that she had come "across the fjords" to marry this unfrozen prince, and was planning to drink this jug of "penguin beer'" with him as a token of their soon to be forever love as he "read aloud to me that last section of that book in your hand: 'Ecumenical Fallacies,' that's my favorite part. My father would read it to me and my sisters as a bedtime story while we fell asleep on the ice shelves beneath the stars years ago. Now, you read it to me, my love."

She explained that the author of the book, the monk, was her uncle and that she had read it at least four times. It was her favorite book and this last part, this last section of the book's last chapter was dedicated to the most interesting cult of all—Protestantism. And that the monk had so artistically explained all the issues between Catholicism and Protestantism and atheism, and had done so via an imaginary dialogue between three characters named Jason, Paul, and Bill was very cool. Alabama Pie had hardly heard a word. He couldn't stop staring at her and everyone knows you can't stare and pay attention at the same time. Mesmerized by her beauty he offered no resistance. Yes, I'll read this to you. Yes, we will be married. Yes, I will drink as much penguin beer as you want me to.

The penguin beer was disgusting. It was the worst thing he had ever tasted. And he kept doing his utmost best to gulp down sip after sip of what tasted to him like warm sewage because, well, she was smiling at him so sincerely, and he wanted to make her happy. That's what mattered. And so faced with the prospect of more penguin beer, or simply starting to read like she had asked him to, he set down the brew and picked up the book once more.

2. Ecumenical Fallacies

Just be Catholic.

"Just be Catholic," that's all it says, he asked?
"Yes."
"Really?"
"Yes."
"Really?"
"Yes."
"Ok."
He took another swig of the penguin beer. Now, now it tasted good. He was soon asleep.

The Necessity of Failure

FAILURE IS A NECESSARY STEP ON THE path to success. Begin at the apex of human experience and work downwards. *Dying you destroyed our death, rising, you restored our life.* The Death and Resurrection of Our Lord, Jesus Christ, on Easter Sunday, is without question, alongside the Incarnation, Christmastime, the most important moment in human history. The most important anything anywhere since a man and a woman who were created in original justice destined to live forever without malady or misery chose the false freedom of their own will, for, indeed, as the serpent who tempted them promised, doing so would ensure they themselves would become "like gods, knowing good and evil."

"Oh happy fault, o *necessary* sin of Adam, which gained for us so great a Redeemer" we hear, twice, during the Easter Vigil. And Easter is happy, it's rapturously joyous, it's elation, ecstasy. But there is no Easter Sunday without Good Friday, without the apparent, when seen through human eyes, "failure" of Good Friday. When a Protestant friend of yours asks you why Catholic Churches are adorned with Crucifixes whereas his or her church has the plain cross—"because He is Risen, the plain cross shows we have our eyes focused on the Risen Jesus," they might say—you don't have to go with the simplest response. "Look, just be quiet. You guys are wrong about most everything. Got sit in the corner as punishment. But, before you do, can you make me a cup of coffee? A latte. Yeah, whole milk is fine. But can you steam and whip the milk for me and then heat it before you pour in the coffee? Thank you."

Instead of the above, you can explain that nothing proclaims the Risen Jesus more forcefully than the Crucifix, for while many poor and nameless men throughout history had been nailed to a cross previously and post-expiration plain, seeing the suffering God-man on the cross is a singular experience. Like the famous Catholic preacher Father John Corapi has said, 'No cross, no Crown.' No Good Friday, no Easter Sunday. We, rightly, thanks to the grace sustained eyes of faith, see all this, the Passion narrative unto the Resurrection, and through the rose-colored glasses of knowing how the story ends. As Father Corapi's super Italian grandmother used to remind him whenever he would waver in his faith, she holding aloft the Bible, "we know how the story ends."

I want you to consider the quality of the Italian food this grandmother must have made. If you've ever felt you were born at the wrong time, this might put you over the edge. Being a part of this neighborhood, playing stickball in the streets of mid-century Hudson, New York until the twilight turned the dial from orange to purple to black, being called to the table by this grandmother, maybe by way of a ringing bell, and then the first bite, the second, soon asking for a second plate, a third. It's sublime. I promise to give you more of Father Corapi's story later on in this talk, but, for now, just focus on us knowing how the story ends, we have that, but those around our Lord did not. For them, Good Friday was nothing but failure and the most abject kind.

"God forbid, Lord! No such thing shall ever happen to you," St. Peter tells Jesus after Christ had told them he must go to Jerusalem and suffer greatly from the elders, the chief priests, and the scribes, and be killed and on the third day be raised. You see Peter, in his understandable distress, doesn't even hear the Good News last part. And so Christ rebukes him, "Get behind me, Satan! You are an obstacle to me. You are thinking not as God does but as human beings do."[1] The Cross here, the Passion, the necessary "failure" of Good Friday is intolerable for the apostles. Peter cuts a guy's ear off so as to try to prevent all this from happening.[2] Judas hangs himself out of despair for his failure and the failure he has led another into. Chanting for Barabbas to be released instead of God is failure. Asking *what is truth* when The Way, the Truth, and the Life stands before you is failure. Denying Christ, three times, is failure. The Chief Priests' tearing their garments

---

1   Mt 16:21–23.
2   Mt 26:51–52.

in rage because God admitted He is God and then accusing God of blasphemy against God is failure.

In short, none of these people and groups of people, and how so often none of us, understand that it is precisely because of, not in spite of, failure that the singular Easter Sunday, and the countless small easters of triumph out of tribulation, can only be had because of the failure first rejected, bitterly, then embraced, then died to with, then, finally, risen into something greater than could have ever been imagined before. No Cross, No Crown. No Good Friday and the Passion, there would be no "do not be amazed! You seek Jesus of Nazareth, the crucified. He has been raised; he is not here . . ."; there would be no "Were not our hearts burning [within us] while he spoke to us on the way and opened the scriptures to us? So they set out at once and returned to Jerusalem where they found gathered together the eleven and those with them who were saying, "The Lord has been raised and has appeared to Simon!"; there would be no and "Afterwards Jesus himself, through them, sent forth from east to west the sacred and imperishable proclamation of eternal salvation."[3]

God works via failure, for, as Saint Paul reminds us, "where sin abounded, grace did more abound. That as sin hath reigned to death; so also grace might reign by justice unto life everlasting, through Jesus Christ our Lord." Out of failure God brings good, an even better good than would have originally arrived for that is God's nature, to endlessly multiply one good onto another and especially in response to injustice and evil. Hence the true meaning of "O happy fall." Hence the famous story of Joseph, thrown into a cistern by his brothers and left to die in the desert, only to because of this, not in spite of it, make his way to Egypt and ascend to the post of Chief of the Egyptian granary. When his brothers came to him begging for bread in a time of famine, Joseph penned a great definition of the *necessity of failure.* "Fear not: can we resist the will of God? You thought evil against me: but God turned it into good, that he might exalt me, as at present you see, and might save many people."[4]

---

3   Luke 24:32–34; Mark 16:20.
4   Romans 5:20–21; Genesis 37, 50:19–20.

And, so, hopefully having convinced you, even in the slightest, and with the smallest amount of evidence owing to our short time, of the necessity of failure—defined as in order for something great or greater to come we must first pass through suffering, trail, testing. We must be willing to, and in fact end up, falling flat on our face, only rising and resuming our work will lead to triumph and appreciation of its value—I aim to continue this topic along two tracks onto a final terminus, that being surrender. The two tracks are the aforementioned story of Father John Corapi, the second smaller, very brief as in brief-mentioned examples of everyday things and experiences in this paradigmical reality. But first I present to you a list, certainly not exhaustive, definitely not scientific, but probably accurate and true, of things that are, by definition, failure. I don't know if they are necessary or not. I do know each gets assigned the grade F, written in bolded, red ink.

- Marriage advice given by Catholics 25 years old or younger; **F.**
- Marriage advice given by Catholics 30 years old or younger; **F.**
- Marriage advice given by anyone under 40 or who hasn't been married for 20 years; **F.**
- Volunteering, unprompted, to give relationship advice, one on one or in groups; **F.**
- Thinking more ecumenism and more dialogue will eventually solve all the ills; **F.**
- Making up nicknames for yourself; **F.**
- 66 book Bibles; **F.**
- Dating advice given by some 23 year old Catholic podcaster about questions like "what are women looking for" and "are there any good Catholic guys out there" but she is unmarried, currently single, and especially, 23; **F.**
- Singing Aladdin to a young woman on a first date in response to 3 Mississippi, 4 Mississippi seconds of silence you feared would soon turn awkward so you burst into *I can show you the world . . .* ; **F.**
- Not understanding the appeal of monarchy would be stability and the surpassing of partisan politics and that things might actually get accomplished; **F.**
- Calling anyone on the right a "fascist"; **F.**

• Calling anyone who points out that Catholic economics does not = pure capitalism a "socialist" or "communist"; **F.**

• Not trying to understand what's actually been going on these past decades, in the Church, in society, all these problems, these problems our problems, but relying on easy answers not because they're easy but because we're scared of the potential of the search; **F.**

• Thinking *Mere Christianity* is a deep theological work; **F.**

• 99% of "Catholic Twitter"; **F.**

• Using the following pick-up line: "So, I'm working my way through the Bible, currently in the Old Testament, Book of Numbers, and I just realized I don't have yours"; **F.**

• Not understanding that all the STEM courses and focus on careers and long term earnings potential won't matter when we can no longer read, or critically think, or do things like give and hear speeches and so we're basically begging for a true demagogue to come around and tell us what to do and what to believe and then one day you wake up and, poof, it's all over, your freedoms, everything, bye bye; **F.**

• Calling yourself a "thought leader"; **F.**

• Calling yourself a "wordsmith"; **F.**

Not failure, but always a win, and necessary because this is a talk about necessary things, necessary see: needed as a break from all the above points on failure, winning, triumph, triumphs, plural, triumphant, the emotion and the reality, always on point and ever welcome, no less than that second cup of homemade hot chocolate next to the fire as the feet come un-asleep pins and needles see yourself out post ski boots removal after a long day on the hills; Mike Leach quotes.

For anyone who needs an introduction, Mike Leach, currently the head football coach at Mississippi State University, was head coach of the WSU Cougs for seven years ending in 2019. His presence on the Palouse is both noted and missed. He has appeared in previous *Hippo Lectures* and most likely will continue to do so in future ones. I once smoked cigars and drank beer in a hot tub with Mike Leach while we discussed the meaning of life. I, in vain, tried to convince him to do nothing but onside kicks in the upcoming game. That's not true, none of that, but I wish it was.

#lifegoals.
#squadgoals.

Mike Leach, who once taught a college course at WSU entitled "Insurgent Warfare and Football Strategies," holder of a Juris Doctor law degree from Pepperdine, who, despite being a highly paid college football coach did not himself play football in college. He played rugby.

The very antidote to, and opposite of, failure, Mike Leach quotes.

"I mean, I completely hate Candy Corn."

"How can it be that we laugh about England's obsession with the royal family? At least the royal family has college degrees and military service."

"You know, buffalo are significantly bigger than elk. I grew up near Yellowstone so I've been near buffalo. Buffalo are huge."

"I'm proud to say I had a bet with a guy from Chicago who said Chicago is windier and colder than Wyoming. Wyoming dominated them."

In a post-game interview with an ESPN sports reporter, in response to her inquiry concerning marriage advice, for she is currently engaged and in the process of planning the wedding, Leach said the following:

As soon as the season is over or even an off week, go elope. Trust me on that, go elope. 'Cause basically every female in the family is going to terrorize you guys until it's over. Once it's over, I mean, they'll be upset for a few days, but it'll be over and then you'll cruise along and have a happy marriage, have a happy life.

His dating advice—directed at young men—comes in four parts

1. Go to a place where she cannot order a salad but must eat real food.[5]
2. Use a coupon to see how she reacts.

---

5 "Try to have somewhere where there's not salad, because girls will try to show off and act like all they eat is salad, so try to put them somewhere where they're in a position where they have to put real food in their mouth."

3. Stop using technology, it will end the human species.
4. Actually have a conversation.[6]

Most profoundly of all, Leach reached deep into the philosophical bag echoing both G. K. Chesterton, who claimed that the only two acceptable reasonable positions are Catholicism or atheism, either accepting it all or rejecting it all, and Robert Cardinal Sarah, he of the book *God or Nothing,* when stating, Leach, that

> [I don't get] atheists that want to believe in ghosts. Wait,
> wait, wait. You can't have a two-way go on that. You want
> to be agnostic, be an atheist, fine. But you don't bring
> ghosts along with you.

Speaking of eternal realities summed up in pithy quotes, a rector of a seminary, this priest originally from the South—this story told to me by the recently retreat present priest Father Chase Hilgenbrinck, this Father Chase an absolute and total legend every bit the legend as our own legend himself pastor Father Chase Hasenoerhl, the two of them, these two Father Chase's, let me state for the record, legends—this Southern priest once opined this in response to Bible Belt Protestants who do not want to convert now to the fullness of Christianity. "Well, they-a, they gon be Catholic in Heaven." He also apparently once said, on the eve of a hunting trip or lesser sojourn to the range seeking clay pigeons, and it's just so perfectly Southern, he said, "Boys. We gon shoot some guns, ain't we."

Okay. So having traced a sketch of the component parts of failure, not failure, and begun the path of asking if and why failure might be necessary, and certainly I am affirming that it is, I present to you the case of track one, example one, Father John Corapi.

Father John Corapi is one of the greatest preachers, homilists, in recent Church history. You can see for yourself by simply entering his name into a Google or YouTube search engine box and clicking from the many selections that pop up. I suggest starting with "Humility: Spiritual Nuclear Weapon." Corapi's life is a testament to the necessity of failure. His preaching is powerful because he's

---

6 "I would go enjoy the incredible college life on College Hill at WSU but make sure you have the opportunity to talk to her a lot."

a gifted orator, having almost actor like command of the tempo of his speech and a knack for both under and overstated delivery, and that's awesome, that does make for good preaching. But he's especially a must hear priest because of the colorful nature of his life, pre-ordination, a life of abject, and often times scandalous, epic, failure.

Corapi made a lot of money in his early years. You cannot worship God and mammon, Our Lord says, and, early on, Corapi committed to the latter. He did lots of drugs. Was present for drug deals themselves, in dark alleys, on dark docks, tooling about forsaken nooks and crannies in many a big city's seedy underbelly. He did drugs, got plastered, got filthy rich, duck taping money to people's bodies at penthouse party's Wolf of Wall Street style rich, caroused with many a woman of ill repute, he more ill repute than maybe all of them combined, and did Fast and Furious impressions driving fancy cars at many digits over one hundred miles an hour on the desert highway connecting Las Vegas to Los Angeles. The place, as he once said in a talk, where, quote, "you can go real fast if you're real stupid."

He repented, praise God, came back to the faith, praise God, and became a priest, praise God. And that God might be praised all the more, and forever more, finally started using the talents the Good Lord had given him for good, his preaching—and those of you that have heard him know what I mean—helping literally millions, millions of Catholics in America, and not a few beyond our borders, grow in their faith. And the crucial thing is this: and I call it the Las Vegas Catholic Church orthodoxy paradigm. Why do you find, in places like Las Vegas, the self-proclaimed "City of Sin," some of the most orthodox and reverent and beautiful Masses? It's the necessity of failure. These people are surrounded by, submerged in sin, submerged in failure, and so look to the Mass as we should, as a refuge from the fallen world, a slice of Heaven and it's *because* not *in spite of* the sin around them that they then take extra care to give Our Lord his devotional due in the way they celebrate Mass. The Las Vegas Catholic Church orthodoxy paradigm; the necessity of failure.

Or, as St Paul put it: where sin abounds, grace all the more.

Precisely because Corapi had lived a bad life of the worst failures he had no tolerance for anything but the unvarnished, non-watered down, dark chocolate 95% straight black coffee Catholic faith. Corapi would often say, "here's an in your face statement," and then proceed to beautifully and powerfully defend a Catholic dogma sure to make any quote "liberal Catholics" in the surrounding area big mad and mad triggered. Catholic parishes in the middle of nowhere Vermont or Indiana often suffer from liturgical abuse. They perhaps haven't plumbed the rancid depths of failure and so want to "live dangerously" which often means act lukewarm and watered down and be freefloat cringe in the most non-attractive way possible. But like so many of these churches in necessity of failure Las Vegas, and San Francisco, and Oakland and Miami, where sin is palpable, in your face, and not hard sought after, have some of the most beautiful Masses, so too do necessity of failure priests, like Father Corapi, feel free to go 100% Catholicism no artificial flavors no added sugars because they know, from experience, that the wages of sin is death.

Necessity of failure Corapi also, and of course, had a lot of credibility with sinners, both soft and of the most hardened variety, when trying to convert them to the one True Faith. When he told stories from his past life it was powerful because it was real, because he has lived it. Stories like this, drawn from Father Corapi's talk entitled "God's Name is Mercy." It's a long talk, over one hour, and you can watch it all on YouTube and I think you should and I hope you do.

Corapi begins by explaining having to go to a bad part of town in some big city and how—necessity of failure—it was his former life that had perfectly equipped him for this mission. The mission was to retrieve a priest who had fallen into a few sins in a whorehouse slash drug den and so Corapi goes there and just walks in and finds the priest and puts him over his shoulder and readies to leave. Soon he's staring at a gun, pointed directly at him. Corapi—necessity of failure, former life, you get it by now—is unfazed. He recounts that, quote, "when I was a younger man, I might have done one thing, but now, being older and hopefully more wise, I did precisely the same thing. I told him what I would do with the gun, down to the exact details, down to where I would stick it into his body, if he didn't get it out of my face immediately." Corapi reported being able to leave without further problems.

Father Corapi had a lot of failure before his priesthood and he's had some recently too. He mentioned this, to his credit, that he might fall back, in some form or another, into his old life, his old ways, and so we should be vigilant in praying for him, in praying for all priests. And he did. Some kind of scandal; women, drugs, maybe, I don't know. The details really are hazy. For a while it seemed like he might even leave the priesthood. Recently, praise God once again, it has been officially stated that he was back with his order, fully reconciled, and committed to living a quiet life of prayer and penance for the remainder of his days. He will never speak publicly again. This last fact a cause for great joy for Corapi, while he was at his best was the best, was, by the grace of God doing the Matthew 5:48 be perfect as your Heavenly Father is perfect in preaching to the maximum. For him to preach now might taint something, the bad sequel to that great film that should have been left alone.

And so we too will now leave Father Corapi alone.

The necessity of failure is necessary in all pursuits because of the fruit it bears and that is the great Catholic virtue of perseverance. Perseverance: fruit of the final mystery of the twenty decade run, The Coronation of Our Lady as Queen of Heaven and Earth, the grace of perseverance and trust in Our Lady's intercession. Perseverance: not quitting, not giving up. That's ultimately why failure is necessary. It breeds humility and a certain hunger, a true desire for greatness. For we have something in mind and then we start out. We fail, fail, and fail some more. Once we've failed enough we try again and probably fail scores times more. But only by going through a necessary period of failure, of failures, do we, via perseverance, finally, and truly then only by God's grace, achieve our goal. No cross, no crown.

Anyone who has learned a language, seen a diet through to completion, earned a medical degree, played a collegiate sport, opened a business, learned how to cook, overcome some type of social anxiety, learned to control their anger, their lust, the lack of charity, their passions in sum, read the Bible cover to cover, kept on loving family members who don't love them, kept praying for people who do not pray for them maybe even hate them, knows about the necessity of failure, knows about the perseverance that's therein born and about the sweet victory found a long ways down a rocky road strewn with setbacks but one which he or she did not stop walking.

And that—not quitting when having failed countless times—makes all the difference. For while preserving in the face of the necessary failure that is natural to our post-Eden fallen nature helps in small things like languages, sports, baking, and business, it really is, as all things are, about Christ, about turning to him and saving our souls. Father Corapi liked to open his talks with "In the end, you and I will be in Heaven or Hell, winners or losers for all eternity. Period." Yes, he's right. So when you fail, and you will fail, don't fret but understand how necessary that and these, all these, failures are and will be. Failure is necessary. Without the apparent failure of Good Friday there is no empty tomb on Easter Sunday. So too in our lives. When you fail, offer it up to God, surrender fully to God, and as the Divine Mercy Chaplet encourages us to say: Jesus, I trust in You. Despite my failures, despite the necessary and inevitability of my failures, I offer and surrender them, I offer myself, I abandon them and me and everything to you, Jesus. Jesus, I trust in you. And then: keep going. Then: persevere. And then, finally, take heart and sublime confidence in the sacred words of Scripture which tell us, all of us failed people saddled with all our countless flaws and failures, "But the one who preservers to the end, will be saved."

On Scholasticism and Saint Thomas

SCHOLASTICISM IS A PHILOSOPHICAL school emphasizing the use of reason and logic, especially in common sense deductions replete with postulations, objections, and responses aimed at a singular and simple but most noble goal: the Truth. Not *a* or *one* or *your* or *mine,* simply *the,* the Truth, the truth of all things. And all things indeed, for from the most abstract speculations—the famous quip inquiring as to how many angels can dance on the head of a pin—to the most lowly objects such as dirt, bugs, algae on a pond, the shape and size of rocks, rocky cliffs suffering erosion from the constant battering of ocean waves, the Scholastics were convinced, St. Thomas Aquinas chief among them, that studying then finding the truth of all things points to the singular Truth about God, God Incarnate, He who is Himself the Way, the Truth, the Life. In other words, the Scholastics saw no conflict whatsoever between faith and science, between faith and reason, between the secular and sacred spheres for God is the unique author and authority everywhere. John Paul II spoke of this in his 1998 encyclical *Fides et Ratio* saying faith and reason are "two wings on which one rises to the contemplation of truth." One is well served to fly with two wings, to fly with faith and reason, certainly the balance is better this way, the intellectual flight and later landing smoother. On a side-note I have no idea, not for the life of me, can't make heads or tails of the consternation, why people claim the supposed puzzle about angels and pinheads is some kind of inscrutable, uncrackable conundrum. How many angels can dance on the head of a pin? I assume you'll ask next, what is 2+2, or how do you spell Idaho. The obvious answer is an infinite amount. Angels are disembodied spiritual creatures that therefore take up no physical space. The head of a pin, no matter how small it is, is a physical space which loses no room no matter how many angels take up residence upon it. There you go, problem solved, as many angels as you want. See how fun Scholasticism is?

Scholastics argue truth is true wherever it is found, hence St. Thomas' deep love, and reliance, upon the philosopher Aristotle, hence his eagerness to read Jewish, Muslim, and pagan authors for he was confident, and please do remember this, that the truth is always the truth and is always converging, always meeting up as if spilling into a river delta upon the source and truest true thing in existence: God. And so, the Scholastics believed, since God is the Truth behind all things, all things are themselves intelligible and engineered, by God, to a specific purpose. In a post-modern world of so much chaos and confusion the Scholastics today sound like radicals in declaring that eggs are eggs, grass is green in reality not by way of an illusion, water is wet, fire is hot and so touching it will burn you, a dog is a dog but not a cat a cow or a horse. And so you see, we can therefore close our initial introductory remarks by summing up Scholastic philosophy as taking God given reality as a starting point and, knowing all truth converges on the singular truth of God and his divinely fashioned order, use logic and reason and the very science this school gave birth to to learn more about the wonderful world around us. And I'm going to close this talk by talking about how St. Thomas Aquinas is the beau ideal star of this school and that while he certainly touched the most cloud rimmed heights of heavenly speculation he is, ultimately, a patron saint of the commonest common sense, of the most logical, rational, obvious points that when we point them out gain so much profundity and clarity for perhaps we had overlooked them before.

But, before I do that, before I focus on St. Thomas, I need to comment upon the historical rooting of this, the Scholastic period. Last month we covered the Patristic Fathers from the time of Christ up past St. Boniface to Charlamagne's crowning as Holy Roman Emperor in 800 AD. So that is not the scholastic period: 0 to 800 AD. And post 1517 AD is not the Scholastic period either. Martin Luther's 95 theses usher in, very much, the modernity that would later give birth to our post-modernity. For from Luther's challenge to whole-Christendom Catholic unity you soon see Henry VII and Calvin follow; then many religious wars; soon atheist usurpation altogether in the tragic and often blasphemous French Revolution of the late 18th century unto more nonsense in the form or nationalism as religion, communism as utopian pseudo-salvation, and Freudian confession aping psychoanalytics to round out the 19th century. As for the 20th century onwards, let's save that for another time. Suffice to say, just as 0–800 AD is not the Scholastic period neither is 1517 onward.

Left with, by simple deductive logic, the approximate period between 800 and 1517, or if you like centuries more, the 9th to the 16th century, let's talk about some points of interest here for the purpose of thoroughness and framing and then return to the 13th century man born in the smack dab middle of this time, St. Thomas.

The Scholastic period is about God as the source of Truth, one Truth, and logic and reason and science, ultimately even common sense, helping us see and live the truth. This time period has a lot of good things like this, things that fit the proverbial bill. Great thinkers besides Thomas like Albert the Great, St. Bonaventure and the, to purposely use an anachronistic term, "Christian feminist" figure Hildegard of Bingen who proved via her polymathematical genius in philosophy, theology, herbal medicine, and maybe most of all sacred music that women, from time immemorial, are every bit as capable as men for both men and women are equally made in God's image and likeness. Postmodernity tells us how enslaved and disrespected and on the periphery of power and influence women have been until the 1960s showed up and made things right. 12th century, Scholastic era Hildegard would like you to hold her beer. And I mean this literally, as a good German woman she probably loved beer, so another feather in her cap that.

Good things like the birth of modern science—once more a shout out to Albert Magnus, tutor and nickname giver of St. Thomas—by way of the birth of the university system. Some of the still-greatest universities in the world today were founded during the Scholastic period: Bologna in 1088, Oxford in 1117, Cambridge in 1209 and the University of Paris in the year 1200.

Good, no, great Catholic artists like Dante whose *Divine Comedy* explains to us that God, God's love, divine charity, is the glue and motive power binding the world together as it makes it go round. Great saints in the very imitation of Christ, St. Francis of Assisi the most famous and striking example. And good leaders like the Saint King and Crusader Louis IX of France. Louis liked to fight, I mean he was good at fighting, he was great with a sword, led men on campaign, liked to brawl, was super hyper-masculine in the classic way of he likes to fight, he's a fighter, don't mess with him, you'll regret it, mark my words you will. Okay. Fine. But Louis' court was frequently upset with him because they viewed him as more of a monk than a monarch. He was often to be found at Mass, in front of the Blessed Sacrament, praying, praying, praying.

Would that we had this Scholastic reality in our leaders today. "Sir, where is the president? Where is Biden?" "Well, we've been trying to fetch him but he's currently occupied. He's been doing Eucharistic Adoration the past two hours and said it will be a little while longer, my apologies." Yes, would that we had Louis IX type leaders today. Maybe America would be a better place, I don't know.

But for all the good of the Scholastic period there was quite enough bad to go around as well. Please let us not frame our Catholic collective memory in rose-colored glasses. The Scholastic period was not Eden. Eden was Eden and then Adam and Eve did their thing and since then here we are, here we've been, woe is us, fallen humanity. So, the Scholastic period was in no way some perfect utopia; see: the 1054 East-West Schism, see: the fourth Crusade of 1202–1204 when Christians were killing Christians in Constantinople until blood was up to past the ankles flowing freely in the streets. One might imagine them stopping to catch their breath only to ask each other: "Hey, aren't we supposed to be on the same team?" See: perhaps worst of all, the 10th century *Saeculum Obscurum* more commonly known as the "pornocracy." Maybe that says it all. At the so-called Cadaver Synod of 897 Pope Stephen VII had the late Pope Formosus' body exhumed, dressed in papal garb, and placed on a throne to face charges of having been pope unworthily. Found guilty, garments and digits—three fingers—were ripped from his body before he was dumped into the Tiber River. The infamous Marozia, mistress of Pope Sergius III, would not be outdone by her lover who, purportedly, ordered the murder of his two immediate predecessors and fathered an illegitimate son who later on became pope himself. That Sergius III's pontificate has been described as "dismal and disgraceful" is a gross understatement. Sort of like saying mass murdering rampager Genghis Khan "wasn't exactly a nice guy," or describing Joseph Stalin as a "problematic historical figure."

The Scholastic period is about God as the source of Truth, one Truth, and logic and reason and science, ultimately even common sense, helping us see and live the truth. And no one better embodies this than St. Thomas Aquinas. And before I comment on three ways in which he does, I'll encourage you to fall in love with Aquinas by reading him, yes read his most famous *Summa* for sure, but, and this only a humble suggestion, start with Chesterton's biography, regarded, even by Thomistic specialists like Etienne Gilson and Anton Pegis, as one of the finest works telling his story.

So who was he, Aquinas? He was born in 1225 and died in 1274. Born into a well-off family, more so on the very edge of "purple," his cousin being Holy Roman Emperor, Aquinas' parents wanted him to become abbot of a local Benedictine monastery but he wanted to enter the new, begging and preaching Dominican order. For outrage level here, a modern analogy would be New York high society lawyer wants his son to enter Harvard Law before taking over the family business and the son tells him "I'm going to Hollywood, dad, gonna wait tables then get famous. By the way I'm hitchhiking my way there, Sprinter Van, bunch of people say they're trying to live the deep meaning of Woodstock, good people." Aquinas' brothers locked him in a tower for two years, even tried breaking his call to the Dominicans by way of a prostitute but they, she, all his opponents failed. He arrived at the university of Paris and was immediately branded the class dunce; the big, silent, dumb, probably rocks in his head slow on the uptake moron.

How true Christ's words that we never judge. It takes one to know one and only the genius Albert the Great recognized Aquinas' true talent hidden by modestly answering, when having learned that the class had nicknamed him "the Dumb Ox," "you call him the Dumb Ox. I tell you this ox will one day bellow so loud his bellowing will fill the whole world." And so one day the Dumb Ox had consented to be tutored by a well-meaning peer who thought he was doing Thomas a favor and Thomas listened patiently until the guy made a mistake and Thomas not only corrected him but explained it to such an impressive level the guy fell to his knees and begged, yes *begged,* for Thomas to tutor him henceforth. The secret was out and the rest is history.

The Scholastic period, for a final time, is about God as the source of Truth, one Truth, and logic and reason and science, ultimately even common sense, helping us see and live the truth. Here are the three ways I mentioned before in which Thomas lived, rather teaches us, even today, the Scholastic truths we might properly call timeless.

1. By the foundation and beating heart of his philosophy, a philosophy, simply put of "Being." That God being pure Being—see Exodus 3:14 I am WHO AM; see John 8:58 when Christ says "Before Abraham was I AM"—means everything else is in its proper order, its logical and to be understood by grace-infused rationality common sense. This common sense

2. That common sense is in fact that most noble theology. God being God means all things are ordered by God to be as God wants them to be. And so rather than break our heads pretending eggs are dogs or dogs are grass or grass is the sky we say, as any blue collar worker would readily agree, that eggs are eggs, dogs dogs, grass grass and the sky not just the sky but orange and purple at sunset, and blue on a clear day, and gray when it's cloudy and that, yes, rain comes from clouds. And when you read the most famous part of Thomas' summa, the five proofs for God's existence, you see how rational, how beautiful, how simple and logical and true the real truth can be and is.

3. Finally, equipped with 1. That God is God and His non-contingent Being the source of all contingent being and beings and 2. That logic and common sense are most common in their factual reality, Aquinas was free to look for and find truth wherever it might be found. For he knew, as it would behoove all of us to know, that truth is united, it is one, it converges, ultimately on Christ; for the truth is not some*thing,* it is some*one,* Jesus Christ, our Lord and Savior.

It is therefore quite unsurprising that when at the end of his life Christ appeared to him and told him "You have written well of me, Thomas. What will you have as your reward?"—and talk about an endorsement, that, people brag about this celebrity writing a blurb for their book or being on the *New York Times* bestseller list maybe even being a Nobel Prize Laureate; but, I ask, how about that God Himself, personally, told you "Good job"—quite unsurprising that he responded,

"Nothing but you, Lord."

For it is simultaneously the most common sense logic and the highest theology to know that we cannot desire a higher recompense than God Himself, an eternity beholding the grandeur of God in Heaven enraptured in heavenly bliss. May God grant us the grace to live lives where God might one day tell us, "God job," and when asking what we'd like as a reward we might respond, without hesitation, "Nothing but you, Lord."

A Brief, Biblical Exegesis on Three Principles for Perfection[1]

ANCIENT TRADITION HOLDS THERE ARE two *senses* of Scripture, the literal and the spiritual. Little need to expound much on the former, it's obvious enough. But in the latter there are three sub-categories: the *allegorical*, crossing the Red Sea as a prefiguring of Christian baptism, the *moral*, those things we are to find instructive for our own, personal behavior, "how we should act," and the *anagogical*, being able to see Scriptural entities in light of where they are leading, within the optic of the eternal, the Church on earth being a sign of the heavenly Jerusalem to come, for example.[2]

The two senses of Scripture are therefore in reality four properties perhaps best summed up in the medieval couplet, "The Letter speaks of deeds; Allegory to faith; The moral how to act; Anagogy to our destiny." These four analytical tools, if you will, are helpful in assisting us Catholics today arrive at deeper, better, and more fruitful reflections upon the Word of God. Tonight I'm going to be employing two of these four senses, the literal and the moral, in a brief inspection of a singular passage from the Gospel of St. Matthew.[3]

Now, there is certainly no shortage of passages I could have picked for tonight's talk. The great discourse on the Real Presence of the Eucharist, in the sixth chapter of St. John's Gospel, where we hear that "unless you eat the flesh of the Son of Man and drink

---

1 Lecture presented at the St. Thomas More Catholic Student Center on the campus of Washington State University (Pullman, WA), March 12, 2020.
2 CCC, 115–117.
3 CCC, 118.

his blood, you do not have life within you," but, conversely, Christ's Body, Blood, Soul, and Divinity being "true food" and "true drink [,] Whoever eats my flesh and drinks my blood remains in me and I in him" would be a good choice; so too the biblical foundation of the papal office in Matthew 16 when St. Peter, the first pope, announces "you are the Messiah, the Son of the Living God," to which Jesus replies that Peter is blessed for "flesh and blood has not revealed this to you, but my heavenly Father. And so I say to you, you are Peter, and upon this rock I shall build my church, and the gates of the netherworld shall not prevail against it. I will give you the keys to the kingdom of heaven"; or perhaps something about Our Blessed Mother; the "woman clothed with the sun, with the moon under her feet, and on her head a crown of twelve stars," the warrior-Queen of Heaven and Earth assigned with "striking the head of the serpent" in the fallen world's ongoing strife between the forces of good and evil, the woman who all generations will call blessed, the one for whom "The Mighty One has done great things for…[for] his mercy is from age to age to those who fear him"; or perhaps something about Baptism, that it must be administered to infants[4] for it is the way the guilt of Original Sin is washed away and we become adopted children of God, and the New Covenant entry point just as circumcision was for the Jews, as St. Paul tells us in Colossians 2:11-12. Baptism, which Saint Mark reminds at the close of his gospel is necessary for salvation: "whoever believes *and is baptized* will be saved" are all, each of them, great examples of the genius, surprise, intellectual rigor, and rapturous joy awaiting anyone who, like Saint Augustine might *tolle, lege.*[5]

Nonetheless, I will not be commenting further on any of the above, aforementioned passages. Instead, my exclusive focus will be on Matthew, chapter nineteen, verses sixteen through twenty-one. We will break open this passage part-by-part via the literal and

---

4   On Saint Paul baptizing "the household of Stephanas," see 1 Corinthians 1:16. On Baptism as entrance into the New Covenant as circumcision was into the Old, see Colossians 2:11-12.

5   *The Holy Bible* (New American Bible: For Catholics) published for Catholic Extension by the American Bible Society, New York: 1970/1991. John 6:53-55; Matthew 16:16-19; Revelation 12:1, Genesis 3:15, Luke 1:46-55; Colossians 2:11-12, Mark 16:16.

moral biblical senses considering first what it means and, secondly, how we should act in response. For, as many of you know, this section of Saint Matthew's gospel begins with an all-important inquiry. As if standing in for all of us, a young man asks Jesus, "Teacher, what good must I do to gain eternal life?" Does any more pressing question exist for us poor pilgrims exiled in this vale of tears? Is there anything more important than knowing how to live a good life so as to inherit life eternal? For those not familiar with this passage, and for the purpose of possessing the whole before delving into what I call "three principles for perfection" Christ offers in response, here is the text in full following the young man's question.[6]

> Why do you ask me about the good? There is only One who is good. If you wish to enter into life, keep the commandments. He asked him, Which ones? And Jesus replied, You shall not kill; you shall not commit adultery; you shall not bear false witness; honor your father and mother; and you shall love your neighbor as yourself.
>
> The young man said to him, All of these I have observed. What do I still lack? Jesus said to him, If you wish to be perfect, go, sell what you have and give to the poor, and you will have treasure in heaven. Then come, follow me.[7]

The answer to the young man's question, ultimately our own question, comes in three parts. Christ presents three principles that, if by the grace of God we can follow, ultimately lead to perfection and eternal beatitude. The three principles of perfection are, in order,

1. 1. *Keep the commandments.*
2. 2. *Detachment from material wealth and goods.*
3. 3. *complete commitment to Christ.*

Let's look at these more closely, and how we can implement these lessons into our daily lives.

First, *keep the commandments.* "If you love me, you will keep my commandments," Christ tells us in John 14:15. It is insufficient

---

6   Matthew 19:16.
7   Matthew 19:16–21.

to claim a one-time profession of faith exempts us from anything further, that our salvation is therefore and henceforth assured—Christ's explains near the end of the Sermon on the Mount that "not everyone who says to me 'Lord, Lord' will enter the kingdom of heaven, but only the one who does the will of my Father in heaven"—for what we do, how we respond to God's call, matters. To keep and live the two greatest commandments, in fact, to love God above all and your neighbor as yourself, is the foundation upon which "the whole law and prophets" depend; "worth more than all burnt offerings and sacrifices."[8]

The first principle towards perfection lies in the realm of personal action. What does Christ say constitutes "keeping the commandments"? "You shall not kill; you shall not commit adultery; you shall not bear false witness; honor your father and mother"; and "you shall love your neighbor as yourself." Don't murder, don't participate in abortion or genocides, yes, period and above all with before the period the words bolded, in CAPS, and double-underlined; yes, these, and these like these first and without false equivalencies but, in striving for the perfection Jesus calls us all to too, what about extending that to avoiding trafficking in hatred and hateful comments, to avoiding useless conflicts, to avoiding slowly killing personal relationships and family relations with anything opposed to that great principle from the Beatitudes, *blessed are the peacemakers, for they will be called children of God?*[9]

Don't cheat on your spouse, yes, of first order importance—period and above all with before the period the words bolded, in CAPS—but how can we Catholics also maintain and promote sexual purity in all aspects of our life beyond simply keeping to marital fidelity? To not bear false witness might be one of the most challenging demands, for we're not usually talking about your word being the difference between a condemned man going free or getting the electric chair, so to speak. And to honor your father and mother, that eternal commandment asking us to see our parents in the light of God's lieutenants on earth, also commands us to respect all variants of lawful authority to which we

---

8   John 14:15; Matthew 7:21; Matthew 22:36–40; Mark 12:33.
9   Matthew 5:9.

are subject. It is no easy task in a current culture whose highest virtues seem to be protesting, piling vitriol on, and pushing back against any and all authority that might restrict our imagined unlimited license to self-determination. The first principle to perfection is in the realm of personal behavior, moral choice, and in case we're just too stupid, *that stupid,* to not understand fully, Christ ends this first part with the catch all, all-encompassing requirement to love others as we do ourselves. Do this and you're on the right track.[10]

The second principle, "go, sell what you have and give to the poor" so as to inherit "treasure in heaven" calls for an explicit *detachment from material wealth and goods.* There are some people that argue this only calls for a certain attitude towards money, poverty in spirit and just use of material goods. I agree. I wish the best people in the world were the richest because perhaps they could authentically do good things with their earthly blessings, like some holy medieval monarch emptying the royal purse for the betterment of his or her subjects. And does not the Beatitude in Matthew's gospel say blessed are the poor *in spirit*? See, it is about attitude, not depleted numbers in a bank account.

Well, hold on, attitude, yes, and first and foremost, but that same just quoted beatitude reads as such in Luke's account of the Sermon on the Mount: "Blessed are you who are poor, for the kingdom of God is yours. Blessed are you who are now hungry, for you will be satisfied." No qualifiers, Christ seems to be speaking of bread and butter daily necessities. Just like when he recounts Moses condemning the rich man for not assisting Lazarus with his daily material needs rather abandoning him to the shame of not even being able to eat scraps fit for dogs. Just like when Christ tells us, plainly, "you cannot serve God and mammon." One of the litmus tests of salvation, recounted in Christ's judgment of the nations in Matthew 25, depends upon whether or not we quenched the thirst of the parched, satisfied the hunger of those without a thing to eat, whether or not we clothed and sheltered the naked and forlorn. None of these things are "in spirit" lofty

---

10   Ibid.

and abstract ideals, rather, being concrete, we may, along with Saint James, rightfully ask "if a brother or sister has nothing to wear and has no food for the day, and one of you says to them, 'Go in peace, keep warm, and eat well' but does not give them the necessities of the body, what good is it? So also faith in itself, if it does not have works, is dead." Ask yourselves, am I both poor in spirit and willing to be poorer materially, even a little bit more personally impoverished, so as to help the truly poor among us? What have I been doing during this Lenten season of praying, fasting, and giving alms? And am I doing enough? Perfection and salvation hang in the balance.[11]

Only once we have been keeping the commandments and helping the poor a final question comes into focus. Are we ready for the third, most simple and yet most demanding command, the *complete commitment to Christ* embodied in Jesus' simple request to "come, follow me." The third principle of perfection is true devotion to Jesus, forsaking all and everything for His sake, truly having Him, God, be the epicenter of your life and daily existence, and for as long as you live, it's supposed to never end, this "following," never end unto everlasting life itself in the Kingdom to come. Like the beautiful story of St. Thomas Aquinas before the Cross in prayer and Christ telling him that he had written well of Him and so what would he, Thomas, have as his reward? "Nothing but you, Lord."[12] Are we ready, more so willing because with our own will we will that it and our whole selves be united perfectly with the Divine Will, for anything else, to paraphrase the one and same Dumb Ox, would be like straw? Are we ready to give the same answer, ready for perfection?

Lots of people today want to skip steps one and two and proclaim to anyone who has ears to hear how much they love Jesus, how right they are with Jesus, how Jesus is their friend, their Lord, their Master. If you love him, you'll keep his commandments. And if you really serve him, you'll serve the poor, for in serving the

---

11   Matthew 5:3; Luke 6: 20–21; Luke 16:19–30; Matthew 6:24; Matthew 25:31–46; James 2:15–17
12   "Dio o Niente: parla il cardinale Robert Sarah." Talk posted to YouTube December 17, 2015. https://www.youtube.com/watch?v=0mw2vTUiu1w

poor you really are serving the Master who came to serve, not to be served. "Then the righteous will answer him and say, 'Lord when did we see you hungry and feed you, or thirsty and give you drink? When did we see you a stranger and welcome you, or naked and clothe you? When did we see you ill or in prison and visit you?' And the king will reply, 'Amen I say to you, whatever you did for one of these least brothers of mine, you did for me.'" [13]

---

13 Matthew 25:37–40.

ABOUT THE AUTHOR

Gracjan Kraszewski is the author of three books: the novels *The Holdout* and *Thermonuclear Mirth* and the Civil War history *Catholic Confederates*. He earned his PhD in history from Mississippi State University and taught at the University of Illinois. He is currently Director of Intellectual Formation at the St. Augustine Center in Moscow, Idaho, while also teaching at the University of Idaho and in Washington State University's history department and School of Design + Construction. Played baseball in college, professionally in Europe, and for the Polish National Team. Fluent in English, Polish, and French, he possesses intermediate ability in Russian, Italian, and Spanish.

9 781990 685811